Making Freedom
African Americans in U.S. History

SOURCEBOOK 4

⟶⽊⟵

Our New Day Begun
1861–1877

OTHER BOOKS IN THIS SERIES

SOURCEBOOK 1

True to Our Native Land: Beginnings to 1770

SOURCEBOOK 2

A Song Full of Hope: 1770–1830

SOURCEBOOK 3

Lift Ev'ry Voice: 1830–1860

SOURCEBOOK 5

March On Till Victory: 1877–1970

Making Freedom is a beautifully crafted five-volume sourcebook for classroom use. In its presentation of primary sources and learning strategies it has no rival in the area of African American history. This handsome, thought-provoking series belongs on the desk of every middle and high school United States history teacher who knows that without African American history there is only a partial and unbalanced United States history.

GARY B. NASH
*Director, National Center for History in the Schools
University of California, Los Angeles*

The Making Freedom *Sourcebooks and CDs are a treasure trove of documents, analysis, and resources guaranteed to inspire lively classroom discussion and thoughtful student research. This original collaboration between teachers and scholars offers extraordinary access to the historical and continuing role of African Americans in the shaping of our nation.*

MARILYN RICHARDSON
*Former Curator, Museum of Afro-American History and
the African Meeting House, Boston, Massachusetts*

Making Freedom *offers teachers of American history a powerful and compelling teaching tool to help broaden their focus curriculum. The lessons are well crafted and provide students an opportunity to sharpen historical and critical thinking skills in a dynamic, meaningful, and relevant fashion. In the hands of teachers,* Making Freedom *will make a difference.*

JIM PERCOCO
Author, Divided We Stand: Teaching
About Conflict in U.S. History

Developed through a skillful collaboration between scholars and experienced social studies teachers and curriculum specialists—and covering a span of time from medieval Jenne-Jeno to 1970—this excellent five-volume set is built around firsthand evidence (mostly written documents but also many visual materials). Undoubtedly it will be a valuable classroom resource for students and teachers alike.

ROBERT L. HALL
*Department of African-American Studies
Northeastern University, Boston, Massachusetts*

For many students, the fact that the past was made up of real people who made real decisions about issues that are not far different from ones that we face today rarely comes through in the textbooks that they use. Primary Source's Making Freedom *helps open the history classroom to the lives of many different types of people. The range of documents and the tips on how to use them creatively give a real opportunity for teachers to help their students understand the past and its relevance to today.*

STEVEN D. COHEN
Education Department, Tufts University

The curricula within these sourcebooks was developed by some of the most creative educators I have ever met. We are truly excited about sharing them with you.

Rachel Zucker wrote "Paul Robeson" and "The Black Press" in Sourcebook 5

I have found as both an educator and an administrator that I have learned more of my own history by being involved in this historical project. For teachers of color, it will be most helpful in the classroom where we can share the true stories of African American culture and help to correct some misinformation of the past. After all, African American history IS American history.

Deborah Ward contributed to "The Exodusters—Ho for Kansas!" in Sourcebook 4

I use primary sources in my curriculum because the students become more engaged in the process of discovering history for themselves. They are fascinated by reading and deciphering the art, documents, letters, diary entries, and law codes written in centuries past. I feel these exercises encourage students to empathize with people of the past and to better understand complex aspects of history. History comes alive!

Laurel Starks wrote "The Slave Experience: Their Words and Others" and "Slavery and Resistance" in Sourcebook 3

I recall deciding in the fourth grade that history was not for me or about me. It definitely did not make me feel connected to anything. The lessons I wrote in the Primary Source Black Yankees Seminar (subsequently a part of the series) gave me an exciting rebirth experience that forged a connection for me and turned on my search for historical truth. The Making Freedom *series empowers teachers to make history come alive for students of all ages.*

Deborah Gray wrote "Slave Literacy" and contributed to "Schooling of Free Blacks—The Roots of 'Separate But Equal'" in Sourcebook 3

I found that using these primary source materials with my students helped them understand more thoroughly the issues and complexities of the time periods being studied. Students and I use the key questions and organizing ideas to focus and guide our thinking through the many activities and assessments provided by the Sourcebooks. Students are engaged in the work and seek additional information to increase their knowledge of history.

Leslie Kramer wrote a number of lessons in Sourcebook 1, including "Sugar and Slaves," "Riverine Craft—Bringing the Skills Over," and "Resistance and Rebellions"

Writing lessons for the Making Freedom *series represented the ideal scholarly endeavor: I could use my research and analytic skills to get to the heart of the topic and then draw on my teaching experience to present the material in a meaningful way to students. I appreciate being able to give students this opportunity to immerse themselves in the richness and subtlety of history.*

Mark Meier wrote "Urban Disturbances" and "Many Roads to Freedom" in Sourcebook 5

Making Freedom

African Americans in U.S. History

SOURCEBOOK 4

Our New Day Begun
1861–1877

COMPILED AND EDITED BY
THE CURRICULUM SPECIALISTS AT
PRIMARY SOURCE, INC.

FOREWORD BY
JAMES OLIVER HORTON

Education Resource Center
University of Delaware
Newark, DE 19716-2940

HEINEMANN
PORTSMOUTH, NH

T 92816

Heinemann
A division of Reed Elsevier Inc.
361 Hanover Street
Portsmouth, NH 03801–3912
www.heinemann.com

Offices and agents throughout the world

© 2004 by Primary Source, Inc.

All rights reserved. No part of this book may be reproduced in any form or by any electronic or mechanical means, including information storage and retrieval systems, without permission in writing from the publisher, except by a reviewer, who may quote brief passages in a review.

Acknowledgments for borrowed material begin on p. 244.

Library of Congress Cataloging-in-Publication Data
Making freedom : African Americans in U.S. history / compiled and edited by the curriculum specialists at Primary Source, Inc. ; foreword by James Oliver Horton.
    p.   cm.
   Includes bibliographical references.
   ISBN 0-325-00515-X (v. 1 : acid-free paper) — ISBN 0-325-00516-8 (v. 2 : acid-free paper) — ISBN 0-325-00517-6 (v. 3 : acid-free paper) — ISBN 0-325-00518-4 (v. 4 : acid-free paper) — ISBN 0-325-00519-2 (v. 5 : acid-free paper)
   1. African Americans—History—Study and teaching.   2. African Americans—History—Sources.   I. Primary Source, Inc.

E184.7.M34 2004
973'.0496073'0071—dc22   2003024628

Editor for Heinemann: Danny Miller
Editor for Primary Source: Liz Nelson
Production service: Lisa Garboski, bookworks
Production coordinator: Vicki Kasabian
CD production: Marla Berry and Nicole Guay
Interior and cover design: Catherine Hawkes, Cat & Mouse
Typesetter: TechBooks
Manufacturing: Steve Bernier

Printed in the United States of America on acid-free paper
08 07 06 05 04   VP   1 2 3 4 5

The Making Freedom *series is dedicated to the memory of*
Clara Hicks,
a former school principal in Newton, Massachusetts,
and a colleague at Primary Source.
She served briefly as a Project Administrator for this series
and has left us a legacy of wisdom and joy.

Primary Source has created the Making Freedom *Sourcebooks*
thanks to the generosity of these contributors:

National Endowment for the Humanities
Germeshausen Foundation
LEF Foundation
Massachusetts Foundation for the Humanities
Wellspring Foundation
and many individual donors

Lift Ev'ry Voice and Sing

JAMES WELDON JOHNSON

Lift ev'ry voice and sing,
Till earth and heaven ring,
Ring with the harmonies of Liberty;
Let our rejoicing rise
High as the list'ning skies,
Let it resound loud as the rolling sea.
Sing a song full of the faith that the dark past has taught us,
Sing a song full of the hope that the present has brought us;
Facing the rising sun of our new day begun,
Let us march on till victory is won.

Stony the road we trod,
Bitter the chast'ning rod,
Felt in the days when hope unborn had died;
Yet with a steady beat,
Have not our weary feet
Come to the place for which our fathers sighed?
We have come over a way that with tears has been watered,
We have come, treading our path through the blood of the slaughtered,
Out from the gloomy past,
Till now we stand at last
Where the white gleam of our bright star is cast.

God of our weary years,
God of our silent tears,
Thou who hast brought us thus far on the way;
Thou who hast by Thy might,
Led us into the light,
Keep us forever in the path, we pray.
Lest our feet stray from the places, our God, where we met Thee,
Lest our hearts, drunk with the wine of the world, we forget Thee;
Shadowed beneath Thy hand,
May we forever stand,
True to our God,
True to our native land.

Contents

Foreword by James Oliver Horton, George Washington University xiii
Project Staff xv
Introduction xix

CONTEXT ESSAY "Who Freed the Slaves? The Civil War and Reconstruction" by Dr. Patrick Rael, Bowdoin College *1*

Part I ⸭ Initial War Aims

To what degree was the war about freeing slaves? At the start of the war, what was Abraham Lincoln's primary goal? How did his purposes evolve as the war progressed? What did African Americans think were the goals for the war?

LESSON 1   Lincoln and Slavery *12*
LESSON 2   Enslaved People Force the Issue *22*

Part II ⸭ The Soldiers' Experience

The war was not the quick suppression of Southern rebellion that the Union had anticipated. Battlefield stalemates and tremendous loss of lives forced the Union to consider what had once been unthinkable—arming black men. Many African Americans jumped at the chance to fight for their freedom. What prejudices did they face in government policies and in the day-to-day realities of serving in the army? What were the limits of the Union's commitment to complete equality?

LESSON 3   Who Should Fight? *38*
LESSON 4   The Decision to Enlist *56*

Part III ※ Wartime Reconstruction

Union successes often seemed to pose as many problems as they solved. As slavery withered in the wake of the Union army, what would replace it? What were the variety of solutions explored by black people, their allies, and their enemies during the war?

LESSON 5 Sustaining a Living *71*
LESSON 6 How to Rebuild the Union *77*

Part IV ※ The Dawn of Freedom

The end of the Civil War in April of 1865 heralded a new world of freedom for African Americans. But, as the assassination of Abraham Lincoln just days after the Confederate surrender symbolized, conflict and tension were not over. The new president, Andrew Johnson, permitted many former Confederates to return to power. But Congress, in the hands of antislavery legislators, provided the Freedmen's Bureau to assist with the transition to freedom. Freedpeople's hopes for freedom developed in the midst of this conflict between Congress and the White House.

LESSON 7 Hopes and Obstacles *85*
LESSON 8 The Black Codes and Presidential Reconstruction *101*
LESSON 9 The "Misrepresented Bureau" *113*

Part V ※ Labor

With freedom, one important thing did not change: African Americans were still expected to perform the bulk of the manual labor in the South. But with the institution of slavery gone, how would the reconstruction of southern agriculture proceed? Would formerly enslaved African Americans be given the opportunity to become prosperous independent farmers? Or would they be limited to the status of semiservility?

LESSON 10 Occupations and Obstacles *129*
LESSON 11 The Rise of Sharecropping *144*

Part VI ※ Building a Free Community

Freedom provided African Americans new opportunities to build community institutions. The family, the schoolroom, and the church became the centers around which African American life coalesced. How did these institutions work to create a sense of community among the freedpeople? What obstacles did they help African Americans to overcome?

LESSON 12 Reuniting and Protecting Family *154*
LESSON 13 Knowledge Is Power *164*
LESSON 14 The Role of the Church *181*

Part VII ⚜ Politics and the End of Reconstruction

Reconstruction was as much a political as a social revolution. By 1870, the constitution legally guaranteed the right to vote to all African American men. Starting with the Military Reconstruction Acts of 1867, the enfranchisement of black men transformed southern politics. Nonetheless, by 1877, Reconstruction's fragile experiment in biracial democracy had failed. Why were African American men given the right to vote? How, despite that African Americans were armed with the ballot, did Reconstruction fail to guarantee the freedpeople equality? Why did some African Americans choose to head West in search of work and community?

LESSON 15   Voting and Representation   *191*
LESSON 16   The Undoing of Radical Reconstruction   *208*
LESSON 17   The Exodusters—Ho for Kansas!   *221*

Glossary   240
Credits   244

Foreword

JAMES OLIVER HORTON
GEORGE WASHINGTON UNIVERSITY

The most exciting thing about history is the likelihood of discovery. Documents from the past—official papers, letters, diaries, newspapers, and maps—are windows into the public and private worlds of those who came before us, those who prepared the society that has shaped our lives.

The documents, lessons, and context essays in this book focus on the lives and experiences of African American people in the history of the United States. They make clear the importance of race in the formation of American culture and society. Through these documents and the interpretive essays that place them in historical context, *Making Freedom* illustrates a more inclusive American history, revealing the interracial, multicultural historical experience that Americans lived. It makes the critical point that African American history is American history made by Americans in America.

Every American has been—and continues to be—shaped by African and African American cultural heritage and its interaction with the multitude of other cultural heritages that have combined to form American culture. These documents help us to see the world of the past through the eyes of those who lived in that world and to understand the events of their time as they did. They enable us to appreciate the role of race in shaping American assumptions and expectations and understand the interconnection between the meaning of American freedom and the limitations Americans imposed on that freedom. If we are ever to have a successful conversation on race in today's society, it is essential that we come to terms with these issues.

Historical documents can bring history to life at a time when America needs a historical context for its contemporary concerns. Unfortunately, Americans are undereducated about their past, and our public school system has not successfully addressed this problem. If, as Thomas Jefferson believed, an educated citizenry is essential for the maintenance of democracy, America is in trouble.

Recent surveys make clear the critical need for better history education. The U.S. Department of Education reports that 60 percent of the nation's high school seniors cannot demonstrate even a fundamental knowledge of U.S. history. This ignorance is especially glaring on the subject of race. More than half of the students could not identify Africa as the continent from which people were brought to be enslaved in the Western Hemisphere. Almost two-thirds could not correctly identify the term "Jim Crow" as the set of laws that enforced racial segregation, and less than one quarter could explain the purpose of the Fifteenth Amendment as a Constitutional protection against discrimination in voting, even when the wording of the amendment was provided to them.

If there was ever a time to enhance history education, that time is now. The documents in this book do just that, and the accompanying lesson plans suggest effective teaching strategies. From first-hand accounts of the Atlantic slave trade, to descriptions of black seafaring communities after the Revolution, to the wartime experiences of black Civil War soldiers, to the emergence of the Harlem Renaissance, *Making Freedom* presents a compelling and dramatic American story. It introduces the major concerns and events of the African American experience and the significance of race in America. These documents transport students back in time and allow them to discover the past in its own words and on its own terms.

Standard history textbooks provide information about the past that is important, but too often less than engaging. These documents and lessons are as lively and interesting as the human struggles they portray. Whereas textbooks frequently separate African Americans from the general American experience, *Making Freedom* places African American history at the center of the broad sweep of national history.

Most important, it helps us to evaluate America's past through a reading of direct historical evidence. Students will come to understand history through their personal investigation. This critical component of learning can add excitement and meaning to the educational experience. Students become more than simply consumers of historical information. They move closer to being historians and begin to understand the excitement of historical discovery.

Most of us who have become professional historians remember the moment when history became something more than a list of names and events, when it became an adventurous search for meaning. At the moment when facts become not simply significant in themselves but inspiring bits of evidence to be used in building a case for historical interpretation, we started to feel like real historians, detectives on the trail of history.

When students feel like historical detectives they will have less trouble remembering the significant fundamentals of history and they will appreciate the importance of the past.

Those who understand how exciting history is and understand its meaning for the present and the future never find it boring. Instead, they become lifelong learners of history. The documents in *Making Freedom* open a new and exciting world of the past and provide a greater appreciation of the full range of American history and of the lives of the people who made it.

Project Staff

Primary Source Staff

Anna Roelofs, Project Director
Kathy Bell, Librarian
Renee Covalucci, Picture Research
Abby Detweiler, Program Associate
Jim Diskant, Curriculum Specialist
Kathleen M. Ennis, Executive Director
Betty Hillmon, Kodaly Music Consultant
Eve Lehmann, Permissions Editor
Roberta Logan, Education Director
Rachel Margolis, Program Associate
Brande Martin, Program Associate
Liz Nelson, Editor
Charles Rathbone, Board of Directors
Jesse Ruskin, Music Researcher
Kelly Scott, Program Associate
Martha Shethar, Photo Researcher
Ann Vick-Westgate, Editor

Interns

Lucia Carballo
Kendra Carpenter
Jessica Kyle Ellis
Mike Fearon
Tracey Graham, Mellon Fellow
Imani Hope
Meredith Katter
Nina Miller
Sam Schwartz

PROJECT STAFF

Special thanks to James Jones of Northeastern University for his musical expertise, to Marvin Karp, Benjamin Kendall, Jill Minot-Seabrook, and Anthony Parker for their advice, to The Lovejoy Society, DeKalb, Illinois; and to Pam Matz, librarian at Harvard University.

Advising Scholars

Frances Smith Foster, Emory University
V. P. Franklin, Columbia University Teachers' College (Evaluator)
Paul Gagnon, Emeritus, Boston University
Gerald Gill, Tufts University
Robert Hall, Northeastern University
Emmett Price, Northeastern University
Heather Cox Richardson, Suffolk University
John Ross, National Center of Afro-American Artists, Boston

Contributing Scholars

Robert Allison, Suffolk University
Edmund Barry Gaither, Museum of the National Center for African American Artists, Boston
Robert Hayden, Independent Scholar
Betty Hillmon, Park School
James Oliver Horton, George Washington University
Lois Horton, George Mason University
Grey Osterud, Historian
Patrick Rael, Bowdoin College
Marilyn Richardson, Independent Scholar
Julie Richter, Independent Scholar

Teacher-Authors

Wendell Bourne, Cambridge Public Schools
Phyllis Bretholtz, Teacher/Educational Consultant
Ilene Carver, Boston Public Schools
Monny Cochran, Weston Public Schools
Julie Craven, Cambridge Public Schools
Andrea Doremus Cuetara, Boston Public Schools
Inez Dover, Newton Public Schools
Kathleen Drew, Cambridge Public Schools
Sharon Fleming, Abington Public Schools
Linda Forman, Framingham Public Schools
Richard Berry Fulton, Boston Public Schools
Deborah Gray, Community Educator

Andrea Gross, Westwood Public Schools
Jennifer Hames, Boston Public Schools
Deborah Hood-Brown, Cambridge Public Schools
Leslie Kramer, Cambridge Public Schools
Roberta Logan, Boston Public Schools
Peter Lowber, Malden Public Schools
Mark Meier, University of Virginia
Nicole Miller, Westborough Public Schools
Martin Milne, Eaglebrook School, Deerfield
Edward Morrison, Winthrop Public Schools
Melisa Nasella, Lincoln-Sudbury Public Schools
Karl Netter, Boston Public Schools
Catherine O'Connor, Newton Country Day School
Alexandria Pearson, Metro Director, Natick High School
Gwynne Alexandra Sawtelle, Westborough Public Schools
Andrew Shen, Lincoln-Sudbury Public Schools
Laurel Starks, Milton Academy
Sandra Stuppard, Boston Public Schools
Deborah Ward, Wellesley Public Schools
Joseph Zellner, Concord Public Schools
Rachel Zucker, Burlington Public Schools

Introduction

Making Freedom: African Americans in U.S. History grew out of the synergy and vision of a group of Boston-area teachers, several scholars, and the program staff of Primary Source. Beginning in 1995 with a series of seminars on "Black Yankees" of the eighteenth and nineteenth centuries, the project grew and expanded to reach across the country and over time, up to the last quarter of the twentieth century.

Fortunately for all of us who see history as discovery, continuing scholarship is illuminating almost four centuries of African American thought, creativity, and activism in the social, political, and cultural development of our nation. Although work has been going on for years at the university level to understand the ways in which African American ideas and experiences influenced the development of our national culture and political ideology, little of this new thinking has yet become part of the standard school curriculum. The traditional historical narrative forming the basis of content for precollege students often relegates the study of African American history to separate units on slavery or to the struggle for civil rights. *Making Freedom* offers precollegiate teachers and their students exposure to exciting and informed scholarship on 400 years of history, thus strengthening the content and adjusting the lens through which African American history is viewed and understood.

The *Making Freedom* sourcebooks contain information and materials that demonstrate at least two important phenomena: the social agency and intellectual achievement shown throughout African American history from the colonial period forward and the inextricable relationship of African Americans to the collective history and cultural development of the United States. The primary sources contained in these sourcebooks reveal a diversity of perspectives and experiences among African Americans from their first arrival in British North America. In contemporary textbooks, slavery is often presented as a singular experience that shaped the character of all African Americans. *Making Freedom* intentionally illuminates the variety of the slave experience for African Americans, focusing both on individual ideas and actions and on collective efforts to hold America accountable to the ideals of freedom and equality.

Through the speeches and writings of scholars and activists, slave narratives, poetry, fiction, music, and fine arts, revealing agency in the face of repression,

Making Freedom illumines the ways in which Africans and African Americans have influenced American thought and cultural expression, as well as our traditions of freedom and democracy.

Making Freedom:

- ❖ provides teachers with multidisciplinary scholarship, primary source materials, and lesson plans concerning African American history from fourteenth-century Africa through the Civil Rights Movement of the 1970s
- ❖ presents this new material in ways that stimulate teachers and students to ask questions about how the intellectual history of African Americans relates to mainstream history and provokes a deeper understanding of the achievements and frustrations of African Americans in the pursuit of a lived freedom
- ❖ inspires teachers, who in turn inspire students, to become active learners, engaged in the process of historical research and community exploration, to tolerate both conflict and ambiguity in the historical narrative, and to learn more about themselves and others in an increasingly complex, pluralistic world
- ❖ addresses a variety of issues—scholarship, teaching strategies, and diverse student preparations for understanding history—and pulls them all together into a useful resource
- ❖ increases understanding and teaching capacity of both experienced and novice teachers for presenting the powerful and integral role of African American intellectual history in American history

The history of minorities *is* American history—to leave it out or mention it peripherally deprives students and teachers alike, giving an incomplete and often a false view of our past. Both majority and minority students gain from learning a more holistic story. Because mainstream history is often restricted to the story of one dominant group, complicating what is taught as history becomes a vital and legitimate goal for anyone seriously concerned with historical accuracy.

How This Series Was Created

In the summer of 1998, with financial support from the National Endowment for the Humanities, an enthusiastic group of teachers and scholars met to imagine and then to begin to create a multipart series of curriculum sourcebooks. We formed into working groups, each with a scholar, teachers, and a curriculum specialist.

Since its inception, the project has been informed by emerging scholarship in African American history and the growing availability of primary source materials to the general public. History has been described as a funnel—lots of stories go in, but only a few emerge to be told. Our goal is to enlarge the mainstream narrative for teachers and students, offering an inclusive history that places African Americans among the founders and shapers of our culture. *Making Freedom* uncovers stories of African American agency and intellectual vision and demonstrates how this intellectual history catalyzed movements such as abolition and civil rights and contributed to new interpretations of the Constitution. Recognizing that some of the primary source testimony of African Americans is in nonliterary form, primary source documents may be in the form of original artworks and musical scores that illustrate African American contributions to the development of American art, folk culture, and religious traditions.

Although one major thrust of this curriculum initiative is related to content, there are pedagogical objectives as well. Teachers and students need tools and strategies to enable the process of discovery and to encourage investment in learning. By using these sourcebooks, teachers can help their students become active participants in history. Through reading firsthand, authentic accounts of moments in history, looking at an engraving or listening to a piece of music, students are moved to ask questions and learn to formulate their own opinions about a person, an issue, or an event.

As we designed *Making Freedom* and began to draft materials, we drew heavily upon James Banks' paradigm for transforming curriculum. Banks' model shifts the perspective away from a conventionally focused study to reveal a more inclusive and far more interesting array of interrelated content. Offering a variety of activities and nontextbook, original source material, this approach lays the groundwork for teachers to transform their teaching goals and methods.

Who We Are

Primary Source, a teacher resource center in Watertown, Massachusetts, promotes education in the humanities that is historically accurate, culturally inclusive, and explicitly concerned with ethical issues such as racism and other forms of discrimination. Its services link university and school and combine scholarly research from original sources with practical knowledge of how adults and students learn. Through institutes, seminars, and conferences, Primary Source models an active, interdisciplinary approach to teaching. Primary Source offers educators intellectual enrichment and opportunities to participate in serious, professional dialogue with scholars and other classroom teachers.

Primary Source supports teachers' efforts to restructure their social studies teaching by serving as a conduit for primary source materials that reveal the voices of people from various ethnic, racial, and cultural groups within the United States and from countries around the world. Once these original source documents are brought to light and their intellectual and creative accomplishments are revealed, curriculum content is necessarily more inclusive of both genders and all racial and ethnic groups. Students may then see themselves in the curriculum and feel more connected to the educational process, to a cultural past, and to a civic future.

Using Primary Sources

The organization Primary Source takes its name from the same term used by historians to distinguish original, uninterpreted material from secondary or third-hand accounts. Thus a photograph, a memoir, or a letter is a primary source; an essay interpreting the photograph or memoir is usually, though not always, a secondary source. A textbook, still further removed, is a tertiary source.

In some instances, the same document or other piece of evidence may be a primary source in one investigation and secondary in another. For example, Henry Wadsworth Longfellow's poem "Paul Revere's Ride" is a primary source when it is considered as a reflection of how nineteenth-century citizens romanticized the Revolutionary War. It is not, however, a primary source that provides information about the events of April 18–19, 1775. (Paul Revere never did arrive in Concord.)

Making Freedom utilizes a range of primary sources. Included are maps, travel journals, letters, illustrations, engravings and other kinds of art, business records, diaries, wills, autobiographies, contemporary biography, advertisements (including those for the sale or recapture of slaves), music (including folk songs), and photographs of artifacts.

Although it is imperative to read secondary sources in order to understand context and background, introducing students to "the real stuff" raises student interest and curiosity and offers opportunities for students to make discoveries on their own. The closer students get to real people's lives, the better chance they have to formulate real questions and to care about people and events from another time and place. In a March 2002 speech to members of the Boston Athenaeum, historian David McCullough advised, "To understand the people of a particular historical period, you have to read what they read, not just what they wrote. You have to listen to the music, look at the paintings . . . ."

When textbooks are used as the only source of information, it is much more difficult for students to take ownership, both of their own learning and of a particular body of knowledge. It is very difficult to remember other people's generalizations or conclusions. Original source material provides students with rich opportunities for inquiry, the chance to move from concrete to abstract thinking and back again.

Teaching About Race

In the 1990s, a national dialogue about race was initiated by the Clinton administration. This endeavor was not widely covered in the media, and it is difficult to assess what was accomplished. The creators of this series believe that in order to bring about healing of a shameful national past, a dialogue about race needs to begin at the classroom level and be carried out into the world by students grounded in an honest study of history and committed to social justice.

We Are All Involved

The seeds of ignorant, biased, and racist opinions and feelings are often sown in children as they grow up, through families, the media, friendships, and even schools and religious institutions. Although students are not to blame for bringing ignorant opinions into the classroom, we must all now be accountable for attitudes and actions we take into the future. Discussions of racism often focus on blacks and other people of color as victims, essentially making it a black problem. The question of racism's cost to white people is rarely raised. Yet racism presents a serious challenge to any individual's ability to reason, make sound judgments, and develop perspective.

Individual Discovery

In studying the racial history of this country, we see that many painful things have happened in the past and continue to happen today in many communities. In general, students lack accurate information, ways to analyze this information as well as their own feelings and experiences, and an ability to articulate their analysis. Our job as teachers and students is to uncover the prejudices that exist in our institutions, our culture, and ourselves and to revisit our history in a careful, inclusive, and truthful manner. As a more accurate understanding of our complicated racial history is achieved, students can express their new knowledge in a variety of ways, as the activities in the lessons suggest. Finally, they can be encouraged to take action to address issues of unfairness in their schools and communities.

Depending on the composition of the class, there may be students who feel particularly vulnerable or targeted by the material discussed on a given day. Typically, students of color become angry and aggressive, while white students feel guilty and defensive. In addition, students who are of mixed race may feel conflicted. All students should be encouraged to express their thoughts and feelings; students learn a great deal from each other.

Giving students ample time to reflect in writing on what they have learned is a good outlet for feelings and is also a way to discover a student who may be having an especially difficult time. A piece of private reflective writing may reveal conflicts appropriate for the whole class to discuss or individual conflicts that need to be responsibly addressed by the teacher.

Class Discussion

Students seldom have the opportunity to engage in critical, analytical discussions about race. Our role as educators is to provide them with the information and tools to do so constructively. Students can be engaged in setting class guidelines for discussion of controversial subjects. Some examples follow.

1. All opinions and expressions of feelings and emotions are accepted and respected in class, whether other students share them or not.
2. Opinions and feelings expressed on sensitive topics should be kept within the confines of the classroom, not discussed elsewhere.
3. Students should speak from their own experience, using "I-statements" as much as possible. This simply means that students should start with, "I think, I heard, I believe, I feel . . ." rather than "You're wrong because . . ." The former prompts reflection, whereas the latter can feel like a direct attack on another speaker.
4. Students should know also that it is fine to choose *not* to speak.

How to Use This Book

Making Freedom is intended for use as a resource in all American history classes at the middle and high school levels. This series enables teachers to weave the African American story into and throughout the wider narrative. We have purposely emphasized individuals and events that are not often included in standard American history textbooks. Our purpose is to widen and deepen the narrative, not to repeat the few names and incidents already familiar to most teachers and students.

The five *Making Freedom* curriculum sourcebooks provide innovative, intellectually compelling curriculum materials that fit into the conventional scope and sequence. The sourcebooks specifically examine the African American intellectual tradition in the context of the following historical eras: (1) Colonial America; (2) Revolution and Forging the Nation; (3) Antebellum Reform; (4) Civil War and Reconstruction; and (5) The Gilded Age into the Twentieth Century. The five sourcebooks, with titles from "Lift Ev'ry Voice and Sing" by James Weldon Johnson, are:

True to Our Native Land: Beginnings to 1770

A Song Full of Hope: 1770–1830

Lift Ev'ry Voice: 1830–1860

Our New Day Begun: 1861–1877

March On Till Victory: 1877–1970

Each book contains the following:
- a table of contents for the series
- one or two context essays written by scholars
- lesson plans, including primary sources
- a glossary

The accompanying CD-ROM includes all primary source materials, supplementary materials, and a time line and annotated bibliography for the entire series.

Each lesson contains
- Introduction
- Organizing Idea
- Student Objectives
- Key Questions
- Primary Source Materials
- Vocabulary
- Student Activities
- Further Student and Teacher Resources
- Contemporary Connections

Several lessons also include music selections.

Together, the **context essays** at the beginning of each book and the **introductions** to individual lessons provide background information necessary for understanding the primary sources and engaging in the activities. Teachers can use this introductory material in a variety of ways. For example, they can have the students read the introductions in their entirety, present the information in a brief lecture, create background information sheets with key points, or ask students working in groups to research the answers to questions that create a context for the lesson.

Vocabulary lists with topical words are included, and the words are defined in the **glossary**. In many instances, given the historical period of the documents, additional vocabulary lists are provided under supplementary materials to help students better understand what they read.

Each lesson includes a variety of teaching strategies designed to engage student interest. Suggested **activities** include study and analysis of primary sources, mapping, research and writing, debating, creating graphic displays, and role-plays that involve assumption of a particular perspective, sometimes an unpopular or (in the twenty-first century) an unacceptable one. This activity needs to be understood as an attempt to see things as they were in a particular time in the past. The challenge is to try not to view all events from the perspective and values of today. When an activity calls for speculation or analysis, it is important to have verifying information available close at hand—in the classroom, the school library, or online. A speculation exercise is not a standalone activity, but, together with research to clarify information and verify a theory, it gives students the opportunity to act as historians.

Because the context essays and lessons were written by a group of scholars and teachers, they offer a variety of writing and instructional approaches. Although the format for all the lessons is the same, we have respected the authors' voices and have not edited them to a uniform length or style. The lessons vary in length and level of detail and offer a choice of activities.

We would not expect teachers to use every activity in every lesson. Rather, they should choose those lessons—and, within the lessons, those activities—that dovetail best with their instructional plan and meet the needs and learning styles of their students. We have set out a buffet—we do not intend for all of it to be consumed by each teacher.

A list of **further resources** is provided with most lessons. Although every effort has been made to ensure that references to websites are current, they do change. Teachers may wish to check URLs before giving students assignments. Students should also be cautioned to evaluate information found in a website carefully, checking who is the author and who sponsors the site.

Each lesson includes a **contemporary connection**. Our intent is to demonstrate that the issues raised by studying the primary sources do not pertain only to the past. Some remain the same; others have been transmuted a little. This feature gives resources and often asks open-ended questions for further exploration.

Some of the **primary source materials** are difficult for students to read. They have been set in type, but no changes have been made to the original language. As a result, the documents contain syntax with which students may not be familiar, as well as vocabulary no longer in active use or for which meaning has shifted. Sometimes words are spelled differently. Each teacher knows best how to adapt a lesson to students' skill levels. The books include suggestions, such as having students work in pairs or small groups, reading the documents aloud to the class, and/or providing vocabulary definitions before students tackle the documents.

The lengthier documents have been abbreviated in the sourcebooks. All **primary source materials** appear in full on the accompanying CD-ROMs and can be printed out for classroom use.

This *Adinkra* symbol represents the Akan belief that we must look at and learn from the past in order to move with wisdom into the future. It teaches people to value and protect their cultural heritage.

Who Freed the Slaves? The Civil War and Reconstruction

DR. PATRICK RAEL, BOWDOIN COLLEGE

Preface

On March 4, 1861, President-elect Abraham Lincoln became the sixteenth president of the United States of America. Between the November election and Lincoln's March inauguration, the seven states of the Deep South had seceded from the Union. Eight more slaveholding states had threatened to secede. With the crucial exceptions of Fort Pickens in Pensacola, Florida, and Fort Sumter in Charleston, South Carolina, federal property throughout the seceded South was in the process of being transferred to Confederate hands. Popular feeling in the North was running high. While *New York Tribune* editor Horace Greeley argued that the Confederate states should be free to "leave in peace," for others secession confirmed the need to take arms against the "slave power," which they believed sought to impose its tyrannical will on free white men.

In the midst of this crisis Lincoln took the oath of office, and issued what was undoubtedly the most important inaugural speech in American history. "I have no purpose, directly or indirectly, to interfere with the institution of slavery in the States where it exists," he stated, echoing a claim he had made many times before. Despite the pervasive discussion of slavery throughout the sectional crisis of the 1850s, secession itself did not pose an immediate threat to the institution of slavery. The same held true into the war. In July of 1861, Congress passed two resolutions which proclaimed that the war would not be one to abolish slavery. The resolutions did not mention slavery by name, merely stating that the Union would not prosecute the war with the "purpose of overthrowing or interfering with the rights or established institutions of those States."

Yet a few years later, by time the Thirteenth Amendment was ratified in December of 1865, the four million African Americans who had been held in chattel bondage before the war were freed. In 1868, their status as citizens would be affirmed by the Fourteenth Amendment, and in 1870 male African Americans would be universally enfranchised by the Fifteenth. Thus concluded one of the most remarkable transformations in modern times, an event singular throughout the experience of slavery's demise in the New World—in the United States, all slaves became legally entitled to all the rights of citizens.

The transformation of the Civil War, from a struggle to retain or sunder the union to one to destroy or maintain slavery, did not proceed as the product of a conscious design on the part of those who effected it. Rather, it happened haltingly, with hesitation and paradox, through the acts of hundreds of politicians and generals, many of whom worked at complete cross-purposes. Most importantly, though, it happened through the will and behavior of thousands upon thousands of African Americans themselves.

Emancipation from the Bottom Up

The process of emancipation began during the war, as a consequence of the Union's inexorable creep toward victory. Since their earliest arrival in America, Africans had registered their dissent toward enslavement. The conditions of war, however, lent new significance to the enslaved's act of defiance. Old patterns of day-to-day resistance, designed to withhold work from masters, dealt innumerable small blows to the war effort. Open acts of insubordination, for example, diverted Confederate energies to the home front. Of particular importance was the practice of escape. Especially as the conflict stalemated into a war of attrition between Union and Confederate economies, Confederate leaders considered the enslaved a vital source of labor, and hence crucial to the war effort. When enslaved African Americans fled southern farms and plantations, they not only sought to free themselves and their families, they also struck a blow for the Union by depriving the Confederacy of labor.

Union leaders quickly divined the value of slave labor to the Confederate war cause. In the field, as Union lines slowly encroached into Confederate territory in Virginia, the Carolina low country, and Louisiana, army officers encountered fugitive slaves from nearby plantations. They reacted in various ways. Some, perhaps responding from the racial prejudice which beset many white Northerners, heeded the requests of slaveowners and returned the fugitives to those who claimed to own them. Others, however, declared the slaves "contraband of war," withholding their labor from the Confederates in the same way they withheld captured arms and ammunition. Most notable in this regard was General Benjamin F. Butler, commander of Fortress Monroe in Virginia. Butler pioneered the government's policy for dealing with slaves who had escaped to Union lines. He refused to return them to their masters, instead putting them to work for the Union war effort.

Emancipation from the Top Down

Enslaved African Americans themselves, by escaping to Union lines, took the initiative in leading the U.S. government toward emancipation. Later, the enslaved posed the same challenges to Union policy by simply staying put as U.S. Army troops steadily began to sweep over lands left behind when planters fled. What should be done with these people? Union leaders believed that if freed, perhaps the former slaves would feel no compunction to work the cotton that fueled the South's economy. Yet if they were kept in a state of servitude, what message would this send to the world about Union war aims?

Once again, the answers were initially eked out in the field, on a case-by-case basis, largely by the generals who controlled Union-held territory in the slave states. In 1861 and '62, Union generals John C. Frémont and David Hunter declared martial law in the areas they controlled and freed slaves owned by Confederate sympathizers. While Lincoln revoked both moves as untimely, he did permit the army to "take possession" of slaves behind Union lines. The use of such phrases suggested the depth of the Union dilemma in dealing with enslaved blacks. Should the Union declare escaped slaves free, it might risk the fragile loyalty of the border states and alienate political dissidents in the North. Yet if it retained such people as property, it risked participating in the very system of chattel slavery against which it warred.

The slow progress of the war increasingly lent such questions great import. In July 1861, Confederate victory at the first battle of Bull Run demonstrated that the seceded states would not quickly yield to the pressure of Northern numbers and industry. Bloody Union defeats at battles such as Fredericksburg, and costly Union victories like those at Shiloh and Antietam, demonstrated that technological advances in weaponry had made the battlefield a very dangerous place indeed. By increasing the range and accuracy of fire, the rifled barrels of the new muskets gave a large advantage to defenders, making decisive victories difficult, expensive, and rare. As the conflict on the battlefield approached stalemate, and as the war steadily became a protracted struggle of societies and economies, Union commanders and the President himself sought alternative avenues to victory.

Congress pioneered the first such path through a series of Confiscation Acts, which were designed to enshrine in law what the enslaved themselves were already effecting in practice. These authorized seizure of all Confederate property, including slaves, used in the rebellion and eventually declared all slaves behind Union lines free. They also prohibited army officers from returning fugitive slaves to their masters, and provided for the compensated abolition of slavery in the District of Columbia. The Confiscation Acts marked a turning point in Union perceptions of the purposes of the war. More than Sherman's March to the Sea through Georgia in 1864, this breaking of the unspoken consensus on the sanctity of private property signaled an important shift in the war. As the conflict turned into what scholars have termed a "total war," Union war aims came to include the abolition of property in slaves.

The second path to victory the Union pursued was still more profound. In July of 1862, as the Union war machine ground to a halt against well-led Confederates in Virginia, at the Mississippi, and in Tennessee, Lincoln began to imagine changing Union war aims. Abolitionists such as Horace Greeley and black activists such as Frederick Douglass had from the start called for the inclusion of universal emancipation of the slaves as a primary war aim. But Lincoln feared that such a move would alienate the wavering slave states still in the Union (Missouri, Kentucky, Maryland, and Delaware) and energize Democratic political opponents in the North who sympathized with the Confederacy. In the summer of 1862, however, Lincoln decided that widespread emancipation had become "a military necessity, absolutely essential to the preservation of the Union."

In September of 1862 Lincoln thus issued a preliminary draft of the Emancipation Proclamation, declaring that on January 1, 1863 "all persons held as slaves within any State or designated part of a State the people whereof shall then be in rebellion against the United States shall be then, thenceforward, and forever free." While the Proclamation applied primarily to slave property still under Confederate control, and thus affected few blacks immediately, it had an enormous impact on the nature of the conflict. It instantly transformed the war for union into a war against slavery.

The Proclamation had three major effects. First, issuing it guaranteed that the Union's worst fear would not come to pass. Great Britain's "Lords of the Loom" sympathized heavily with southern "Lords of the Lash" who supplied the booming British industry with cotton. Union leaders feared that Britain, the strongest naval power on the planet, would recognize the legitimacy of the Confederacy in order to protect its own trade interests, and perhaps even enter the war on the Confederacy's side. The Emancipation Proclamation, however, tapped into popular feeling in England—the same abolitionist sentiment which had propelled that nation to abolish slavery in its empire (in 1831) and to champion the destruction of the international slave trade. Once the Proclamation was promulgated, virtually no chance remained that Great Britain would recognize the Confederacy as a legitimate independent nation.

Perhaps more importantly, the Emancipation Proclamation set a precedent for action on slavery which would not easily be countermanded. Having made the momentous decision to begin emancipating blacks en masse, Lincoln could hardly go back. When asked if he would consider revoking the Proclamation in order to bring the war to a speedy, victorious conclusion, Lincoln replied: "I should be damned in time and in eternity for so doing. The world shall know that I will keep my faith to friends and enemies, come what will." With only slight wavering, Lincoln from 1863 on steadfastly retained universal emancipation as one of the two key prerequisites for the cessation of hostilities. (The other was the recognition of U.S. sovereignty and consequent dismantling of the Confederate government and armed forces.)

Thirdly, the Proclamation expedited the process through which former slaves became Union soldiers. The Proclamation contained a clause which declared that those freed by the Proclamation "will be received into the armed service of the United States." From the beginning of the war, black activists had called for the enlistment of black troops, and the battlefield stalemates which led to the war's protraction did nothing to quell their voices. Editorialized Frederick Douglass: "One black regiment in such a war as this is . . . would be worth to the Government more than two of any other. . . . While the Government continues to refuse the aid of colored men, thus alienating them from the national cause, and giving the rebels the advantage of them, it will not deserve better fortunes than it has thus far experienced." As the war deepened, others—particularly white abolitionists and antislavery moderates—began seeing the utility, and indeed the necessity, of enlisting black troops.

The Proclamation put behind such voices the weight of White House authority, and the recruitment of black soldiers proceeded steadily after its promulgation. Some joined northern regiments composed primarily of antebellum free blacks, such as the exemplary 54th Massachusetts, the famous "Glory" regiment led by Colonel Robert Gould Shaw. Most black soldiers, however, were recruited from the ranks of former slaves into southern regiments such as the 1st South Carolina Volunteers. By the end of the war, 189,000 African Americans had served in the Union army and navy, many in key battles which demonstrated time and again blacks' willingness to sacrifice their lives, if necessary, for the cause of freedom.

Black soldiers, who suffered disproportionately high casualty rates, helped turn the tide for the Union. Army life was not without its own hardships and experiences of prejudice, and many black soldiers faced nearly as much privation and racism as they had on the plantations. Yet, in a way few Union generals appreciated, military service unwittingly served as an important mechanism for socializing former bondsmen to a new life in freedom, and for preparing many for the rigors of post-war leadership.

The Reconstruction of Black Labor

It is notable that the evolution of Union war aims—from mere preservation of the Union to the abolition of slavery—resulted from military exigency rather than from liberalized racial sentiments in the North. Slavery may have been dead, but prejudice certainly had not perished. When the war ended in April of 1865, the first priority of many in the nation was not to secure a meaningful freedom and equality for the freedpeople, but to restore the integrity of the union as quickly and as painlessly as possible.

This certainly seemed to have been Lincoln's top priority. Though his assassination in April of 1865 confounds any attempt to fully divine his plans for Reconstruction, his "10 percent plan" of December 1863 offered some hints. Under this "Proclamation of Amnesty and Reconstruction," former Confederate states would be permitted back in the Union under lenient terms (just ten percent of the population had to swear an oath of loyalty to the Union). As for the freedpeople, the new state governments had to ratify the Thirteenth Amendment abolishing slavery, but could otherwise institute any measures found to be "consistent . . .with their present condition as a laboring, landless, and homeless class."

As this vague language underscored, the fate of the freepeople remained very much in question as the war ended. Deeply imbued with centuries of prejudice, most whites both north and south feared the specter of four million landless blacks, lacking formal education and employment. Many whites claimed that African Americans would work only under compulsion. Few understood that the freedpeople themselves desired not freedom from work, but freedom from oppression. As one freedman reflected: "We thought we was going to be richer than the white folks, cause we was strong and knowed how to work, and the whites didn't, and they didn't have us to work for them any more." Unfortunately, it did not work out that way. As this man continued, "We soon found out that freedom could make folks proud, but it didn't make 'em rich."

Even abolitionist allies misunderstood the freedpeople's goals in freedom. Early in the war, as the Union Army came to occupy the Sea Islands of South Carolina and Georgia in 1861, free labor advocates from the North went south to begin what became known as the "Port Royal Experiment." Abolitionists such as James Miller McKim and Edward S. Phillsbrick hoped to vindicate arguments they had been making for many years—that freedpeople would respond to a competitive capitalist economy with free labor markets. Unfortunately, the Port Royal reformers had too little faith in their own ideology. Rather than loose the freedpeople into the economy as true equals, they treated them as apprentices, limiting their participation in the market economy in an effort that set important precedents for the post-war years.

For their part, the freedpeople did not wish to work the abolitionists' plantations on terms little better than enslavement. Rather than grow cotton, which they could not consume themselves and which was the hated master's crop, they wanted to grow food for themselves and local exchange. Rather than work for the paltry wages offered by the abolitionists, they preferred to work for a share of what they grew. And rather than work in gangs, they preferred to work in families.

The Port Royal experiment foreshadowed the deeply qualified nature of the freedom that resulted from the destruction of slavery and Union victory in the Civil War. Throughout the South, wherever the reconstruction of southern agriculture began, experience echoed that of the failed Port Royal experiment. Union officials and white southerners sought to establish the freedpeople as an immobile, exploitable agricultural workforce. The freedpeople themselves sought to work in families, for their own subsistence, and for a share of the crop. With the oversight of the Bureau of Freedmen, Refugees, and Abandoned Lands (a.k.a. the Freedmen's Bureau), an agency of the Federal Government established in 1865 to help negotiate the reestablishment of southern agriculture, freedpeople entered into thousands upon thousands of individual negotiations with white landowners. In these negotiations, blacks faced opponents with far more power than they had. Sometimes prejudiced agents of the Freedmen's Bureau even worked against the interests of those they were charged to protect.

Yet blacks were not utterly without leverage. Southern planters, devastated by the war, depended on the speedy cultivation of their cotton crops for their very survival. Under such circumstances, blacks threatened to withhold their labor until they received terms for work more favorable to themselves. They often refused to work for former masters, and sometimes refused to work at all, unless planters made important concessions to their desires. They never received the "forty acres and a mule" frequently rumored to be in the works, but they did influence the terms of their labor. Rather than working for wages, they chose to work for a share of the crop they raised. And rather than work in gangs, they chose to live and work in family units. Though it was not without its own contests and tensions, the reconstitution of black family and community life permitted by this system of sharecropping was perhaps the greatest triumph of the African Americans who lived through the war.

Despite freedpeople's success in putting their agency to work, the deck was stacked against them. Persistent efforts by southern whites to exploit black labor went beyond merely negotiating the terms of labor contracts. Though sharecropping initially reflected the freedpeople's success in bargaining for favorable labor terms, hostile whites turned their control of law and the economy against the freedpeople. They established local credit monopolies which artificially raised the cost of necessary goods and credit, rendering blacks' meager profits still more marginal. And white planters' frequent collusion with local white officials defrauded the freedpeople, reducing sharecropping to little more than a system of debt peonage.

The Rise of the Radicals

With the end of the war in 1865, the new governments of the former Confederate states took the lead in continuing to deny equality to the freedpeople. Under the lenient hand of Andrew Johnson, who had succeeded Lincoln to the Presidency, the former Confederate states had been brought back into the Union on terms favorable to the old slaveholding elite. Widespread political amnesty insured that many of the prime instigators of southern secession became important political figures in the first Reconstruction governments. The legislatures of these Reconstructed states quickly passed a series of laws which codified the opprobrious labor terms planters sought to enforce in individual contracts. These "Black Codes" frequently forced the freedpeople into unfavorable contracts, controlled the hours and terms of their labor, restricted freedpeople's freedom of movement, and imposed strict penalties for vagrancy. The freedpeople were to be reduced to a state of semi-free peonage, steeply at variance with the free labor ideology propounded by antebellum antislavers. More than this, by failing to extend full civil rights to the freedpeople, the codes excluded blacks not simply from the benefits of full participation in the market economy, but from the promises of democratic civil society. In unmistakable language, the codes signaled that even in "freedom" black people still had no rights the white man was bound to respect. As if to emphasize the point, whites in Memphis, Tennessee and New Orleans, Louisiana engaged in vicious racial massacres against blacks in the summer of 1866.

These denials of black civil rights did not go uncontested. A powerful group of Republicans in Congress—"Radicals" such as Thaddeus Stevens, who had been a pre-war abolitionist—rejected what they viewed as efforts by former Confederates to secure in defeat what they could not win on the battlefield. Having defeated the Confederate "Slave Power" at the cost of 620,000 American lives, the Radicals were not about to permit the re-institution of slavery in all but name. The Radicals often expressed a paternalistic attitude toward the freedpeople that heavily qualified their approach to black rights, and their proposals often suggested that they were constitutional conservatives rather than revolutionary Jacobins. Nonetheless, their fierce political battles with former Confederates and with Johnson, whom they finally reduced to lame duck status through impeachment in 1868, pushed them ever closer to supporting the civil rights of freedpeople.

It was in this context that Congress enacted sweeping legislation to put its own plan for Reconstruction into effect. The Reconstruction Act of 1867 removed all the former Confederate states (except Tennessee) from the Union, and placed them under temporary military rule. It then established requirements for the readmission of these states into the Union. The states had to call new state constitutional conventions, the delegates to which were to be elected through universal male suffrage. These constitutional conventions were to draft new state constitutions, permitting black men to vote and hold office. Finally, the conventions had to ratify the Fourteenth Amendment, which guaranteed blacks the rights of citizenship.

Because of its shaky constitutional foundation, military reconstruction was a move distasteful to many Americans, including the Radicals who spearheaded it. After all, the imposition of British military rule on the American colonies had been one of the root causes of the American Revolution. The risk to the liberties of southern whites was made necessary, the Radicals argued, by the dire imperative of securing the rights of defenseless freedpeople from the incursions of hostile southern whites bent on returning blacks to slavery. By permitting blacks the vote, Congress hoped to give the freedpeople (or at least black men) the means to protect themselves. It would thus minimize the need for continued federal intervention into state affairs, and avoid the risks to individual liberties federal intervention implied. Frederick Douglass explained the case for black enfranchisement with characteristic cogence: "The arm of the Federal government is long, but it is far too short to protect the rights of individuals in the interior of distant States. They must have the power to protect themselves, or they will go unprotected, in spite of all the laws the Federal government can put upon the national statute-book."

Local Politics and the Unraveling of Reconstruction

The Radicals' efforts failed. The new state governments produced by the Reconstruction Acts at first looked promising. Dominated by Republicans, they were comprised of an unprecedented mixture of African Americans and whites. These governments achieved many successes, providing free public schooling, establishing a host of beneficial social institutions, and fostering economic development. Yet none of the Reconstructed state governments lasted for more than a decade. In the long run, Republican Reconstruction failed.

Some of the Reconstruction state governments foundered on internal divisions between northern "carpetbaggers" and southern "scalawags," and perhaps even among blacks themselves. In addition, among the southern white populations which would ultimately determine their success or failure, the new governments faced a tough sell. The social costs of the Old South had been borne primarily by the wealthy, paternalistic elites of southern society. Under the Republican governments, social expenses were spread more equally throughout society. They had also risen considerably. Four million formerly enslaved blacks, all entitled to services as free people, had been added to the citizenry. Throughout the South, however, the crucial southern white "swing" vote saw not a more egalitarian social order, but increasingly greater burdens of taxation, with few benefits in return. A storm of Democratic propaganda declaring the Reconstruction governments corrupt took root, and the southern whites who had initially supported the Reconstruction governments turned against them.

Neither of these factors alone would necessarily have spelled defeat for the Republicans. Together, though, they weakened them, creating vulnerabilities easily exploited by a widespread and persistent southern commitment to white supremacy. Underlying whatever problems the Reconstruction governments faced was the overwhelming desire on the part of many in the South to return blacks to a position in which they would be socially subordinate and economically exploited. From the first efforts to secure meaningful rights for blacks, white supremacy fought back through terrorist vigilante organizations such as the Ku Klux Klan, White League, and Knights of the White Camilla. In carrying out their dual roles of imposing on blacks political intimidation and controlling their labor, such groups acted not on their own, but as grass-roots manifestations of racial attitudes widely held throughout the South. Often they served as the military wings of the Republicans' political rivals, the southern Democrats.

The federal government tried persistently to halt the lawlessness perpetrated by the Klan and similar groups. Despite the good faith of these efforts, however, they were limited by restraints on the acceptable bounds of federal activity. Contrary to the view that the Civil War represented a victory for forces of centralization, even Radical Republicans in Congress during Reconstruction viewed federal intervention in local affairs as a violation of the spirit of American democracy. Black activists like Frederick Douglass feared "a despotic central government, with power to control even the municipal regulations of States, and to make them conform to its own despotic will." The use of federal troops in the South was greeted with particular dismay.

Rather than manifesting a firm intention to subject local government to national control, the great pieces of Reconstruction legislation resulted from cautionary sentiments. They were all alternatives to the unthinkable option of a continued federal presence in the South. The Fourteenth Amendment, which guaranteed the national citizenship of all blacks; the Fifteenth, which secured the franchise for all black men; and the Civil Rights Act of 1875, which prohibited racial discrimination in public places all stemmed from Congress's desire to arm the freedpeople themselves with the tools necessary to protect themselves.

Efforts to resolve the crisis of racial democracy in the South through purely constitutional mechanisms failed. Emboldened by the federal government's reluctance to enforce black rights, the spirit of the Klan lived on to win the day. In 1876, the last of the Reconstruction state governments fell to a campaign of voting fraud, political terror, and outright violence. In many instances blacks fought valiantly for their rights, sometimes engaging in armed conflict. With the continued support of the federal government, their actions may have sufficed to secure a meaningful equality. In the contested Presidential election of 1876, however, the Republicans traded a promise to leave the South to its own devices for an electoral victory for their candidate, Rutherford B. Hayes. The Party had sacrificed its commitment to racial democracy on the altar of political expediency. Never again could it sell itself as a "friend to the Negro." Left as a disempowered minority in the South, the freedpeople lost their champion, and fell under the power of the class which had formerly claimed to own them.

Conclusion

In recent years historians have debated the question of "who freed the slaves?" Lincoln, say some, was the crucial factor without which freedom could not have happened. Perhaps it is true that Lincoln was a necessary factor in the abolition of slavery. He certainly was a remarkable figure who played an immensely important role. He was not, however, a sufficient cause in the destruction of slavery. When searching for the *sine qua non* of the "who freed the slaves?" question, it is important to remember that no one could have freed slaves who did not yearn to be free. Since their enslavement began, Africans in America registered their yearning for freedom through daily acts of resistance. Before the Civil War, such acts reminded the nation that black people were neither brutes nor pets, but human beings. During the war, African Americans' acts of resistance collided with the Union war effort, challenging the government to craft policies which translated blacks' yearning for freedom into Union victory.

In the long run, blacks' loyalty to the Union went largely unrewarded. Freedom, though unquestionably a benefit, foundered on the rocky shoals of labor control, white supremacy, conservative constitutional thinking, and northern indifference. Yet for a decade the issue hung in the balance. The Union, having achieved victory at such cost, was loathe to lose the peace. Radical Republicans in Congress sought time and again to arm African Americans with the tools necessary to protect themselves. While in the end popular understandings of the limits of government interference in local affairs prohibited a more strident defense of black rights, African Americans did their best to avail themselves of the means at their disposal. Throughout, African Americans themselves created their own realities, by reconstituting families, negotiating the terms of their labor, and participating in the political process. Their efforts signaled that, regardless of the shifting contexts of power around them, blacks would never relinquish the struggle to assert their humanity. Just as their resistance to slavery had served as a constant, crucial source of pressure before and during the Civil War, their resistance to prejudice, segregation, and disenfranchisement served as the steady refrain for their activities after it.

The gains of Reconstruction were soon lost in a campaign of lynching, race riots, and disenfranchisement—a period which historian Rayford Logan has termed "the Nadir." Once the ally of blacks, the federal government became a neutral or hostile force, reneging on its promise to secure the blessings of liberty for all Americans, and leaving blacks to the will of the capricious mob. In the late nineteenth and early twentieth centuries, federal courts overturned much of the Reconstruction legislation as unconstitutional, or chose to interpret it in ways which did little to benefit blacks. Such actions suggested that it would take far more than the letter of the law to produce meaningful equality for blacks—it would take a revolution in popular sentiment. The story of Reconstruction and its horrific aftermath should remind us that history, even American history, does not inevitably move forward toward a greater justice. However, it is not the product of inevitable forces beyond the control of individual actors. As we have seen and shall see again, even the most oppressed may still craft much of their own reality.

Finally, in assessing the legacy of Reconstruction, we must consider how the motives behind the great changes it entailed influenced their outcomes. Neither emancipation nor the enfranchisement of black men happened as the result of a revolution in national sentiments. Emancipation had stemmed from military necessity, while enfranchisement had resulted from the perceived need to minimize federal incursions into states' rights by permitting blacks to protect themselves through participation in the political process. Undoubtedly the travails of the Civil War and Reconstruction had altered popular sentiment on issues of race, and many Radical Republicans supported civil rights for blacks as much from a fervently held belief in blacks' humanity as from a desire to minimize the federal presence in the South.

Yet it would be a great mistake to assume that black liberation and enfranchisement had resulted from an America which had become more racially tolerant. Racial prejudice sturdily withstood the forces which destroyed slavery, emerging triumphant in the post-Reconstruction years. A new generation of race-baiting southern leaders could look back on the failure of Reconstruction, using it as "evidence" of blacks' incapacity for self-government. African Americans, however, could look to Reconstruction as a failure, but, as W. E. B. Du Bois qualified it, a "splendid failure." For the activists of the twentieth century, Reconstruction would always serve as a reminder that there had been a moment in American history when blacks had participated fully and importantly in the political system, and one when the federal government had spearheaded efforts to realize the dream of a true biracial democracy. Nearly a century after the first Reconstruction ended, a second Reconstruction would begin.

LESSON 1

Lincoln and Slavery

Abraham Lincoln, the great emancipator, was elected to the office of president of the United States in 1860. It was a time when the issue of slavery was on the minds of many Americans. However, the controversy surrounding slavery was not so much moral as political. The United States had recently expanded to the West Coast, and there was much disagreement over the slavery question in the western territories. Some politicians wanted territories and newly created states to be allowed to decide for themselves whether or not they wanted slavery to be legal. Many southern politicians disagreed with this idea because they believed it would tilt the balance of slave states verses free states against them in Congress.

During his campaign, Lincoln followed the Republican platform and pronounced that slavery should be left undisturbed where it existed and that it should be excluded from the new territories. Lincoln easily won in all the free states except New Jersey. In addition, split factions within the Democratic party allowed Lincoln to win, even though he had only a plurality, not a majority, of the national popular vote.

Problems arose for Lincoln even before he took the oath of office in March 1861. The South deeply resented his policies on slavery in the territories. As a result, South Carolina, Mississippi, Florida, Alabama, Georgia, Louisiana, and Texas (the "Deep South") joined together and voted for secession, stating that the Constitution was a contract among sovereign states, which had been broken when the federal government failed to enforce the Fugitive Slave Law and denied Southern states their equal rights in the territories.

Unlike many northerners who agreed with General Winfield Scott when he said, "Wayward sisters, depart in peace," President Lincoln believed that secession was unconstitutional and was determined to find a solution, even if it meant going to war. Although a number of compromises were proposed, none succeeded, primarily because Lincoln was unwilling to give in on the issue of slavery in the territories. It appeared as though Lincoln was, as many southerners feared, attempting to ease America away from slavery. Publicly, however, his speeches were centered on the preservation of the basic democratic principle that the will of the majority should prevail. This meant that he believed secession was not a legal option in a disagreement over the policies of a democratically elected president.

War broke out, and as it progressed, it became clear that Lincoln believed emancipation of slaves in the Confederacy was paramount from both a strategic and moral standpoint. His Emancipation Proclamation, announced on September 22, 1862, freed slaves in rebelling states as of January 1, 1863. However, because Lincoln did not want any of the northern border states, which had kept slavery legal, to turn on him and side with the Confederacy, he did not free the slaves in states that had not seceded from the Union at the same time. Many people, both contemporaries and historians looking back on his actions, believe that he planned to do so shortly after the war, but he was assassinated in April 1865, before he could put any such plan into action. The Civil War ended with slavery still legal in the border states.

It is worth noting that African Americans enslaved in the South and in the border states did not wait for the federal government to decide its official policy but took action, freeing themselves by the thousands. Many made their way to Union lines to help out in the war effort in any way that they could.

Organizing Idea

Union policy regarding slavery evolved over the course of the war. At the start, President Lincoln insisted that the war was about preserving the union. But as the war progressed, Lincoln and the federal government made the freeing of slaves in the South an integral part of Union war objectives.

Student Objectives

Students will:

- understand Lincoln's official and personal views on slavery and the goals of the war
- explore reasons for the shifts in his official views on slavery and the goals of the war
- practice the skill of exploring documents to trace evolution of ideas

Key Questions

- Was Lincoln personally opposed to slavery?
- What was Lincoln's official stand on slavery? How did that change as the war progressed?
- What was Lincoln's motivation in taking such a gradual approach to ending slavery?

Primary Source Materials

DOCUMENT 4.1.1: Excerpts from President Abraham Lincoln's Reply to an Open Letter from Horace Greeley, *New York Tribune*, 1862

DOCUMENT 4.1.2: Excerpts from Confiscation Act of 1862
DOCUMENT 4.1.3: The Emancipation Proclamation, January 1, 1863
DOCUMENT 4.1.4: President Lincoln's Second Inaugural Address, March 4, 1865
DOCUMENT 4.1.5: Lithograph, "Free!" 1863

Supplementary Materials

ITEM 4.1.A: Additional vocabulary lists for primary sources
ITEM 4.1.B: Concept Map handout

Vocabulary

| emancipate | perpetuate | territory |
| insurgent | proclamation | |

Student Activities

Activity 1 — **Engaging the Students—Why Fight a Civil War?**

Ask students for their thoughts on these questions:

- ❖ What was the goal of the Civil War? How do you know this?
- ❖ What were President Lincoln's views on slavery? How do you know this?
- ❖ What sources could you look at for evidence to support answers to these questions?

Activity 2 — **Reading and Analysis—Lincoln's Views**

Tell students that they will look at three documents that present President Lincoln's official statements about the goal of the war and give insight into his thoughts about slavery, both official and personal. Emphasize that these documents alone are not enough to answer thoroughly questions asked in Activity 1, but that they can provide a solid starting point.

1. Hand out Document 4.1.1, Lincoln's reply to an open letter from Horace Greeley, editor of the *New York Tribune*. Make sure students note the date of the document, as well as its historical context. As a class, go over the document, highlighting any words or phrases that give insight into the following:

    - ❖ Lincoln's position on the goal of the war
    - ❖ Lincoln's position on freeing slaves
    - ❖ Lincoln's personal feelings about slavery

2. Now tell the class that they will be creating a Concept Map. A Concept Map is a visual road map connecting one concept or idea to another, thereby presenting graphic information on subjects that are not always easily connected by the printed word. It describes steps in a process, sequences of events, or the goals, actions, and outcomes of a person, group, or organization. Give the Concept Map handouts (Item 4.1.B) to students. On an overhead, fill out the Concept Map, with students filling in their own maps from the overhead.

3. Now hand out Document 4.1.3, Lincoln's Emancipation Proclamation. Again, make sure students note the date of the document, as well as its historical context. This time, have students work alone or in pairs to do Step 1 of the process, highlighting key words and phrases just as they did for the first document. Have students report what they highlighted, and then use those ideas to complete the next section of the Concept Map as a class.

4. Finally, hand out Document 4.1.4, Lincoln's Second Inaugural Address, noting the date and context. Then, ask students to fill in and highlight the third section of the Concept Map on their own. When they are done, ask them to share answers. (*Note:* This sequenced activity should help students build skills and confidence in examining documents for key ideas. Be sure that they know they can change their answers at any time as they listen to the class discussion.)

5. Ask students to use the Concept Map that they have created to write a two- to three-sentence summary of Lincoln's positions on the goal of the war and on the freeing of slaves. Share their summaries and discuss which ones seem to best capture the ideas presented in the concept map.

Building Theories and Exploring Answers—The Shift in Policy

Activity 3

Have students read Document 4.1.2. Ask them to theorize on reasons for the shift in official policy in regard to freeing enslaved African Americans. Probe to see if they can identify the sources of their theories. Again, ask them where they would look for evidence. Tell them that this time, instead of looking at primary source documents, they will look at a secondary source to compare their theories with those of historians. Have students find and read excerpts from their textbook and another source. Then, discuss the reasons that historians present for Lincoln's policy shifts. Ask students if they think that Lincoln would have eventually freed all slaves, even those in border states. Encourage them to base their answers on information and words they see in the documents (or that they know from other sources).

Debrief the Lesson—Does It Matter?

Activity 4

- ❖ Does it matter that people know that the freeing of slaves only gradually became a focus of the government's war effort? Explain.

❖ Whose voices are missing from all these documents? How would knowing the words and actions of thousands of escaping African American slaves shape your understanding of the shift in government policy? (See Lesson 2.)

Activity 5 **Reflecting on the Hopes for Emancipation**

Human beings can sometimes get lost among official documents. Students should examine "Free!" (4.1.5). Have them describe their feelings as they examine the image of an African American reaching up. What do they think he is reaching for? Students should return to this image after learning about Reconstruction.

Activity 6 **Creative Extensions—A Cartoon**

Ask students to make a three-panel political cartoon that captures the evolution of Lincoln's policy toward freeing slaves. Encourage students to use their own opinions on Lincoln's policies to shape their cartoons. Have them evaluate each other's cartoons, based in part on how well they incorporate evidence from the documents.

Further Student and Teacher Resources

Burchard, Peter. *Lincoln and Slavery.* New York: Athenaeum Books, 1999.

Music Connection

On the final night of December 1862, black men and women, enslaved and free, gathered across the nation. In his book *The Negro in the American Rebellion* (1867), former slave William Wells Brown described the scene at a contraband camp in Washington, D.C. As African Americans waited for Lincoln's Emancipation Proclamation to take effect, they sang over and over again:

> Go down Moses
> Way down in Egypt land;
> Tell old Pharaoh,
> Let me people go.

It is impossible to date accurately many of the songs that enslaved African Americans created. "Before I'd Be a Slave" (also known as "Oh Freedom") may well have been sung beyond the hearing of whites, as a song of resistance. A century after the Emancipation Proclamation, the song was adopted by the Civil Rights Movement. After that, writes Eileen Southern in *The Music of Black Americans: A History*, it became the signature song for people seeking civil rights and equal opportunity throughout the world. As students listen to the song (available on CD-ROM), ask them to identify what makes this song applicable to so many people.

Note: William Wells Brown, once a fugitive slave, is considered the first African American to publish in several literary genres. Prior to the Civil War, he was a tireless worker for the abolitionist movement.

Frankel, Noralee. *Break Those Chains at Last. African Americans 1860–1880. The Young Oxford History of African Americans, Vol. 5*. New York: Oxford University Press, 1996.

Holtzer, Harold, ed. *Abraham Lincoln the Writer: A Treasury of His Greatest Speeches and Letters*. Honesdale, PA: Boyds Mills Press, 2000.

Marrin, Albert. *Commander in Chief: Abraham Lincoln and the Civil War*. New York: Dutton, 1997.

Video

Abraham and Mary Lincoln: A House Divided. A David Grubin Productions Inc. film for American Experience in association with PBS. Alexandria, VA: PBS Video, 2001.

Contemporary Connection

Museum Controversies

Although the Civil War has been over for well over one hundred years, there continue to be divisive issues. Wounds are reopened when museums organize exhibits to interpret the war. In 2002, the Tredegar National Civil War Center Foundation in Richmond, Virginia, began presenting Confederate, black, and Union versions of the war in one all-inclusive exhibit. Alexander Wise Jr., president of the Foundation and himself a descendant of a Confederate general, said, "We need a civil discussion of a very uncivil war... You have to go beyond symbolism and into the facts."

Wise negotiated an agreement with the Philadelphia Civil War Library and Museum to receive Union artifacts such as memorabilia of Ulysses S. Grant, but some scholars and Northern war buffs protested the move, stating that it violated the original donors' intent to keep their Union memorabilia in Philadelphia. Wise was also interested in telling the story of black Americans who participated in the war and who have been ignored in Civil War retellings.

In Richmond, Robin Reed, for fourteen years the director of the Museum of the Confederacy, resigned together with several staff members. Supporters say that Reed was actually forced out because he supported the Tredegar Foundation's efforts to tell a more inclusive story. After two weeks on the job, the new director, J. A. Barton Campbell, unfurled a Confederate battle flag outside the front doors of the museum to, in his words, "teach others about its past." Mr. Reed had this to say, " I don't think (this) is an effective way to educate people... these (flags) are relics and icons from the killing fields themselves." The danger, according to one former staff member, is that the museum will turn back from being a museum *of* the Confederacy to a museum *for* the Confederacy. (Information from Francis X. Clines, *New York Times Service*, *The Richmond Tribune*, and Janet Caggiano and the *Richmond Times Dispatch*.)

Ask students if they can identify a history museum in their community. Can they discover how their local museum has handled a controversial exhibit?

Websites

Abraham Lincoln Presidential Library and Museum. State of Illinois and the Illinois State Preservation Agency
www.ALincoln-Library.com/Apps/default.asp
Website for the Museum and Library, scheduled to open in 2004, it includes access to a beginning collection of Lincoln digitized resources at **www.papersofabrahamlincoln.org/**

A House Divided: America in the Age of Lincoln. Digital History, University of Houston
www.digitalhistory.uh.edu/ahd/resources.html
Extensive resources including maps, images, documents, time lines and other recommended resources for teaching about Abraham Lincoln and the Civil War

The Time of the Lincolns. American Experience, PBS Online
www.pbs.org/wgbh/amex/lincolns/
A companion site to the PBS biography of Abraham and Mary Lincoln, including several segments on the Civil War, particularly the role of newspapers reporting the war

Primary Source Materials for Lesson 1

4.1.1

Excerpt from President Abraham Lincoln's Reply to an Open Letter from Horace Greeley, *New York Tribune*, 1862

My paramount object in this struggle is to save the Union and is *not* either to save or to destroy slavery. If I could save the Union without freeing any slave, I would do it; and if I could save it by freeing all the slaves, I would do it; and if I could save it by freeing some and leaving others alone, I would also do that. What I do about slavery, and the colored race, I do because I believe it helps to save the Union . . . I intend no modification of my oft-expressed *personal* wish that all men everywhere could be free.

4.1.2

Excerpts from Confiscation Act of 1862

AN ACT to free from servitude the slaves of certain rebels engaged in or abetting the existing rebellion against the government of the United States.
 Be it enacted by the Senate and House of Representatives of the United States of America in Congress assembled,
 That all right, title, interest, and claim whatever, of every person comprehended within the following enumerated classes, in and to the service or labor of any other person or persons held to service or labor in any State under the laws thereof is hereby declared forfeited, and such persons so held to service or labor, commonly called slaves, are hereby declared forever discharged from such service or labor, and to be freemen . . .

The full text of Document 4.1.2 is available on the CD-ROM.

4.1.3

The Emancipation Proclamation, January 1, 1863

That on the first day of January, in the year of our Lord one thousand eight hundred and sixty-three, all persons held as slaves within any state or designated part of a State, the people whereof shall then be in rebellion against the United States, shall be then, thenceforward, and forever free; and the Executive Government of the United States, including the military and naval authority thereof, will recognize and maintain the freedom of such persons, and will do no act or acts to repress such persons, or any of them, in any efforts they may make for their actual freedom. . . .

The full text of Document 4.1.3 is available on the CD-ROM.

4.1.4

President Lincoln's Second Inaugural Address, March 4, 1865

The Almighty has His own purposes. "Woe unto the world because of offenses; for it must needs be that offenses come, but woe to that man by whom the offense cometh." If we shall suppose that American slavery is one of those offenses which, in the providence of God, must needs come, but which, having continued through His appointed time, He now wills to remove, and that He gives to both North and South this terrible war as the woe due to those by whom the offense came, shall we discern therein any departure from those divine attributes which the believers in a living God always ascribe to Him? Fondly do we hope, fervently do we pray, that this mighty scourge of war may speedily pass away. Yet, if God will that it continue until all the wealth piled by the bondsman's two hundred and fifty years of unrequited toil shall be sunk, and until every drop of blood drawn with the lash shall be paid by another drawn with the sword, as was said three thousand years ago, so it still must be said, "The judgements of the Lord are true and righteous altogether." . . .

The full text of Document 4.1.4 is available on the CD-ROM.

4.1.5

Lithograph, "Free!" 1863

The color lithograph was created by Henry Louis Stephens (1824–1882).

Library of Congress

LESSON 2

Enslaved People Force the Issue

The coming of the Civil War meant different things for different southerners. For nonslaveholding white families, it meant the removal of young men, many of whom would die. For plantation owners and slaveholders, it meant new threats to their established ways of life. To the enslaved themselves, however, it meant new opportunities to become free.

All black southerners knew of the war and its potential consequences. They overhead the talk of white people and shared information along the informal communication networks that existed within and between plantations. They saw white men go off to war and sensed the anxiety of the women left to manage by themselves. Of course, the nearly four million enslaved African Americans in the South experienced the war in a wide range of ways. One important factor in determining the enslaved's experience of the war was location. Little changed in the daily lives of those well behind Union lines. As one former slave from Texas recalled, "The war didn't change nothin'. Sometimes you didn't knowed it was goin' on." Those nearer the front lines, however, experienced vastly different conditions. Confronted with the extra privations of war, some faced starvation, because planters prioritized ill-fed Confederate troops above lowly slaves. Others helped rebuild in the aftermath of marauding troops from both North and South, whereas still others marched off to war (and sometimes died) in the service of their masters.

Whatever their condition African Americans took advantage of the circumstances of war to expand their freedom and even to destroy slavery. The mere fact that the institution of slavery was maintained only through the ever-present threat of violence helped undermine its stability in time of war. White southerners feared that they had long been sitting on a powder keg of resentment, which the chaos of war might help ignite. Slaves, as long years of servitude had taught them, kept their own council, concealing their thoughts and plans from masters. As Mary Chesnut, the wife of a prominent planter and politician in South Carolina, declared, "Not by one word or look can we detect any change in the demeanor of these negro servants." African Americans' dissemblance led suspicious whites to wonder if "their" slaves might not have been the contented lot they had long hoped they were. When

Chesnut learned that her cousin had been strangled in her sleep by her own slaves, the news shook to its foundations her faith in slaves' loyalty. "Hitherto I have never thought of being afraid of Negroes," she confided to her diary. But now she did not know whether she could trust her own servants or not. "Why should they treat me any better than they have done Cousin Betsey Witherspoon?" she asked. "If they want to kill us, they can do it when they please, they are noiseless as panthers." Although Chesnut survived the war with her self intact, her experience mirrored that of many slaveowners who had thought they knew their own slaves' minds.

Far more typical of wartime patterns of slave resistance, though, were much subtler acts of day-to-day disobedience. The old tactics of daily resistance—feigning ignorance, pretending to misunderstand orders, working slowly or carelessly, mishandling livestock or produce—gained new efficacy as the traditional sources of plantation discipline, planters and their hired overseers, went off to war. Slaves had long used such tactics to bargain for small liberties within an oppressive institution; now they raised the ante on their masters, demanding the maintenance of old privileges and the granting of new.

The presence of the Union army vastly enhanced African Americans' capacity to resist. Masters and mistresses often found themselves surprised that slaves they had thought of as loyal and docile had run away to Union lines, sometimes taking with them entire families. Overnight, entire plantations lost their labor forces. Even when masters tried to relocate their slave labor forces to the interior of the Confederacy, simply moving "their" slaves created new opportunities for flight.

The consequences of slave flight to Union lines were serious. As some northern generals quickly learned, each slave removed from the Confederacy and put to work behind Union lines counted as two laborers: one removed from the enemy and one benefitting the North. Additionally, the erosion of the southern labor force badly sapped morale on the Confederate home front. Finally, the presence of African Americans behind Union lines was a crucial force pressuring Union policymakers to confront the fate of slavery. Military labor could be just as brutal as slavery, but—as the experience of black soldiering would more clearly show—once African Americans offered their labor for the Union, few could deny them freedom.

Organizing Idea

According to Union officials, the purpose of the Civil War was to preserve the Union. African American slaves had their own ideas. From the start, slaves recognized that their futures depended on the results of the war. They took actions that pushed the issue of emancipation to the fore.

Student Objectives

Students will:
- know what actions slaves took during the war in support of their freedom

- understand how African American attitudes towards the war sparked these actions
- understand how the actions of slaves influenced decisions in Washington, D.C.

Key Questions

- What did African Americans see as the goal of the Civil War?
- What actions did enslaved people take during the war in support of their freedom?
- What attitudes sparked these actions?

Primary Source Materials

DOCUMENT 4.2.1: Letter from William H. Lee, a barely literate farmer, to President Jefferson Davis, May 4, 1861

DOCUMENT 4.2.2: Letter from John J. Cheatham, an educated Georgian, to the Confederate secretary of war, May 4, 1861

DOCUMENT 4.2.3: Letter from General Ambrose E. Burnside to Secretary of War Edwin M. Stanton, March 21, 1862

DOCUMENT 4.2.4: Excerpt from petition by Robert Q. Mallard and his fellow planters to Confederate General Hugh W. Mercer, August 1, 1862

DOCUMENT 4.2.5: Photo, "Fugitive African Americans Fording the Rappahannock River" in Virginia, August 1862

DOCUMENT 4.2.6: Engraving, "Stampede of slaves from Hampton to Fortress Monroe," 1861

DOCUMENT 4.2.7: Drawing of "Contrabands Coming into Camp," January 1863

DOCUMENT 4.2.8: Photo, "Contrabands," Camp Brightwood, Washington, D.C., 1863

DOCUMENT 4.2.9: Engraving, "Slaves from the plantation of Confederate President Jefferson Davis arrive at Chickasaw Bayou, Mississippi," 1863

DOCUMENT 4.2.10: Letter from General Ormsby M. Mitchel to Secretary of War Edwin M. Stanton, May 4, 1862

DOCUMENT 4.2.11: Testimony to a federal commission by former slave Samuel Elliot, McIntosh, Georgia, July 17, 1873

DOCUMENT 4.2.12: Obituary for Whitfield Ross, Olathe, Kansas, newspaper, March 1926

DOCUMENT 4.2.13: Narrative of the life of Margaret E. Ross, as told to a family member, Kansas, 1942

DOCUMENT 4.2.14: Photograph of Whitfield Ross

DOCUMENT 4.2.15: Photograph of Margaret E. Ross

Supplementary Materials

ITEM 4.2.A: Supplementary vocabulary lists for primary sources
ITEM 4.2.B: Stations Guide, a student handout
ITEM 4.2.C: Map of Confederate states

Vocabulary

afford aid	dispatch	fugitive
depredation	emissary	

Student Activities

Engaging the Students—Why Go to War? *Activity 1*

Engage students in a discussion of the following questions: If you want to know the purpose of a war, whom do you ask? Why those people?

Write the following statement on the board: "At the outset, the North was fighting the Civil War with the goal of preserving the Union. The war did not become a war to free slaves until President Lincoln issued the Emancipation Proclamation in 1863." Tell students that this statement represents a common interpretation of the purposes of the war. Yet, if you had asked African American slaves what the war was about, you might have got a very different answer. What is the best answer to the question: What was the purpose of the war? How does one go about trying to answer it? Students will look at documents to help them decide how, if at all, they would modify the opening statement.

Stations Activity—Answering Questions on Primary Sources *Activity 2*

Students will look at the documents through an activity involving different stations. Divide students into four groups. Hand out the Stations Guide (Item 4.2.B). Students should answer the questions for each station at that station. The order of the stations does not matter; what matters is that each group gets to each station at some point during the activity. Students should have with them a map of the Confederate states (Item 4.2.C). As they move from station to station, they should plot on the map the locations referred to in the primary source. (This activity can also be done as a class, using an overhead to project a map onto a screen.) When all groups have completed all stations, discuss the activity.

First, ask students to share their answers to the questions at the different stations. Where there is disagreement, have students ground their answers in evidence from the documents themselves. Then return to the statement: At the outset, the North was fighting the Civil War with the goal of preserving the Union. The war did not become a war to free slaves until President Lincoln issued the Emancipation

Proclamation in 1863. Based on what students have seen and discussed, how would they modify the original statement, if at all? Look back at the questions with which the lesson opened. Would they answer differently now that they have gone through this activity?

Activity 3 **The Ross Family Papers**

Students should read the obituary for Whitfield Ross (4.2.12) and the narrative of the life of Margaret E. Ross (4.2.13) and then study the photographs of Mr. and Mrs. Ross. Have them consider the following questions:

- How are these family papers similar and how are they different from the other documents in this lesson?
- What specific information can you obtain about events, issues, and choices in the lives of these two people? How does that information add to your knowledge of the lives of enslaved African Americans?
- How does this biographical information enlarge your general understanding of U.S. history?
- Based on these documents, what can you conclude was held in high value by the Ross family? How do you know that?
- If you could interview Whitfield or Margaret Ross, what would you ask them?

Further Students and Teacher Resources

Berlin, Ira, Barbara Fields, Steven Miller, Joseph P. Reidy, and Leslie S. Rowland, eds. *Free At Last: A Documentary History of Slavery, Freedom and the Civil War*. New York: The New Press, 1992.

Friedheim, William. *Freedom's Unfinished Revolution: An Inquiry into the Civil War and Reconstruction*. New York: The New Press, 1996.

McPherson, James M. *For Cause and Comrades: Why Men Fought in the Civil War*. New York: Oxford University Press, 1997.

Seidman, Rachel F. *Civil War: A History in Documents*. New York: Oxford University Press, 2001.

Tackach, James. *The Emancipation Proclamation: Abolishing Slavery in the South*. San Diego, CA: Lucent Books, 1999.

Tenzer, Lawrence C. *The Forgotten Cause of the Civil War: A New Look at the Slavery Issue*. Manahawkin, NJ: Scholars' Publishing House, 1997.

Video

The Civil War. Episode 1, 1861, The Cause. Florentine Films in association with WETA-TV, Washington; produced by Ken Burns and Ric Burns; written by

Geoffrey C. Ward, Ric Burns, and Ken Burns. Alexandia, VA: PBS Video, 1989.

Websites

Index of Civil War Information on the Internet. United States Civil War Center, Louisiana State University, Baton Rouge, LA
www.cwc.lsu.edu/cwc/civlink.htm#cwres
A rich collection of resources on all aspects of the Civil War

The Valley of the Shadow: Two Communities in the American Civil War. Virginia Center for Digital History, University of Virginia, Charlottesville, VA
http://jefferson.village.virginia.edu/vshadow2/
Archival information from two communities in Pennsylvania and Virginia before, during, and after the Civil War

---

Contemporary Connection

Juneteenth—Celebrating Emancipation

Juneteenth is the oldest known celebration of the ending of slavery. The first Juneteenth was held on June 19, 1865, the day that Union soldiers liberated Galveston, Texas, thereby ending the war and freeing the slaves. It was a time for reassuring each other, for praying, and for gathering together remaining family members. Throughout the late nineteenth century, Juneteenth continued to be highly revered in Texas, with many former slaves and descendants making an annual June 19th pilgrimage back to Galveston.

In the early 1900s, the Juneteenth celebration declined as more and more African Americans migrated to cities where their employers were unwilling to give them the day off. In the urban setting, July 4 eclipsed Juneteenth in importance because it was already recognized as a holiday of independence and it served as a way for African Americans to show their patriotism. The Civil Rights Movement of the 1950s and 1960s led to a rebirth in Juneteenth celebrations. Young activists used the celebration to link their current struggle with earlier struggles of their ancestors. For example, student demonstrators involved in the Atlanta civil rights campaign in the early 1960s wore Juneteenth freedom buttons.

On January 1, 1980, Juneteenth became an official state holiday in Texas through the efforts of the African American state legislator, Al Edwards. This marked Juneteenth as the first emancipation celebration to be granted official state recognition. Throughout the 1980s and 1990s, Juneteenth became an increasingly popular event in African American communities. In the larger community, institutions such as the Smithsonian, the Henry Ford Museum, and others have begun sponsoring Juneteenth-centered activities that promote knowledge and appreciation of the past and respect for others. Students can research if and how this holiday is celebrated in their state. They may want to find a way to participate in such a celebration or to launch this event in their own community.

Primary Source Materials for Lesson 2

4.2.1

Letter from William H. Lee, a barely literate farmer, to President Jefferson Davis, May 4, 1861

The State of Ala. Monroe County Bells Ldg May th 4/1861

Dear Sir i havs to in form you that thire is a good meny pore men with large famely to susport. An if they have to go in to the Army there famelys will sufer. thire is a Nother question to rise with us the Negroes is very Hiley Hope up that they will soon Be free so i think that you Had Better order out All the Negroe felers from 17 years oald up. Ether fort them up [imprison] or put them in the army and Make them fite like good fells for wee ar in danger of our lives hear among them. So I Will close with my Best love to you.

Wm H Lee

4.2.2

Letter from John J. Cheatham, an educated Georgian, to the Confederate secretary of war, May 4, 1861

Dear Sir

Some of our people are fearful that when a large portion of our fighting men are taken from the country, that large numbers of our negroes aided by emissaries will ransack portions of the country, kill numbers of our inhabitants, and make their way to the black republicans; There is no doubt but that numbers of them believe that Lincoln's intention is to set them all free. Then, to counteract this idea, and make them assist in whipping the black republicans, which by the by would be the best thing that could be done, could they not be incorporated into our armies, say ten or twenty placed promiscuously in each company? In this way there [sic] number would be too small to do our army any injury, whilst they might be made quite efficient in battle, as there are a great many I have no doubt that would make good soldiers and would willingly go if they had a chance. They might be valued as you would a horse or other property, and let the government pay for them provided they was killed in battle, and it should be made known to them that if they distinguish themselves by good conduct in battle, they should be rewarded. Could some plan of this sort be thought expedient and be carried out with propriety, it would certainly lessen the dangers at home, and increase our strength in the field, and would I have but little doubt, be responded to by large numbers of our people in all the States. It is however only a suggestion, but one that I have thought might merit your consideration. Very Respectfully your humble Servant

John J. Cheatham

4.2.3

Letter from General Ambrose E. Burnside to Secretary of War Edwin M. Stanton, March 21, 1862

Newbern [*N.C.*] Mch 21/62

I have the honor to report the following movements in my department since my hurrid report of the 16" inst—

The detailed report of the Engagement on the 14" is not yet finished but I hope will be ready to send by the next mail—

As I reported, our forces occupied this city & succeeded in restoring it to comparative quietness by midnight on the 14", and it is now as quiet as a New England village—I appointed Gen Foster Military Governor of the city & its vicinity, and he has established a most perfect system of guard & police—*nine tenth* of the depredations on the 14", after the enemy & citizens fled from the town, were committed by the negroes, before our troops reached the city—They seemed to be wild with excitement and delight—they are now a source of very great anxiety to us; the city is being overrun with fugitives from surrounding towns and plantations—Two have reported themselves who have been in the swamps for *five* years—it would be utterly impossible if we were so disposed to keep them outside of our lines as they find their way to us through woods & swamps from every side—By my next dispatch, I hope to report to you a definite policy in reference to this matter, and in the mean time shall be glad to receive any instructions upon the subject which you may be disposed to give—

A. E. Burnside

4.2.4

Excerpt from petition by Robert Q. Mallard and his fellow planters to Confederate General Hugh W. Mercer, August 1, 1862

They [former slaves] have proved of great value, thus far, to the Coast operations of the enemy, & without their assistance, he could not have accomplished as much for our injury & annoyance as he has done; and unless some measures shall be adopted to prevent the escape of the negroes to the enemy, the threat of an Army of trained Africans for the coming fall & winter's campaigns may become a reality. Meanwhile the counties along the Seaboard will become as far as possible for the raising of provisions & supplies for our forces on the Coast.—

In the absence of penalties of such a nature as to ensure respect and dread, the temptations which are spread before the negroes are very strong, and when we consider their condition, their ignorance and credulity & love of change, must prove in too many cases decidedly successful. . . .

The full text of Document 4.2.4 is available on the CD-ROM.

4.2.5

Photo, "Fugitive African Americans Fording the Rappahannock River" in Virginia, August 1862

This photograph, taken by Timothy H. O'Sullivan, shows African Americans escaping to freedom behind Union lines. It was taken during the second battle of Bull Run in 1862.

Library of Congress

4.2.6

Engraving, "Stampede of slaves from Hampton to Fortress Monroe," 1861

This image was published in Harper's Weekly, *August 17, 1861. Escaping at night, slaves carry their belongings as they run along a river bank.*

Library of Congress

4.2.7

Drawing of "Contrabands Coming into Camp," January 1863

Alfred R. Waud took the photograph and then created the drawing for Harper's Weekly, *January 31, 1863. He wrote: "There is something very touching in seeing these poor people coming into camp—giving up all the little ties that cluster about home, such as it is in slavery, and trustfully throwing themselves on the mercy of the Yankees, in the hope of getting permission to own themselves and keep their children from the auction block."*

Library of Congress

4.2.8

Photo, "Contrabands," Camp Brightwood, Washington, D.C., 1863

Initially called "contraband," black slaves fled to Union lines by the thousands. The unidentified African Americans were captured on film when the white officers of the 2nd Rhode Island Camp hired a photographer to create a calling card (cartes de visite) for them.

Library of Congress

4.2.9

Engraving, "Slaves from the plantation of Confederate President Jefferson Davis arrive at Chickasaw Bayou, Mississippi," 1863

The image was published in Frank Leslie's Illustrated Newspaper, *August 8, 1863.*

Library of Congress

4.2.10

Letter from General Ormsby M. Mitchel to Secretary of War Edwin M. Stanton, May 4, 1862

Huntsville [*Ala.*] May 4, 1862

I have this day written you fully embracing three topics of great importance. The absolute necessity of protecting slaves who furnish us valuable information—the fact that I am left with out the command of my line of communications and the importance of holding Alabama north of the Tennessee. I have promised protection to the slaves who have given me valuable assistance and information. My River front is 120 miles long and if the Government disapprove what I have done I must receive heavy re enforcements or abandon my position. With the assistance of the Negroes in watching the River I feel my self sufficiently strong to defy the enemy.

O. M. Mitchel

4.2.11

Testimony to a federal commission by former slave Samuel Elliot, McIntosh, Georgia, July 17, 1873

[*McIntosh, Ga. July 17, 1873*]

My name is Samuel Elliott I was born in Liberty County a Slave and became free when the Army came into the County. I belonged to Maybank Jones. I am 54 years old. I reside at Lauralview in Liberty County. I am a farmer . . .

I resided from the 1st of April 1861 to the lst of June 1865 where I live now at Lauralview. I worked for my master all the time. I changed my business at one time when I was with my master as a waiter—in the rebel service I was with him Eleven month. I came home with him. I told my son what was going on—he with 11 more ran off and joined the Army (the Yankee Army) on St Catherine Island. I dont remember the Year but it was soon after the battle at Williamsburgh Va, and before the 7 days battle near Chickahomony. I mean that was the time I came home with my master. I was with him at Yorktown— Soon after I came home My Son with 11 others ran away & joined the Union Army. My Master had me taken up tied me and tried to make me tell "What made them ran off" I had to lie about it to keep from getting killed. the 11 slaves belonged to My Master Jones that stoped the slave owners from sending or taking slave into the Army as waiters or anything else. it stoped it in Our neighborhood

his
Samuel X Elliot
Mark

4.2.12

Obituary for Whitfield Ross, Olathe, Kansas, newspaper, March 1926

Whitfield Ross Dies

Whitfield Ross was born a slave near Vicksburg, Va., about 90 years ago. He was sold away from his mother when a mere child and lived at different times at Mobile, Ala., New Orleans, La., in Texas, in St. Louis and at Tipton, Mo. He was sold as a slave seven times and belonged to as many different owners.

Whitfield ran away from his slave master at Tipton in 1862 and fell in with a regiment of Union soldiers on their way to Kansas and finally reached Topeka. He enlisted in company F, 79th Kansas, or the first Kansas colored regiment, and served until the close of the war. He was mustered out at Pine Bluff, Ark., in 1865 and returned to Leavenworth where he received his discharge October 12, 1865.

The full text of Document 4.2.12 is available on the CD-ROM.

4.2.13

Narrative of the life of Margaret E. Ross, as told to a family member, Kansas, 1942

Mrs. Margaret E. Ross was born in Butler County, Kentucky, March 10, 1852, on the plantation of Billy Carson. When she was four years of age, she with her mother, four brothers, and two sisters, was sold away from her father into Missouri. This group was settled on the Chapman farm at Kingsville in Johnson County, near the present town of Holden. Mrs. Ross recalls that her slave duties were many— as picking up the thread, spools, thimbles, or anything that might drop as her mistress sewed, weeding the garden, washing the dishes, and many others. She said, "If I became sleepy during the day, I was sent into the yard to pick feathers from the grass." . . .

Then in October 1861, before Lincoln issued his famous emancipation Proclamation, there came an opportunity to reach the free State of Kansas. Jim Lane and his Union soldiers came through that section of the country making this offer to the Negro slaves: "I'll take you if you want to go, or you may stay if you wish." Mrs. Ross, her mother, her uncle, two sisters, and a brother went along with Jim Lane, as did many other slaves. With these soldiers, they finally reached Kansas, after watching Kingsville, Harrisonville, and many other Missouri towns burn.

The full text of Document 4.2.13 is available on the CD-ROM.

4.2.14

Photograph of Whitfield Ross

Courtesy of Janice Ross Lorenz, great-granddaughter of Margaret Elizabeth Ross

4.2.15

Photograph of Margaret E. Ross

Courtesy of Janice Ross Lorenz, great-granddaughter of Margaret Elizabeth Ross

LESSON 3

Who Should Fight?

African Americans played an active, critical role in the Civil War, which eventually abolished slavery. Yet this undeniable fact has not always been woven into the historical narrative. In his 1928 biography of General Grant, W. E. Woodward states that, "the American Negroes are the only people in the history of the world, so far as I know, that ever became free without any effort of their own." Many articles and books have since appeared that provide ample evidence to the contrary. Thanks in large part to the movie *Glory*, even most nonhistorians know that, indeed, there were African American soldiers who fought bravely for the Union. Yet the story of the wartime contributions of African Americans is much richer, more complex, and ultimately more inspiring than a movie can capture.

The more one listens to the voices and learns the stories of African American soldiers, the more one can appreciate, as historian James McPherson does in *The Negro's Civil War:* "perhaps . . . most important of all, the contribution of Negro soldiers helped the North win the war and convinced many Northern people that the Negro deserved to be treated as a man and an equal" (p. xi).

All told, 178,985 African American enlisted men served in black regiments, accounting for about 10 percent of the total Union army. Approximately 33,000 came from the northern free states, 42,000 from the border, slaveholding states of Delaware, Maryland, Missouri, and Kentucky; 20,000 from Tennessee; 24,000 from Louisiana; 18,000 from Mississippi; and 40,000 from the remaining states of the Confederacy. Although it was government policy not to commission African American soldiers, white commanding officers did make commissions on their own in recognition of extraordinary bravery and leadership. In 1862, General Butler commissioned seventy-five black officers in three regiments. (General Banks later replaced most of them with white officers.) Six sergeants in the Massachusetts 54th and 55th Regiments were promoted to lieutenant, and all three officers of an independent battery of light artillery in Kansas were African American.

African American regiments participated in 449 engagements, 39 of which were major battles. In the final year of the war, African American troops fought in every major Union campaign except Sherman's invasion of Georgia. The black soldiers distinguished themselves in these battles with their bravery, ferocity, and camaraderie. Secretary of War Stanton told a newspaper reporter that in the fighting around Petersburg, Virginia, in June of 1864, "the hardest fighting was done by black troops. The forts they stormed were the worst of all" (as quoted in McPherson, p. 223). Such accounts can be found concerning almost every engagement these soldiers had with the enemy.

One of the hardest battles African Americans fought, however, was in overcoming government reluctance to allow them to enlist at all. At the war's start, African Americans flooded local and federal governments with impassioned offers to volunteer. Yet the Union refused their offers. Initially, northern leaders insisted that the war was being fought for the Union, not against slavery. It was a white man's war. In addition, they were concerned about alienating border states. Few commanders or politicians made the connection between slavery and secession. They ignored the degree to which the South's war effort depended on free black and slave labor. Public prejudices in the North outweighed abolitionist pleas. Indeed, many white men insisted that they would refuse to fight next to a black man.

Yet African Americans forced a gradual shift in Union policy with their own actions and bravery. Escaped slaves flocked to Union lines, offering their assistance. General Benjamin Butler was one of the first to recognize the military significance of giving asylum to these people. Labeling them "contraband of war," he put them to use in supporting his army. Other commanders followed suit. The Confiscation Acts of 1861 and 1862 followed, providing for the seizure of all property used "in aid of rebellion," including slaves. Yet although the government and general public were starting to recognize that attacks on slavery needed to be a central part of the war effort, the majority still balked at the idea of African American soldiers.

Despite this reluctance to enlist African Americans, battlefront realities brought pressure from below to change Union policy. In 1862, several Union generals took the initiative to enlist black men. Positive reports of the bravery and discipline of the black men by their commanders began to dispel the white public's image of the African American as an inferior man, unsuited for soldiering. The northern public was also growing more war-weary. The war, which most had expected to be over quickly, was now in its second year; accounts of the horrifying reality of battle were displacing the romantic images many had first held. Casualties were mounting rapidly, and the numbers of volunteers were dropping off dramatically. It was in this atmosphere that Congress passed two acts on July 17, 1862, which paved the way for African American enlistment. Part of the Second Confiscation Act empowered the President "to employ as many persons of African descent as he may deem necessary and proper for the suppression of the rebellion." The second, the Militia Act, repealed a provision of a 1792 law that banned black men from the military and authorized the mobilization of blacks in "any military or naval service for which they may be found competent." In November 1862, the first South Carolina volunteers were mustered in, led by Thomas Wentworth Higginson, a Massachusetts abolitionist.

When Lincoln issued his Emancipation Proclamation in January 1863, the move to enlist black troops gained momentum. Northerners began to insist that black blood be shed as well as white blood in a war now being fought for black freedom. In early 1863, Secretary of War Stanton authorized the governors of Massachusetts, Rhode Island, and Connecticut to organize black regiments. Massachusetts Governor John Andrews, Frederick Douglass, and many other prominent abolitionists who had long been agitating for African American enlistment, quickly mobilized recruiting officers and soon mustered the Massachusetts 54th and then the Massachusetts 55th Regiments. Strikingly, Stanton refused a request by Ohio for a "corps d'Afrique." The Union was still not ready for widespread enlistment of black soldiers, so men from Ohio and other states had to travel to New England to volunteer.

Well-publicized accounts of the valor of African American troops in battles at Port Hudson and Millikens Bend, Louisiana, and at Fort Wagner, South Carolina, further shifted public opinion in favor of black enlistment. Draft resistance was also increasing among whites. The Enrollment Act of March 1863 allowed wealthy men to, in essence, hire a draft substitute for $300.

As states realized that black enlistees would be counted toward their state draft quotas, they requested—and were granted—authority to raise their own regiments. The War Department had institutionalized black enlistment with the establishment of the Bureau of Colored Troops in May 1863. By the end of October 1863, there were 58 African American regiments, with a total of 37,482 men, mustered in eight Northern states, including Maryland, seven Confederate states, and the District of Columbia.

Organizing Idea

There was great debate in the North over whether or not to enlist African American soldiers in the Union war effort. It took the combination of extreme war weariness in the North and of African American bravery in the war to bring about a policy shift toward enlistment.

Student Objectives

Students will:

- understand government policy toward African American enlistment at the start of the war and the reasons for this policy
- identify some of the reasons offered in support of African American enlistment
- recognize African American contributions during the war
- use what they learned in the documents to reflect upon the question: Does government lead the people or do people lead their government?

Key Questions

- What arguments were made for and against black enlistment in the war?

❖ What factors helped bring about a shift in government policy to allow black enlistment in the army?

Primary Source Materials

DOCUMENT 4.3.1: Letter from William A. Jones, a freeman in Ohio to Secretary of War Simon Cameron, November 18, 1861

DOCUMENT 4.3.2: Letter from Michigan black physician to Secretary of War Simon Cameron, October 30, 1861

DOCUMENT 4.3.3: "Fighting Rebels with Only One Hand," by Frederick Douglass, *Douglass' Monthly IV,* September 1861

DOCUMENT 4.3.4: Excerpts from a letter from Maryland's Governor Thomas H. Hicks to Secretary of War Simon Cameron, November 18, 1861

DOCUMENT 4.3.5: Excerpt from "The President and Colored Soldiers," *The Pacific Appeal,* September 27, 1862

DOCUMENT 4.3.6: Excerpt from "Negroes in the Army," *The Pacific Appeal,* September 27, 1862

DOCUMENT 4.3.7: Excerpts from a letter from General David Hunter to the House of Representatives, June 23, 1862

DOCUMENT 4.3.8: Excerpt from the Emancipation Proclamation, January 1, 1863

DOCUMENT 4.3.9: Photo of African American soldiers standing in front of what was once a slave auction house, Alexandria, Virginia, 1862

DOCUMENT 4.3.10: Illustration, "Colored troops, under General Wild, liberating slaves in Camden County, North Carolina," *Harper's Weekly,* January 23, 1864

DOCUMENT 4.3.11: Photo of 29th Regiment from Connecticut at Beaufort, South Carolina, 1864

DOCUMENT 4.3.12: Photo of Congressional Medal of Honor recipient Christian A. Fleetwood, on a carte de visite, 1884

DOCUMENT 4.3.13: Excerpts of Official Report from Colonel Thomas W. Higginson to Brigadier-General Saxton, Military Governor, &c., February 1, 1863

DOCUMENT 4.3.14: Excerpts from a letter by Lydia Maria Child, April 22, 1864

Supplementary Materials

ITEM 4.3.A: Additional vocabulary for primary sources

Vocabulary

artillery	degraded	fraternizing
cavalry	enlistment	regiment

PART TWO: THE SOLDIERS' EXPERIENCE

Student Activities

Activity 1   **Engaging the Students—Who Leads Whom?**

Ask students to reflect on the question: Does government lead the people or do people lead the government? Have them provide evidence and explanations for their points of view. Tell students they will look at the Union policy toward enlisting African Americans in the Civil War and use what they learn to reflect on how that question should be answered regarding this historical issue.

Note: For the following activities, teachers may wish to divide the class into groups that will work on clusters of documents and share their findings with the class.

Activity 2   **Examination of Freedmen's Views**

Have students read the letters from freedmen (4.3.1. and 4.3.2) and Douglass' editorial (4.3.3). Then discuss these questions:

- Based on these documents, what was existing government policy on using African American troops?
- What reasons do the writers give as to why enlisting African American troops is a good idea?

Activity 3   **Analysis of Black Enlistment Issue**

Students should read the letter from the governor of Maryland (4.3.4) and articles from *The Pacific Appeal* (4.3.5 and 4.3.6) and address the following questions.

Document 4.3.4

- What happened at the Union army camp in Annapolis?
- Was the individual who sought refuge there a "servant"?
- What is Governor Hicks' attitude toward African Americans?
- What was the purpose of the letter? Do you read any message between the lines? On which side was Maryland?

Document 4.3.5

- Explain the statement "all that is done adversely to [the colored race] is so much done in support of traitors." Who are the traitors?
- Why, according to this article, is the president not enlisting black men?
- What does the writer suggest be done?

Document 4.3.6

- What were the prevailing opinions about what the "problems" might be should African Americans be allowed to enlist in the army?

❖ What does historical evidence suggest really happened when African Americans enlisted?

Understanding the Shift in Policy
Activity 4

After reading General Hunter's letter in response to a congressional inquiry (4.3.7) and the short excerpt from the Emancipation Proclamation (4.3.8), students should prepare a written summary, which includes discussion of the following points.

Document 4.3.7
❖ Why is General Hunter writing?
❖ What is the tone of his letter?
❖ How does he justify his actions?

Document 4.3.8
❖ Explain the change in the enlistment policy.

Reflecting on Images of African American Civil War Soldiers
Activity 5

Students should examine the images 4.3.9–4.3.12. As a group, have them brainstorm all the information they gather by looking at the documents. Have them consider the changes for African Americans. Ask them to consider what they thought they knew about black troops in the Civil War and what they now know. Students can also go online and read Christian Fleetwood's diary, in which he describes his actions during a battle in Richmond, Virginia, which led to his being awarded the medal (see *http://memory.loc.gov/ammem/aaohtml/exhibit/aopart4b.html*).

Reading of African American Soldiers in Action
Activity 6

Have students read Colonel Higginson's report (4.3.13) and Lydia Maria Child's letter (4.3.14). Both these documents make clear that the government had indeed shifted its policy toward enlistment of African American soldiers. Discuss these questions:

❖ How does Colonel Higginson describe the performance of his African American troops?
❖ What reasons does Colonel Higginson give for their exceptional performance?
❖ What reasons does Child's account suggest for a shift in attitude?
❖ How do these compare with your ideas about what could bring about a shift?

Essay—Reflecting on Causes of Policy Shift
Activity 7

Using information from the documents, students should write an essay explaining the reasons for the change in Union policy.

Activity 8: Class Discussion—Who Leads Whom?

- In this case, did the government lead the people or did the people lead the government?
- Some people see Lincoln as a master politician who was able to move the country through radical changes because of a keen insight into what to change and when the public could tolerate it. What do you think of this assessment? Where can you find information to help you answer the question?
- How much can the government push for dramatic shifts in society's values and structures? How much does it need to wait for the public to indicate its readiness to shift?
- Who do you think should take the lead in promoting social change, the government or the people?

Further Student and Teacher Resources

Berlin, Ira, Barbara Fields, Steven Miller, Joseph P. Reidy, and Leslie S. Rowland, eds. *Free at Last: A Documentary History of Slavery, Freedom, and the Civil War.* New York: The New Press, 1992.

Blatt, Martin H., Thomas J. Brown, and Donald Yacovone, eds. *Hope and Glory: Essays on the Legacy of the Fifty-Fourth Massachusetts Regiment.* Amherst: University of Massachusetts Press, 2001.

Bolden, Tonya. *American Patriots: the Story of Blacks in the Military from the Revolution to Desert Storm.* New York: Crown Publishers, 2003. (Gail Buckley's book, adapted for younger readers)

Brooks, Victor. *African Americans in the Civil War.* Philadelphia: Chelsea House, 2000.

Buckley, Gail. *Black Patriots: The Story of Blacks in the Military from the Revolution to Desert Storm.* New York: Random House, 2001.

Friedheim, William. *Freedom's Unfinished Revolution: An Inquiry Into the Civil War and Reconstruction.* New York: The New Press, 1996.

McPherson, James. *The Negro's Civil War: How American Negroes Felt and Acted During the War for the Union.* New York: Pantheon Books, 1965.

Websites

African Americans in the Civil War. University of North Texas, Denton, TX
www.hist.unt.edu/09w-acwd.htm
A useful list of links to relevant sites, including several with primary documents

Civil War Soldiers and Sailors System. National Park Service, Washington, DC
www.itd.nps.gov/cwss/
Access to a database of records about those who fought on both sides during the Civil War, along with records of regiments, battles, monuments, and other data

Contemporary Connection

⟶✠⟵

African Americans in the Armed Forces

The African American presence in the United States Armed Forces has been the subject of much controversy throughout the history of this country. Students might find it hard to believe that up until the Second World War, the military was, by law, segregated. Despite this fact, black Americans have consistently filled integral roles in wars to preserve American democracy and way of life.

In recent wars, with the stain of segregation washed from the Armed Forces, the true valor and leadership of African American troops has been seen by all. Hundreds of black soldiers were awarded medals of honor and purple hearts during and after the Korean War. Vietnam was the first war in which black men, in large numbers, were promoted to the status of lieutenant, colonel, and general. In the past, they had been able to obtain rank only in the very lowest levels of leadership. During Desert Storm, Army General Colin Powell served as Chairman of the Joint Chiefs of Staff. In 2001, he became the first African American appointed U.S. secretary of state. In 2003, with many black servicemen and women serving in the armed forces, Powell played a key role in planning for the war against Iraq.

What do students know about African Americans from their communities who have served in the military? This topic presents a wonderful opportunity for students to create an oral history project by interviewing local people about their experiences in the armed services—going back as far as World War II if possible. (This information is from: Gail Buckley, *American Patriots: The Story of Blacks in the Military from the Revolution to Desert Storm.*)

Primary Source Materials for Lesson 3

4.3.1

Letter from William A. Jones, a freeman in Ohio to Secretary of War Simon Cameron, November 27, 1861

Oberlin O. Nov. 27th 1861

Sir:— Very many of the colored citizens of Ohio and other states have had a great desire to assist the government in putting down this injurious rebellion.

Since they have heard that the rebels are forming regiments of the free blacks and compelling them to fight against the Union as well as their Slaves. They have urged me to write and beg that you will receive one or more regiments (or companies) of the colored of the free States to counterbalance those employed against the Union by Rebels.

We are partly drilled and would wish to enter active service amediately.

We behold your sick list each day and Sympathize with the Soldiers and the government. We are confident of our ability to stand the hard Ships of the field and the climate So unhealthy to the Soldiers of the *North*.

To prove our attachment and our will to defend the government we only ask a trial. I have the honor to remain your humble Servant.

Wm A. Jones

4.3.2

Letter from Michigan black physician to Secretary of War Simon Cameron, October 30, 1861

Battle Creek {*Mich.*} Oct. 30th 1861

Dear Sir: Having learned that in your instructions to Gen. Sherman you authorized the enrollment of colored persons I wish to solicit the privilege of raising from five to ten thousand free men to report in sixty days to take any position that may be assigned us (sharp shooters preferred). We would like white persons for superior officers. If this proposition is not accepted we will if armed & equipped by the government fight as guerillas.

Any information or instructions that may be forwarded to me immediately will be thankfully received and implicitly obeyed.

A part of us are half breed Indians and legal voters in the state of Michigan. We are all anxious to fight for the maintenance of the Union and the preservation of the principles promulgated by Pres Lincoln and we are sure of success if allowed an opportunity.

In the name of God answer immediately. Yours fraternally

G.P. Miller M.D.

4.3.3

"Fighting Rebels with Only One Hand," by Frederick Douglass, *Douglass' Monthly IV*, September 1861

Why does the Government reject the negro? Is he not a man? Can he not wield a sword, fire a gun, march and countermarch, and obey others like any other? . . . If persons so humble as we can be allowed to speak to the President of the United States, we should ask him if this dark and terrible hour of the nation's extremity is a time for consulting a mere vulgar and unnatural prejudice? . . . We would tell him that this is no time to fight with one hand, when both are needed; that this is no time to fight with only your white hand, and allow your black hand to remain tied . . . while the Government continues to refuse the aid of colored men, thus alienating them from the national cause, and giving the rebels the advantage of them, it will not deserve better fortunes than it has thus far experienced. Men in earnest don't fight with one hand, when they might fight with two, and a man drowning would not refuse to be saved, even by a colored hand.

The full text of Document 4.3.3 is available on the CD-ROM.

4.3.4

Excerpts from a letter from Maryland's Governor Thomas H. Hicks to Secretary of War Simon Cameron, November 18, 1861

Annapolis [Md.], Novermber 18 1861

My Dear Sir A circumstance occurred at one of the Camps in the vicinity of Annapolis, viz. the Massachusetts 25th Regiment, to day, that, calls forth this communication.

The facts, I briefly, but, correctly narrate. I was called on by a Mr. Tucker of this (Anne Arundel) County, who stated that he had a servant, that had left him, and taken refuge in the encampment of the 25th Regt. from Mass, that he had repaired to the ground so occupied, and that Co. Upton, Commanding, at first refused, afterward, said to him go through and see if your man is here, he proceeded, but a short distance, when he *Tucker* was surrounded by quite a number, menaced him, and, applied opprobious Epithets; such as Negro stealer, Negro catchers, and that the negro was better than he, the master was &c &c until he was obliged to leave the ground, without looking after his servant. Now whilst in this there is amusement, I must say there was much to provoke, and altho I care little for what becomes of the negroes, yet these things produce bad feeling and bad effect. . . .

[Y]ou are fully aware sir of the difficulty we have had in Md. things are working right now. let us have no stumbling blocks placed in our way—I care nothing fir the Devlish Nigger difficulty, I desire to save the union, and will cooperate with the Administration in everything tending to that important result, that is proper. I know the difficulties surrounding us, and do not wish to mingle and mix up too much with the main design.

I labored to have Md. roll up a majority, that would smother secessionism. We have given them a heavy dose. I hope to strike them another blow by an early convocation of the Legislature of our state, and if we can keep away outside Issues, and all things foreign from the one, true, great design of all Patriots, we shall save the Union—I will attend early to your Telegram recd this evening. I have the Honor to be with great respect yr obt Servant

Tho. H. Hicks

4.3.5

Excerpt from "The President and Colored Soldiers," *The Pacific Appeal*, September 27, 1862

The President has declared that he will not accept any regiment of colored men as soldiers. They must all be accepted as laborers. There have been several declarations made in the course of this our war which it has been found expedient to revise or forget, and this declaration of war against the black man may soon be found to belong to the list. The President may do his best and his worst to uphold and maintain a wretched prejudice, but it will be all in vain. The war that is directed against the colored race is neither more nor less than a war in behalf of the rebels, and all that is done adversely to them is so much done in support of traitors. Their services are scornfully rejected by persons who have been unable to do much for their country. . . .

The full text of Document 4.3.5 is available on the CD-ROM.

4.3.6

Excerpt from "Negroes in the Army," *The Pacific Appeal*, September 27, 1862

One of the most consistent and liberal journals in this State is the Tuolumne *Courier*. Speaking on the war in question it says:

We know that an opinion prevails that such troops would be unreliable, and that the race is cowardly; which is but a senseless prejudice, derived from our slavery associations, and will not be concurred in by any military or naval commander who has had any experience with them. The French and the English have always used black troops, and so have we ourselves. They were in all the campaigns under Washington, Greene, and Lafayette, and in the cruisings under Paul Jones, Truxton, Decator, Barry, Perry, and McDonough. The testimony of history unquestionably is, that the negroes bore their full proportion of the trials and sacrifices of the Revolutionary War. We may pooh! at the idea—as many doubtless will—but we cannot get over the fact that so history has recorded it.

We know very well that the negroes of Hayti defeated and drove off four of Napoleon's armies, sent under able generals, to subjugate that Island; and we know, also, that Gen. Jackson had two companies at the battle of New Orleans, whom he afterwards complimented in the highest terms, by proclamation, for their steadiness under fire, and their commendable bravery. . . .

4.3.7

Excerpts from a letter from General David Hunter to the House of Representatives, June 23, 1862

Port Royal S.C. June 23rd 1862

Sir: I have the honor to acknowledge the receipt of a communication from the Adjutant General of the Army, dated June 13th 1862, requesting me to furnish you with information necessary to answer...

1st Whether I had organized or was organizing a regiment of "Fugitive Slaves" in this Department.

2nd Whether any authority had been give to me from the War Department for such organization;—and

3rd Whether I had been furnished by order of the War Department with clothing, uniforms, arms, equipments and so forth for such a force?...

To the First Question therefore I reply that no regiment of "Fugitive Slaves" has been, or is being organized in this Department. There is, however, a fine regiment of persons whose late masters are "Fugitive Rebels,"—men who everywhere fly before the appearance of the National Flag, leaving their servants behind them to shift as best they can for themselves.—So far, indeed, are the loyal persons composing this regiment from seeking to avoid the presence of their late owners, that they are now, one and all, working with remarkable industry to place themselves in a position to go in full and effective pursuit of their fugacious and traitorous proprietors.

The full text of Document 4.3.7 is available on the CD-ROM.

4.3.8

Excerpt from the Emancipation Proclamation, January 1, 1863

And I hereby enjoin upon the people so declared to be free to abstain from all violence, unless in necessary self-defence; and I recommend to them that, in all cases when allowed, they labor faithfully for reasonable wages.

And I further declare and make known, that such persons of suitable condition, will be received into the armed service of the United States to garrison forts, positions, stations, and other places, and to man vessels of all sorts in said service.

And upon this act, sincerely believed to be an act of justice, warranted by the Constitution, upon military necessity, I invoke the considerate judgment of mankind, and the gracious favor of Almighty God. In witness whereof, I have hereunto set my hand and caused the seal of the United States to be affixed.

Done at the city of Washington, this first day of January, in the year of our Lord one thousand eight hundred and sixty-three, and of the Independence of the United States of America the eighty-seventh.

By the President: ABRAHAM LINCOLN
WILLIAM H. SEWARD, Secretary of State

4.3.9

Photo of African American soldiers standing
in front of what was once a slave auction house,
Alexandria, Virginia, 1862

Library of Congress

4.3.10

Illustration, "Colored troops, under General Wild, liberating slaves in Camden County, North Carolina," *Harper's Weekly*, January 23, 1864

University of North Carolina, North Carolina Collection

4.3.11

Photo of 29th Regiment from Connecticut at Beaufort, South Carolina, 1864

Library of Congress

4.3.12

Photo of Congressional Medal of Honor recipient Christian A. Fleetwood, on a carte de visite, 1884

Library of Congress

4.3.13

Excerpts of Official Report from Colonel Thomas W. Higginson to Brigadier-General Saxton, Military Governor, &c., February 1, 1863

No officer in this regiment now doubts that the key to the successful prosecution of this war lies in the unlimited employment of black troops. Their superiority lies simply in the fact that they know the country, while white troops do not, and moreover, that they have peculiarities of temperament, position, and motive which belong to them alone. Instead of leaving their homes and families to fight they are fighting for their homes and families, and they show the resolution and the sagacity which a personal purpose gives. It would have been madness to attempt, with the bravest white troops, what I have successfully accomplished with the black ones. Everything, even to the piloting of the vessels and the selection of the proper points for cannonading, was done by my own soldiers. . . .

The full text of Document 4.3.13 is available on the CD-ROM.

4.3.14

Excerpts from a letter by Lydia Maria Child, April 22, 1864

Capt. Wade, of the U.S. Navy, who bought a house for his wife in this town [Wayland, Massachusetts], has been a bitter pro-slavery man, violent and vulgar in his talk against abolitionists and "niggers." Two years ago, he was for having us mobbed because we advocated emancipating and arming the slaves. He has been serving in the vicinity of N. Orleans, and has come home on a furlough, an outspoken abolitionist. He not only says in private; but has delivered three lectures in town, in which he has publicly announced the total change in his sentiments since he has had "an opportunity to *know* something on the subject." A few days ago, he was going in the cars from Boston to Roxbury, when a colored soldier entered the car. Attempting to seat himself, he was repulsed by a white man, who rudely exclaimed, "I'm not going to ride with niggers." Capt. Wade, who sat a few seats further forward, rose up, in all the gilded glory of his naval uniform, and called out, "Come here, my good fellow! I've been fighting alongside of people your color, and glad enough I was to *have* 'em by my side. Come and sit by *me*." Two years ago, I would not have believed such a thing possible of him. So the work goes on, in all directions.

The full text of Document 4.3.14 is available on the CD-ROM.

LESSON 4

The Decision to Enlist

The African American men who enlisted in the Union forces were disillusioned by the racism and oppression they found in the army. For one, they received less pay than white soldiers. A white soldier received $10 a month plus a $3.50 allowance for clothes; a black soldier had $3.00 for clothes subtracted from his $10 pay. Black soldiers, community leaders, and many white sympathizers, including white officers of the regiments, vociferously protested this injustice, but Congress did not grant equal pay until June 15, 1864. Even then, they did so unequally—the order was retroactive to January 1, 1864, for black soldiers who had been enslaved but retroactive to the time of enlistment for those who had been free on April 19, 1861. This differentiation created a painful dilemma for regiments comprised of both free men and freedmen. Colonel E. N. Hallowell of the Massachusetts 54th worked out a solution that allowed a soldier to solve the problem of proving freedom before April 1861. Even though he may have been enslaved at the time, a black man could swear that he "owe[d] no man unrequited labor on or before the 19th day of April, 1861." This became known as the "Quaker Oath" and was copied by several other officers of black regiments.

African American soldiers were also given much greater fatigue duty than white soldiers. They often found themselves relegated to the myriad labor tasks involved with sustaining a war effort. To many, it seemed that they had exchanged one slave master for another. On June 14, 1864, the War Department issued a directive to end this practice, but it still continued in many places. In addition, African American soldiers endured taunts and physical attacks from racist soldiers and officers. For those who came from Confederate and border states, joining up meant exposing their still-enslaved families to abuse as reprisal from angered owners. Even though the U.S. government promised protection to these families, it was not always willing or able to follow through on that promise. Finally, African American soldiers faced much greater danger if captured by Confederate forces.

On May 1, 1863, the Confederate Congress authorized President Jefferson Davis to have captured African American troops "put to death or be otherwise punished at the discretion" of a military tribunal. African American soldiers were to "be delivered to the authorities of the State or States in which they shall be captured to be dealt with according to the present or future law of such State or States," meaning death or sale into slavery.

There were several well-publicized incidences of atrocities committed against captured black troops, including what became known as the massacre at Fort Pillow. Fort Pillow was a Union outpost on the Mississippi River. On April 12, 1864, it was captured in an attack by Confederate troops led by General Nathan Bedford Forrest. Almost three hundred soldiers, the majority of them black, were murdered after they had surrendered, an act that outraged the North and underscored the particular dangers facing black soldiers. Indeed, "Remember Fort Pillow" became a rallying cry for African American soldiers, who in many cases preferred to fight to the death rather than risk capture.

That African American soldiers helped the Union win the war cannot be denied. More significant, perhaps, is the profound impact that their valor had on black and white attitudes. Echoing the sentiments of many white soldiers who fought with black men, an officer of the 22nd U.S. Colored Infantry wrote to a Philadelphia newspaper: "The problem is solved. The Negro is a man, a soldier, a hero . . ." (quoted in McPherson, p. 224). And, as Thomas Long, a soldier in Colonel Higginson's 1st South Carolina Volunteers, observed: "If we hadn't become soldiers, all might have gone back as it was before . . . suppose you kept your freedom without enlisting in this army; your children might have grown up free and been well cultivated so as to be equal to any business, but it would have been always flung in their faces—'Your father never fought for his own freedom'—and what could they answer? Never can say that to this African Race any more" (quoted in Mullane, p. 236).

Organizing Idea

Once the federal government changed its policies to allow African American enlistment, the actual decision to enlist became a very personal one. Unlike many white soldiers, African American men were not drafted into the army, they volunteered. They and their families had to weigh their personal passions against the very real dangers that enlistment entailed.

Student Objectives

Students will:

- ❖ use a range of documents to identify the positive and negative aspects of enlisting for African American men
- ❖ reflect on the strategies used by different people in their efforts to persuade others of their points of view, including choice of language and appealing to emotions
- ❖ recognize that there was a range of experiences among African American men and, thus, a range of attitudes toward enlisting

PART TWO: THE SOLDIERS' EXPERIENCE

❖ practice decision-making skills by using what they learn in the documents to decide whether they would have joined up
❖ develop critical thinking skills by evaluating the soundness of their classmates' reasoning

Key Questions

❖ What realities influenced African American men in their decisions to enlist or not in the Union war effort?
❖ What did enlistees stand to gain and lose by joining?

Primary Source Materials

DOCUMENT 4.4.1: Rhode Island Recruitment Poster for African American Soldiers

DOCUMENT 4.4.2: Excerpts from a letter to the editor, *The Weekly Anglo-African*, October 19, 1861

DOCUMENT 4.4.3: Excerpt from Henry M. Turner, in which he identifies reasons for enlistment, *Christian Recorder*, February 7, 1863

DOCUMENT 4.4.4: Frederick Douglass supporting enlistment, *Douglass' Monthly V*, March 1863

DOCUMENT 4.4.5: Series of three photos entitled: "Contraband, Recruit, Veteran," *Harper's Weekly*, May 4, 1867

DOCUMENT 4.4.6: Series of three photos entitled "A typical Negro: Gordon, under medical inspection; Gordon as he entered our lines; Gordon in his uniform as a U.S. soldier," *Harper's Weekly*, July 4, 1863

DOCUMENT 4.4.7: Illustration, "An incident in the Battle of the Wilderness—the rebel Generals Bradley Johnson and E. Stuart taken to the rear by Negro cavalry," *Leslie's Illustrated Newspaper XVIII*, June 4, 1864

DOCUMENT 4.4.8: Description of violence toward an African American soldier in Washington, D.C., *Christian Recorder*, June 20, 1863

DOCUMENT 4.4.9: Excerpt from letters sent home by Capt. Charles P. Bowditch of the Massachusetts 55th, 1863

DOCUMENT 4.4.10: Letter from a private in the Massachusetts 54th to his sister, printed in the *Christian Recorder*, March 5, 1865

DOCUMENT 4.4.11: A letter from a Missouri slave woman to her soldier husband, Dec. 30, 1863

DOCUMENT 4.4.12: Letter from the Superintendent of the Organization of Tennessee Black Troops Brigadier General Chetlain to Illinois Congressman E. B. Washburn, April 14, 1864

DOCUMENT 4.4.13: Letter from the Superintendent of the Organization of Kentucky Black Troops Col. James S. Brisbin to Brigadier General L. Thomas, the Adjutant General of the Army, Oct. 22, 1864

Supplementary Materials

ITEM 4.4.A: Additional vocabulary lists for primary sources

Vocabulary

brigade	cavalry	Rebel
broadsides	fatigue duty	recruit

Student Activities

Engaging the Students

Activity 1

Put the recruiting poster (4.4.1) on an overhead. Discuss these questions:

- What is the poster asking? To whom is it directed?
- To what emotions is the poster appealing? What techniques does it use to call up these emotions? Point to specific words or phrases as evidence.
- Is it effective? Would it persuade you to join if you were an African American at that time? Explain.
- What is not said on the poster? Why do you think it is not there?

Reflection on Turner's and Douglass' Appeals for African American Enlistment

Activity 2

Documents 4.4.3 and 4.4.4 were originally spoken arguments. Ask two students to read them to the class. Give the students a few minutes to familiarize themselves with the documents. Be sure to give the context for each document before the student speaks and make sure that students know who each of these men is. After the Turner speech, discuss the following:

- To what point was Turner responding? What do you think the protester meant when he said, "Do you suppose I am going to leave my home and comforts to be killed for nothing?"
- What did Turner want people to do? What reasons did he give for why this was the right decision?
- To what emotions was Turner appealing? How did he do this?

After the Douglass speech, discuss these questions:

- To what "unjust and ungenerous barrier" was Douglass referring?
- What did Douglass want people to do? What reasons did he give for why this was the right decision?
- To what emotions was Douglass appealing? How did he do this?
- Were these men convincing? Would you join?

Activity 3   **Deciding Whether to Enlist**

1. Have students look through Documents 4.4.2 and 4.4.5–4.4.13. As they do, they should keep a list of plusses and minuses of enlisting for African American men. Ask students to annotate their lists so they can tell from which document particular plusses or minuses came (to facilitate class discussion later). Students could do this activity individually, in pairs, or in groups.

   Note: There are many documents for students to look at. If time or focus is a concern, one suggestion is that the teacher set a minimum goal, e.g., that everyone (whether an individual, pair, or group) look at five documents at least. The teacher should distribute the documents so that each document is looked at by someone, even if no one group looks at all the documents. Then, before doing the next step, the class should make a list on the board of plusses and minuses of enlistment, with each individual or group being the expert on particular documents. Thus, everyone is privy to the information in all documents without having to read each one.

2. Have students decide, either individually or in their groups, whether they would have been persuaded to join the army if they were an African American man at the time. Ask them to provide at least three concrete reasons for their decision. They should ground their reasons in the information from the documents provided.

   Students could read their decisions to the class, and the class could then discuss the soundness of their reasons or

   students could debate joining or not, with one or two volunteers speaking for each side. Again, the class could discuss the soundness of their reasons.

3. Use the following question for discussion:

   - What conditions in a man's life might have influenced his decision to join the army or not (e.g., whether he lived in a border state or not, his family or employment situation, education level, personal history . . .)?

Activity 4   **Writing Extensions—To Enlist or Not**

Ask students to place themselves in the early 1860s and then to write a journal entry where they weigh the decision to enlist. Alternatively, ask students to write a persuasive letter to a brother or a close friend in which they try to convince them to enlist or not.

Creative Extensions

Activity 5

Invite students to create a poster without words that expresses the opposite point of view to the one they took in their writing assignment (Activity 4).

Further Student and Teacher Resources

Berlin, Ira, and Leslie S. Rowland, eds. *Families and Freedom: A Documentary History of African-American Kinship in the Civil War Era.* New York: Pantheon Books, 1976.

Berlin, Ira, Barbara Fields, Steven Miller, Joseph P. Reidy, and Leslie S. Rowland, eds. *Freedom: A Documentary History of Emancipation, 1861–1867, Series II, The Black Military Experience.* New York: Cambridge University Press, 1982.

"Blacks and the Military," *Footsteps,* October 2003.

Buckley, Gail L. *American Patriots: The Story of Blacks in the Military from the Revolution to Desert Storm.* New York: Random House, 2003.

Clinton, Catherine. *The Black Soldier: 1492 to the Present.* Boston: Houghton Mifflin, 2000.

Friedheim, William. *Freedom's Unfinished Revolution: An Inquiry Into the Civil War and Reconstruction.* New York: The New Press, 1996.

Gooding, James Henry. *On the Altar of Freedom: A Black Soldier's Civil War Letters from the Front.* Edited by Virginia M. Adams; foreword by James M. McPherson. Amherst: University of Massachusetts Press, 1991.

McPherson, James. *The Negro's Civil War: How American Negroes Felt and Acted During the War for the Union.* New York: Pantheon Books, 1965.

Mullane, Deidre. *Crossing the Danger Waters: Three Hundred Years of African American Writing.* New York: Anchor Books/Doubleday, 1993.

Music Connection

No one knows who added the stanzas about radical abolitionist John Brown (see Sourcebook 3, Lesson 16) to the chorus of "Glory, Glory, Hallelujah." It's believed it was a Union army soldier. "John Brown's Body" became the "unofficial theme song for black soldiers," writes Eileen Southern. Col. Thomas W. Higginson of the 54th Massachusetts Regiment described the singing of black troops and wrote "First [they sang] 'John Brown,' of course." After students listen to the song (available on the CD-ROM), ask them to identify what would make this song popular with black soldiers in the Civil War.

Contemporary Connection

⇥✠⇤

Integration of the Military

In 1944 the War Department outlawed discrimination in transportation vehicles on Army bases. Soon after this ruling, Lieutenant Jackie Robinson, who within a few years would become the first African American to break the color bar in major league baseball, refused to sit in the back of a bus on his Texas military base. For doing this, Robinson was court-martialed, but in the end all charges were dropped and the case was dismissed. His action was just one of many acts by African American soldiers and veterans who successfully challenged the discrimination they faced. Their confidence and perseverance would be a driving force for the Civil Rights Movement of the 1950s and 1960s.

The Marine Corps is a good example of how quickly the military integrated. At the start of the Korean War, African Americans made up 1.5 percent of the Marine Corps, and nearly half of them served as stewards. At the close of the war, the Marine Corps was approaching full integration. The last segregated unit was disbanded and full integration was achieved in 1954, the same year that the Supreme Court struck down legally segregated schools.

By 2003, about 21 percent of the U.S. military was black. More black people than white people elect to remain in the military, in part because they believe, perhaps correctly, that the military provides a more egalitarian work environment and that their chances for color-blind success are greater.

Websites

The Civil War. Digital Schomburg Images of Nineteenth-Century African Americans. The Schomburg Center for Research in Black Culture, New York Public Library, New York
http://149.123.1.8/schomburg/images_aa19/cwar.cfm?zprx3992

Selected Civil War Photographs. Library of Congress, Washington, DC
http://memory.loc.gov/ammem/cwphtml/cwphome.html
More than 1,000 photographs of Union and Confederate officers and enlisted soldiers taken under the supervision of Mathew Brady

http://new.blackvoices.com/features/heritage/bl-heritage-military

Primary Source Materials for Lesson 4

4.4.1

Rhode Island Recruitment Poster for African American Soldiers

4.4.2

Excerpts from a letter to the editor, *The Weekly Anglo-African*, October 19, 1861

We have nothing to gain, and everything to lose, by entering the lists as combatants. In the first place the authorities have not called upon us. . . And suppose we were invited, what duty would we then owe to ourselves and our posterity? We are in advance of our fathers. They put confidence in the word of the whites only to feel the dagger of slavery driven still deeper into the heart throbbing with emotions of joy for freedom. We are not going to re-enact that tragedy. Our enslaved brethren must be made freedmen...We of the North must have all rights which white men enjoy; until then we are in no condition to fight under the flag which gives us no protection.

4.4.3

Excerpt from Henry M. Turner, in which he identifies reasons for enlistment, *Christian Recorder*, February 7, 1863

African American leaders across the north recruited men in their communities to join the fighting. Henry M. Turner, a lifelong fighter for racial justice, was at that time pastor of the Israel Bethel Church in Washington, D.C. Turner would later become the first African American chaplain in the Civil War. In response to one of Turner's recruitment efforts, one black man asked, "Do you suppose I am going to leave my home and comforts to be killed for nothing? I am not going to do any such thing." Turner replied:

Ah! That may do for that portion of our people who have no interest South; those who have no sympathy, no friends, no relations, no care, nor no desire for a triumph of freedom and our heaven-chartered rights. But those who have been taught by a God-blessed experience to abhor the monster slavery, and have felt its inhuman crushings, will look from a different standpoint. . . . The cry has long been, Give us the opportunity; show us a chance to climb to distinction, and we will show the world by our bravery what the negro can do, and then as soon as we are invited to stand on such a basis as will develop these interior qualities, for us to deride the idea and scornfully turn away, would be to argue a self-consciousness of incapacity.

4.4.4

Frederick Douglass supporting enlistment, *Douglass' Monthly V*, March 1863

Frederick Douglass was among the leaders encouraging African Americans to enlist. Though he chafed at the restrictions in place, which prevented blacks from becoming officers, he recruited actively. Two of his sons were the first recruits from New York to join the Massachusetts Fifty-fourth.

Shall colored men enlist notwithstanding this unjust and ungenerous barrier raised against them? We answer yes. Go into the army and go with a will and determination to blot out this and all other mean discrimination against us. To say we won't be soldiers because we cannot be colonels is like saying we won't go into the water till we have learned to swim. A half a loaf is better than no bread—and to go into the army is the speediest and best way to overcome the prejudice which has dictated unjust laws against us. To allow us in the army at all, is a great concession. Let us take this little the better to get more. By showing that we deserve the little is the best way to gain much. Once in the United States uniform and the colored man has a springing board under him by which he can jump to loftier heights.

The full text of Document 4.4.4 is available on the CD-ROM.

4.4.5

Series of three photos entitled: "Contraband, Recruit, Veteran," *Harper's Weekly*, May 4, 1867

The Granger Collection

4.4.6

Series of three photos entitled "A typical Negro: Gordon under medical inspection; Gordon as he entered our lines; Gordon in his uniform as a U.S. soldier," *Harper's Weekly*, July 4, 1863

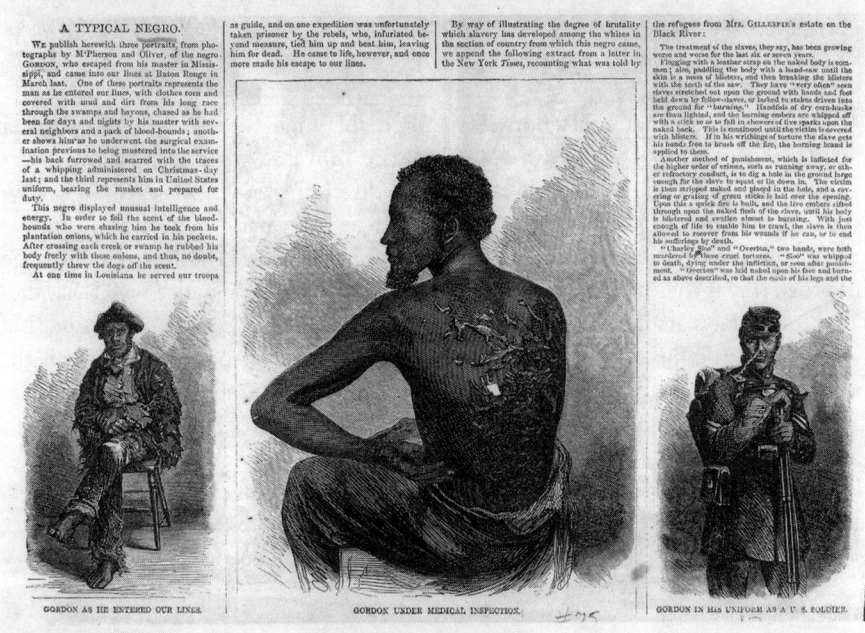

New York Public Library

4.4.7

Illustration, "An incident in the Battle of the Wilderness—the rebel Generals Bradley Johnson and E. Stuart taken to the rear by Negro cavalry," *Leslie's Illustrated Newspaper XVIII*, June 4, 1864

Library of Congress

4.4.8

Description of violence toward an African American soldier in Washington, D.C., *Christian Recorder*, June 20, 1863

Passing along 7th Street, a few evenings ago, I saw an excited rabble pursuing a corporal belonging to the 1st Colored Regiment, District vols., named John Ross. Among the pursuers, was a United States police officer. Ross protested against being dragged away by these ruffians, at the same time expressing his willingness to accompany the police officer to whatever place he might designate; claiming at the same time his (the police officer's) protection from his assailants. But, shameful to say, that officer, after he had arrested Ross, permitted a cowardly villain to violently choke and otherwise maltreat him. After the melee, the corporal received some pretty severe bruises, whether from the policeman's club or from the stones that were thrown by the mob, I will not say. He quietly walked to the central guard house with this conservator of the peace, amidst the clamoring of the mob, their yells and shouts of "Kill the black —— —— ——, "&c., &c., &c., "strip him, we'll stop this negro enlistment," &c., &c., &c.

The full text of Document 4.4.8 is available on the CD-ROM.

4.4.9

Excerpt from letters sent home by Capt. Charles P. Bowditch of the Massachusetts 55th, 1863

Folly Island, South Carolina, Aug. 12, 1863

Dear Charlotte,—Things are going on very quietly here in this camp. Details of men are made nearly every day for fatigue duty on Morris Island. They are erecting batteries on that island continually. . . . I expect to have to go off to-night on fatigue duty, since I have been off for some time and it is my turn. The only trouble about night duty is that it is hard to keep awake all night. The negroes are kept at work digging trenches, hauling logs and cannon, loading ammunition, etc.

The full text of Document 4.4.9 is available on the CD-ROM.

4.4.10

Letter from a private in the Massachusetts 54th to his sister, printed in the *Christian Recorder*, March 5, 1865

My dear sister, it is with pleasure that I write these few lines, to let you know how we are getting along. When we enlisted we were to get $13 per month, clothing and rations, and treatment the same as white soldiers; and now they want to cheat us out of what is justly due us, by paying us off with $10 per month, and taking three dollars out of that for clothing. . . . Why are we not worth as much as white soldiers? We do the same work they do, and what they cannot. We fight as well as they do. Have they forgotten James Island? Just let them think of the charge at Fort Wagner, where the colored soldiers were cruelly murdered by the notorious rebels. Why is it that they do not want to give us our pay when they have already witnessed our deeds of courage and bravery? They say we are not United States soldiers. They want to come around and say we are laborers. If we are laborers, how is it then we do soldiers' duty, such as stand guard, and do picket duty and form a line of battle when the long roll is beat? No, because we are men of color, they are trying to impose upon us. If we had staid at home with our fathers and mothers, wives and sisters, and dear ones at home, we could have received from $1.00 to $1.50 per day.

4.4.11

A letter from a Missouri slave woman to her soldier husband, December 30, 1863

My Dear Husband

I have received your last kind letter a few days ago and was much pleased to hear from you once more. It seems like a long time since you left me. I have nothing but troubles since you left. You recollect what I told you how they would do after you was going. They abuse me because you went and say they will not take care of our children and do nothing but quarrel with me all the time and beat me scandalously the day before yesterday. Oh I never thought you would give me so much trouble as I have got to bear now. You ought not to leave me in the fix I am in and all these little helpless children to take care of. I was invited to a party tonight but I could not go. I am in too much trouble to want to go to parties. The children talk about you all the time. I wish you could get a furlough and come to see us once more. We want to see you worse than we ever did before. Remember all I told you about how they would do me after you left—for they do worse than they ever did and I do not know what will become of me and my poor little children. Oh I wish you had staid with me and not gone till I could go with you for I do nothing but grieve all the time about you. Write and tell me when you are coming.

Tell Isaac that his mother come and got his clothes. She was so sorry he went. You need not tell me to beg any more married men to go. I see too much trouble to try to get any more into trouble too—Write me do not forget me and my children—Farewell my dear husband from your wife

Martha

4.4.12

Letter from the Superintendent of the Organization of Tennessee Black Troops Brigadier General Chetlain to Illinois Congressman E. B. Washburn, April 14, 1864

My Dear Sir

Before this letter reaches you, you will have learned of the capture of Fort Pillow and of the slaughter of our troops after the place was captured. This is the most infernal outrage that has been committed since the war began—Three weeks ago I sent up four companies of colored troops to that place under Major Booth a most brave and efficient [officer] who took command of the Post—Forest and Chalmers with about 3000 devils attacked the place on the 12th at 9 a.m. and succeeded after *three assaults*. And when both Major Booth and Major Bradford of the 13th Tennessee Cavalry had been killed, in capturing the place at 4 p.m.—We had in all less than 500 effective men, 2/3 of which were colored. The colored troops fought with desperation throughout. After the capture our colored men were literally butchered. Chalmers was present and saw it all—out of over 300 colored men, not 25 were taken prisoners and they may have been killed long before [this]. . . .

The full text of Document 4.4.12 is available on the CD-ROM.

4.4.13

Letter from the Superintendent of the Organization of Kentucky Black Troops Col. James S. Brisbin to Brigadier General L. Thomas, the Adjutant General of the Army, Oct. 22, 1864

On the march the Colored Soldiers as well as their white Officers were made the subject of much ridicule and many insulting remarks by the White Troops and in some instances petty outrages such as the pulling off the Caps of Colored Soldiers, stealing their horses etc. was practiced by the White Soldiers. These insults as well as the jeers and taunts that they would not fight were borne by the Colored Soldiers patiently or punished with dignity by their Officers but in no instance did I hear Colored Soldiers make any reply to insulting language used towards [them] by the White Troops. . . .

The full text of Document 4.4.13 is available on the CD-ROM.

Sustaining a Living

LESSON 5

As Union troops slowly secured Confederate territory, pressing questions emerged. What would happen to the southern economy? The war wrought terrible devastation on southern lives, which could be remedied only by the speedy recovery of plantation production. Despite the battles that raged throughout the South, behind Union lines, generals, government officials, and northern reformers sought to reconstruct the southern economy as quickly as possible. The question of African American labor emerged as a key component of this process. Still legally enslaved, most southern blacks existed in a netherworld between slavery and freedom. Their ambiguous status combined with the diverse interests of southern planters and Union officials to create a struggle over the very meaning of free labor. Southern planters desired an inexpensive and controllable labor force such as the one they had enjoyed under slavery. Government agents sought the speedy recovery of the cotton economy and the rapid settlement of slave refugees, who drained Union coffers and manpower. And the freedpeople had their own ideas about what free labor meant. At all points, the shape of black labor in Union-held territories resulted not from a centralized policy, but from a kaleidoscopic array of local conditions and concerns. Several models of wartime labor emerged.

On the Sea Islands off the South Carolina coast, which Union forces occupied early in the war, northern abolitionists and reformers swept down to claim land deemed "abandoned" by planters who had fled to the interior. Former slaves had been working the rich land in the planters' absence, choosing to grow food for local production and exchange rather than cotton for the market. In what became known as the "Port Royal Experiment" (after the main town on the islands), the freedpeople clashed with the abolitionists over the meaning of labor in freedom.

Another model emerged in southern Louisiana, which federal troops occupied in 1862. There, planters remained on the land, thus requiring the Union government to factor them into wartime labor arrangements. Under Union General Nathaniel Banks, the Union Army established a labor system that supplied slave refugees to southern planters. The army paid the African Americans in wages and functioned as the source of discipline. Planters were thus deprived of their traditional rights, but for African Americans the system looked much like slavery.

Other arrangements emerged as well, including efforts to lease abandoned plantations to northern investors. In many cases, freedpeople suffered injustices in seeking fair compensation for their labor. The historical record attests to instances of plantation owners, northern entrepreneurs, and even the Union government itself exploiting freedpeople's precarious economic and political positions for their own gain. In only a very few instances—such as the celebrated example of Sherman's Field Order No. 15, which granted tracts of land to freedpeople in Georgia—did African Americans become landowners themselves.

Far more typical was the experience of African Americans in southeastern Virginia, where government agents settled displaced black people on government-run tobacco and grain farms. Some of these freedpeople rented parcels of land from the government and farmed it on their own. Most, however, worked on a system of "share wages," in which they were paid for their labor with a portion of the crop. In this wartime free-labor arrangement, we can see the roots of the postwar system of sharecropping.

This lesson focuses on evidence of successful examples of free labor in southeastern Virginia, as told through the admiring eyes of Francis W. Bird, a prominent northern abolitionist. The document, Bird's testimony before a War Department commission, is one of many that reveal the respect that freedpeople's determined labor efforts inspired.

Organizing Idea

As the Union Army occupied Confederate states, the issue arose of how to address African American labor. No central policy was created; instead several approaches emerged.

Student Objectives

Students will:

- identify obstacles facing freedpeople seeking to sustain a living farming
- identify ways that the government supported free-labor efforts
- reflect on what constitutes success and use these criteria to evaluate whether these efforts were successful
- use the documents to try to pinpoint reasons for the success freedpeople did achieve

Key Questions

- What does the testimony of Francis Bird reveal about the obstacles that freedpeople faced in their efforts to work their own land?
- What strategies did freedpeople use to overcome these obstacles?

- What support did the government provide to these freedpeople?
- Based on the document, what might it take, from freedpeople and the government, to ensure the long-term success of free-labor efforts?

Primary Source Materials

DOCUMENT 4.5.1: Testimony by Francis W. Bird to the War Department commission recounting his tour of free-labor efforts in southeastern Virginia, Dec. 24, 1863

Supplementary Materials

ITEM 4.5.A: Additional vocabulary list for primary source

Student Activities

Engaging the Students—What Do We Do with the Plantations? *Activity 1*

Discuss the following with students: If you were a Union general, what would you do with plantations that you confiscated as the army moved through the South? Who might be the individuals affected by your decisions? What might it take to ensure the success of your policy? Briefly share and compare ideas.

Reading the Document *Activity 2*

Tell students that there was no coherent Union policy as to what to do with confiscated property. There was, however, a clear drive among freedpeople to own and work their own land. Explain that students will now look at a document that describes some of those efforts. Divide students into smaller groups and have them read Bird's testimony (4.5.1). As they read, each group should develop a list of the following:

a. obstacles facing freedpeople in their efforts to work the land

b. ways that the government provided support

c. any evidence of success of these efforts

When the groups have finished reading and making their lists, ask students to discuss in their groups whether they would call these efforts successful. What criteria are they using to define success?

Class Discussion of Freedpeople's Efforts *Activity 3*

Have groups report on their conclusions. Discuss these questions:

- Were these efforts successful? How did you define success?
- Which obstacles seemed most daunting? Why?

- What do you think accounts for the successes people did achieve, given the obstacles they faced?
- Do you think that these people would have been able to live out their lives on these farms? Explain.
- Bird said in his testimony that "All that is needed to establish . . . a truly loyal and prosperous community is that the men and women who have watered the soil with their tears and blood should be allowed to own it when they have earned it by their own labor." Do you agree? Should this be the basis of Union policy? What might be the cost of such a policy? What would be the cost of not following it?

Further Student and Teacher Resources

Berlin, Ira, Barbara Fields, Steven Miller, Joseph P. Reidy, and Leslie S. Rowland, eds. *Free at Last: A Documentary History of Slavery, Freedom, and the Civil War.* New York: The New Press, 1992.

Edwards, Cheryl, ed. *Reconstruction: Binding the Wounds.* Carlisle, MA: Discovery Enterprises, 1995.

Foner, Eric. *Reconstruction: America's Unfinished Revolution, 1863–1877.* New York: Harper and Row, 1988.

Friedheim, William. *Freedom's Unfinished Revolution: An Inquiry into the Civil War and Reconstruction.* New York: The New Press, 1996.

Hakim, Joy. *Reconstruction and Reform*, Book 7 in *A History of US.* New York: Oxford University Press, 1994.

Hansen, Joyce. *Bury Me Not in a Land of Slaves: African-Americans in the Time of Reconstruction.* Danbury, CT: F. Watts, 2000.

Pressly, Thomas. "Reconstruction in the Southern United States: A Comparative Perspective." *Magazine of History,* Vol IV, No. 1 (Winter 1989): 14–34.

Smith, John David. *Black Voices From Reconstruction, 1865–1877.* Brookfield, CT: Millbrook Press, 1996.

Smolinski, Diane. *The Home Front in the South.* Chicago: Heinemann Library, 2001.

Sterling, Dorothy, ed. *The Trouble They Seen: The Story of Reconstruction in the Words of African Americans.* New York: Da Capo Press, 1994.

Contemporary Connection

⸙

Reparations

Currently a serious legal effort is underway to obtain compensation from the U.S. government and certain corporations for the descendants of slaves. The Reparations Coordinating Committee includes lawyers and academics; factual research will document all claims made in court. The group seeks an apology from the U.S. government, as well as compensation in the form of special scholarship funds for African American students and funding for economic development and education projects in underserved black communities. Not all African Americans agree with this initiative, and even those who do agree acknowledge that getting compensation will take a long time. Ronald Walters, professor of political science at the University of Maryland, puts it this way, "What was taken away (during slavery) was the capacity to do institution building. It's really in this area that most of us believe we should work" (information from *Black Enterprise* magazine, June 2002).

Students can check with local media and online to find out the current status of the reparation efforts and perhaps stage a classroom debate on the issue.

Websites

Freedman and Southern Society Project. University of Maryland, College Park, MD
www.history.umd.edu/Freedmen/home.html
A documentary history of emancipation, 1861–1867

Southern Homefront, 1861–1865. Documenting the American South, University of North Carolina, Chapel Hill, NC
http://docsouth.unc.edu/imls/index.html

Video

Reconstruction: The Second Civil War, 2004, PBS DVD Video, 180 minutes. Available at www.pbs.org

Primary Source Materials for Lesson 5

4.5.1

Testimony by Francis W. Bird to the War Department commission recounting his tour of free-labor efforts in southeastern Virginia, Dec. 24, 1863

Q Were these people men women and children?
A Yes. It is also to be borne in mind that very few able bodied men are now employed upon these farms, nearly all of that class having been drawn either into the army or employed in other labor for the Government. Notwithstanding these drawbacks I think it is safe to say, that on all these farms the laborers have raised crops abundantly sufficient to support themselves and their families until the next harvest.

A portion of the farms are worked "to halves" as it is called, for the Government—the Government furnishing seed agricultural implements and horses and receiving one third or one half of the produce; another portion of the freedmen have managed entirely on their own account. I did not take accurate statistics of many of the Farms; and I was the less anxious to do this as the Superindents [sic] will very soon make reports in full of the results of the season. The facts in the cases of which I took notes are in entire accordance with the results upon the other farms, so far as I learned.

Here is the case of a farm carried on by Gibberty Davis—an old man 70 or 80 years of age. His wife is free. His master is a Captain in the rebel service. He is the only one remaining on the farm out of a gang of thirty slaves He has cultivated with the assistance of two boys who are free thirty acres on which they have raised, besides supporting themselves 250 Bushels of corn and 150 pounds of cotton. They were obliged to replant nearly the whole of the corn. Mr Davis said he should have had four or five hundred pounds of cotton but for the early frost. The corn is worth 90 cts pr bushel and the cotton perhaps 60¢ pr pound; showing that he has now more than enough left to support himself and family until the next crop. . . .

The full text of 4.5.1 is available on the CD-ROM.

LESSON 6

How to Rebuild the Union

By the end of 1863, Union troops were gaining ground. The Confederate army continued to fight aggressively, yet the North's enormous advantage in population and resources seemed to ensure its ultimate victory. Once victorious, how then would the United States deal with the rebellious states? To what extent would former rebels be welcomed back as participants in government? Although slavery in the Confederate states had been abolished with the Emancipation Proclamation in January 1863, what of the plantations and wealth which slave labor had created? To whom did they belong?

Both President Lincoln and Congress had ideas about how the nation should best move forward. Lincoln, in his "Proclamation of Amnesty and Reconstruction" (December 8, 1863) suggested a conciliatory stance toward the Confederate states. Congress, in its Wade-Davis Bill (July 8, 1864), showed a greater inclination to punish and exclude former rebels from the rights and responsibilities of citizenship. The two sides were at loggerheads. Although Lincoln's Proclamation fell within what he believed was his presidential power to pardon, Congress refused to admit representatives from reconstructed states. Lincoln, in turn, prevented the Wade-Davis Bill from becoming law by not signing it.

The lack of agreement on a vision for the postwar former Confederate states contributed to the explosive racial tensions that would test the nation during Reconstruction. This lesson introduces the students to the challenges the government faced following the Civil War.

Organizing Idea

As the war was drawing to a close, the federal government began to grapple with the questions of how to rebuild the union and who should be extended rights of citizenship. President Lincoln was also at odds with the Congress about how to treat the rebellious states once the war was over.

Student Objectives

Students will:

- ❖ understand that citizenship conveys both rights and responsibilities
- ❖ know the different positions held by President Lincoln and the Congress on granting citizenship to former rebels
- ❖ develop critical thinking skills by reflecting on which Reconstruction policy they feel was "best" for the nation and why

Key Questions

- ❖ What questions did Union leaders face as they decided how to allow former rebellious states and individuals to return to the Union?
- ❖ What were the positions held by President Lincoln and by Congress on readmitting former rebellious states into the Union?
- ❖ In what ways were their positions similar? In what ways were they different?

Primary Source Materials

DOCUMENT 4.6.1: President Lincoln's Proclamation of Amnesty and Reconstruction, December 8, 1863

DOCUMENT 4.6.2: Excerpt from the Wade-Davis Bill, July 8, 1864

DOCUMENT 4.6.3: President Lincoln's Second Inaugural Address, March 4, 1965

Supplementary Materials

ITEM 4.6.A: Additional vocabulary lists for primary sources
ITEM 4.6.B: Study Sheet 1
ITEM 4.6.C: Study Sheet 2

Vocabulary

amnesty	inaugural	provisional	reconstruction
citizenship	proclamation	reconciliation	treason

Note: Be sure to explain the concept of equal protection under the Constitution if students are not already familiar with it.

Student Activities

Engaging Students—How Should the Victorious Side Treat the Side That Lost?

Activity 1

Discuss with students: After a war, how should the victorious nation or "side" treat its conquered enemy? What circumstances should the victor take into account when deciding this (e.g., previous relationship, depth of injuries on both sides, goals for future relationship)?

Simulation—How to Restore the Union

Activity 2

Divide students into groups. Tell them that they are going to have a chance to answer the questions posed in Activity 1 for themselves, in the specific context of the Civil War. They are to place themselves in the summer of 1864. The original goal of the North had been to preserve the Union. When the North wins the war, how should the rebellious Confederate states be brought back into the Union? The federal government needs to decide how to deal with the former rebels. It needs to keep in mind both the cause and cost of the war as well as what is best for the nation's future. It also needs to keep in mind the range of people in the Confederacy: rebel officers and soldiers, noncombatants, freedpeople, Union loyalists, to name a few. In their groups, students should come up with their policy by answering the following questions on Study Sheet 1 (Item 4.6.B).

- What does an individual in the Confederate states need to do to regain U.S. citizenship?
- What will a person regain with citizenship (e.g., property, voting rights, right to hold office)?
- Who should not be allowed this opportunity to regain citizenship? (Who, if anyone, should be considered guilty of treason? Confederate soldiers? Officers? Government officials? Others?)
- Does everyone in a state need to abide by the guidelines you have established before a state may reenter the Union as an equal participant in the Union, entitled to the equal protection of the Constitution? If not everyone, then what percentage? Why?
- What will happen to formerly enslaved people?

When students have finished answering these questions, they should answer the reflection questions on the handout.

Reporting—Proposals for Reconciliation

Activity 3

Groups should report on their policies regarding the former Confederate states. As a class, discuss these questions:

- Which group's policy seems the best to you? Why?

- Can you anticipate any problems that might arise from any of the proposals? Explain.
- Which groups' policies seem more conciliatory? Which seem more geared toward punishment?
- Ask each group to share why they chose the tone they did.
- Did any groups run into conflicts as they tried to create their policy? What were the conflicts about?

Activity 4   **Exploring the President's and Congress' Proposals**

Tell students that they will now look at two documents laying out differing visions of what the policy toward the Confederate states should be: President Lincoln's Proclamation of Amnesty and Reconstruction (4.6.1) and Congress' Wade-Davis Bill (4.6.2). Hand out copies of Lincoln's Proclamation to half the groups and the Wade-Davis Bill to the other half. Have students read the documents and determine how the president and Congress answered the same questions they, the students, were just struggling with (Item 4.6.C).

Note: These are long, challenging documents. With support, students should be able to get the key ideas from the documents. Be sure to prepare students for this challenge. Tell them to focus on getting the information to answer the questions on the handout and not to worry about understanding every word and idea.

Depending on the class, there are several ways to have students read through the documents. One is for each group to take a particular part of each document and be responsible for summarizing it for the class and pulling out any answers to the handout questions contained within the section. Another is to have students within each group be responsible for a section and report to their group before the group reports to the whole class. To facilitate reading, Item 4.6.A identifies vocabulary words for each document. Teachers can either provide students with a list of words and definitions or assign individual students to look up words and build a class vocabulary list.

When groups are finished, have them share their results. Discuss these questions:

- What is similar about the two policies?
- What is different?
- Which one seems more conciliatory to you? How?
- Which do you think will be more successful at helping the nation heal and grow strong again as a union? Why?
- Whose rights are not well addressed, if at all, in the documents?

Activity 5   **Research Extensions**

- Both Lincoln and Congress assumed they had the power to decide policy toward the South. Look at the Constitution, Articles I and II, which lay out the powers of Congress and the President. Who do you think had the power? Who do you think should have had the power?

- Have students read President Lincoln's Second Inaugural Speech (4.1.4). Explore it for its content and style. In addition, follow up this lesson with questions that include: What is President Lincoln asking the North to do? Do you think that it is possible to "judge not, lest we be judged" and to move forward "with malice toward none, with charity for all" as Lincoln asks? Explain. Can you have a "lasting peace" without it being a "just" peace?

- After studying Reconstruction in the lessons that follow, return to Lincoln's Second Inaugural Speech. Having seen what was and was not accomplished during Reconstruction, reflect on how history might have been different if Lincoln had lived and had had a chance to try to move the nation toward his vision. Would he have been able to? Would it have been better? Worse? How?

- The class could examine any conflict, contemporary or historic, and explore what the terms of peace were, who decided them, and how "just and lasting" they were.

Further Student and Teacher Resources

Berlin, Ira, et al. *Slaves No More: Three Essays on Emancipation and the Civil War.* Cambridge, UK: Cambridge University Press, 1992.

Edwards, Cheryl, ed. *Reconstruction: Binding the Wounds.* Carlisle, MA: Discovery Enterprises, 1995.

Foner, Eric. *Reconstruction: America's Unfinished Revolution.* New York: Harper and Row, 1988.

Freedman, Russell. *Lincoln: a Photobiography.* New York: Clarion, 1987.

McKissack, Patricia C., and Frederick L. McKissack. *Days of Jubilee: The End of Slavery in the United States.* New York: Scholastic, 2003.

Smith, John David. *Black Voices from Reconstruction, 1865–1877.* Brookfield, CT: Millbrook Press, 1996.

Websites

Black History Pages: Reconstruction
blackhistorypages.com/Reconstruction/

Civil War and Reconstruction. History Matters: A U.S. History Course on the Web, a joint program of the American Social History Project, City University of New York, and the Center for History and New Media, George Mason University
http://historymatters.gmu.edu/
Access to hundreds of relevant sites and other resources for researching history

Contemporary Connection

※

African American Heritage Sites

By the late twentieth century, the National Park Service was committed to expanding their interpretation of African American heritage sites. The network of Underground Railroad sites is one example; another is the proposal before Congress to study certain sites in Beaufort County, South Carolina, relating to the Reconstruction era. In 2001, with the support of historian Eric Foner, the Reconstruction History Partnership—composed of local university and governmental entities—began to explore strategies for preserving and interpreting these sites. Among the sites are: the Penn School for former slaves on St. Helena Island, the Old Fort Plantation where African Americans assembled on January 1, 1863, to hear the reading of the Emancipation Proclamation, and the Beaufort Arsenal, where free slaves voted for the first time. Federal legislation, introduced in 2002 by Senator Ernest Hollings of South Carolina, has a broad base of support. However, there is no funding authorized as yet. There is opposition as well. At the March 2003 convention of the Sons of Confederate Veterans, a resolution was passed opposing any initiative to interpret Reconstruction sites in Beaufort County, South Carolina. Students might take a look at the website for this group (*www.scscv.com*) (click on Resolution Passes Unanimously) to understand the reasons for the opposition. Students can also contact the Washington offices of the legislators from South Carolina to discover the progress of the legislation.

Video

Reconstruction: The Second Civil War, 2004, PBS DVD Video, 180 minutes. Available at **www.pbs.org**

Primary Source Materials for Lesson 6

4.6.1

President Lincoln's Proclamation of Amnesty and Reconstruction, December 8, 1863

Therefore, I, Abraham Lincoln, President of the United States, do proclaim . . . to all persons who have, directly or by implication, participated in the existing rebellion, except as hereinafter excepted, that a full pardon is hereby granted to them and each of them, with restoration of all rights and property, except as to slaves and in property cases where rights of third parties shall have intervened, and upon the condition that every such person shall take and subscribe an oath inviolate, . . . [swearing to "faithfully support, protect, and defend the Constitution of the United States"]. . . .

And I do further proclaim, declare, and make known that whenever, in any of the States of Arkansas, Texas, Louisiana, Mississippi, Tennessee, Alabama, Georgia, Florida, South Carolina, and North Carolina, a number of persons, not less than one-tenth in number of the votes cast in such state at the Presidential election of the year A.D. 1860, each having taken oath aforesaid, and not having since violated it, and being a qualified voter by the election law of the State existing immediately before the so-called act of secession, and excluding all others, shall re-establish a State government which shall be republican and in nowise, contravening said oath, such shall be recognized as the true government of the State, . . .

The full text of Document 4.6.1 is available on the CD-ROM.

4.6.2

Excerpt from the Wade-Davis Bill,
July 8, 1864

Sec. 2. That so soon as the military resistance to the United States shall have been suppressed in any such state, and the people thereof shall have sufficiently returned to their obedience to the constitution and the laws of the United States, the provisional governor shall direct the marshal of the United States, as speedily as may be, to name a sufficient number of deputies, and to enroll all white male citizens of the United States, resident in the state in their respective counties, and to request each one to take the oath to support the constitution of the United States, and in his enrollment to designate those who take and those who refuse to take that oath, which rolls shall be forthwith returned to the provisional governor; and if the persons taking that oath shall amount to a majority of the persons enrolled in the state, he shall, by proclamation, invite the loyal people of the state to elect delegates to a convention charged to declare the will of the people of the state relative to the reestablishment of a state government subject to, and in conformity with, the constitution of the United States.

The full text of Document 4.6.2 is available on the CD-ROM.

4.6.3

President Lincoln's Second Inaugural Address,
March 4, 1965

With malice toward none, with charity for all, with firmness in the right as God gives us to see the right, let us strive on to finish the work we are in, to bind up the nation's wounds, to care for him who shall have borne the battle and for his widow and his orphan, to do all which may achieve and cherish a just and lasting peace among ourselves and with all nations.

The full text of Document 4.6.3 is available on the CD-ROM.

LESSON 7

Hopes and Obstacles

The year 1865 was momentous. The Civil War ended and the Thirteenth Amendment to the Constitution, abolishing slavery in the United States, was ratified, albeit under duress in the South. This freedom did not come to everyone at the same time or in the same form. As William Friedheim writes in *Freedom's Unfinished Revolution:*

> Emancipation happened in different ways and came in different forms. Some slaves seized freedom by sabotaging plantation production, escaping to Union lines, and joining the Union Army to fight for the liberation of their people. For others, freedom had to wait for Lincoln's January 1863 Emancipation Proclamation, for liberating northern armies, or for the ratification of the Thirteenth Amendment abolishing slavery in January 1865 (p. 173).

By 1865, four million former slaves were free Americans. What did it mean to be free? How varied were black responses to emancipation in the single year 1865? No one or even twenty documents can ever fully capture the responses, for every person had his or her own story of becoming free. Moreover, these subtle, yet powerful, responses were difficult to capture in documents. Friedheim explains:

> But once emancipation came, African Americans took the measure of freedom's boundaries, constantly pushing them outward. At freedom's first coming, they defied the physical and psychological barriers created by years of slavery. Discarding the symbols of their enslavement, many rejected names forced upon them by slavemasters and took new ones. Casting aside the drab garments of slavery, they wore new badges of freedom—brightly colored outerwear, fancy hats, ornate parasols, elegant veils.
>
> They held meetings without white permission, supervision, or presence—that is, without the probing eyes of a master or overseer. In everyday encounters, they challenged former masters, mistresses, and overseers. Such defiance was expressed in a variety of encounters—looking an ex-master straight in the eye, talking back to a plantation mistress, refusing to tip a hat or give way to whites on a sidewalk (p. 173).

The documents in this lesson will help orient students to what freedom meant for many African Americans in 1865 given their previous servitude and the reality of the world in which they now lived. This orientation should serve as a springboard for the subsequent exploration of Reconstruction.

Organizing Idea

The goal of this lesson is to allow students to experience a snapshot of responses to emancipation in the single year 1865 in order to get a sense of what freedom meant, some of the hopes freed people had, and the obstacles they faced.

Student Objectives

Students will:

- create a working definition of "freedom"
- learn about freedpeople's initial and varied responses to emancipation
- compare the reality of emancipation to an ideal: the gains that were made, the obstacles that existed, and the resources people could draw upon
- reflect upon the impact white intentions of emancipation had on the reality of emancipation
- practice the skill of making generalizations by synthesizing information from a range of documents

Key Questions

- What does it mean to be free?
- What expectations did African Americans have for being free?
- What did people gain with freedom?
- What obstacles or hardships did they face?
- How did the reality of freedom meet people's expectations?

Primary Source Materials

DOCUMENT 4.7.1: Image of *Forever Free*, sculpture by Edmonia Lewis, 1867

DOCUMENT 4.7.2: Excerpt from interview with former slave Felix Haywood, age 92, of San Antonio, Texas, "Like Freedom Was a Place"

DOCUMENT 4.7.3: Excerpt from interview with former slave Fred James, age 81, of Newberry, South Carolina, "When Christmas Came"

DOCUMENT 4.7.4: Excerpt from interview with former slave Simon Phillips, age 90, of Birmingham, Alabama, "What's Mine is Mine"

DOCUMENT 4.7.5: Excerpts from freedpeople's reactions to emancipation from *We Are Your Sisters: Black Women in the Nineteenth Century*, edited by Dorothy Sterling

DOCUMENT 4.7.6: A freedman's description of Norfolk, Virginia, 1865

DOCUMENT 4.7.7: Excerpts from an interview between African American ministers and lay leaders and Secretary of War Edwin M. Stanton and General William T. Sherman, Savannah, Georgia, January 12, 1865

DOCUMENT 4.7.8: Excerpts from a Protest Memorial sent to President Andrew Johnson, 1865

DOCUMENT 4.7.9: Advertisements seeking relatives in the *Colored Tennesseean*, Nashville, 1865

DOCUMENT 4.7.10: Letter from the wife of a Michigan black soldier to the Secretary of War, May 11, 1865

DOCUMENT 4.7.11: "Emancipation," a wood engraving by Thomas Nast, 1865

DOCUMENT 4.7.12: "Freedom to the Slaves," a print by Currier & Ives

Supplementary Materials

ITEM 4.7.A: Station 1, Worksheet for Documents 4.7.2–4.7.6

ITEM 4.7.B: Station 2, Worksheet for Documents 4.7.7 and 4.7.8

ITEM 4.7.C: Station 3, Worksheet for Documents 4.7.9 and 4.7.10

ITEM 4.7.D: Station 4, Worksheet for Documents 4.7.11 and 4.7.12

Vocabulary

emancipation	jubilee	petition	serfdom

Student Activities

Engaging the Students—Building a Working Definition of Freedom

Activity 1

Students should begin by writing their own definitions of the concept of freedom. They can follow this up by working in small groups to create posters depicting their thoughts on freedom.

Students then look at an image of Edmonia Lewis's sculpture *Forever Free* and research her biography and the subject of the statue. Students then answer the following:

- ❖ Define the "romantic ideal" of freedom that you think Lewis is expressing.
- ❖ Add to that definition ideas you consider part of "being free."
- ❖ Share your answers.

Activity 2 **Exploring Document Stations**

This activity is organized around the use of *stations*, with students moving in groups around the classroom to examine documents and other information displayed at four centers or stations. The order of the stations is not important; what is important is that each group completes each station. Typically, students need 15 minutes per station, but check for progress before having groups rotate from one station to the next. Students should complete the questions for each station on their handouts. Stations enable teachers to use walls, tables, and other spaces to display the materials effectively. In addition, the combination of time limits and a chance to move seem to increase student focus.

Handout: Stations Worksheet (Items 4.7.A–D) Explain to students that they will do a stations activity in which they will study documents from the year 1865, the year the Civil War ended and the Thirteenth Amendment abolishing slavery was enacted. They will use these documents to compare the ideals expressed by Lewis and by themselves with the reality of freedom as expressed by the people experiencing it. Prepare students for the appearance of the word "nigger" in the documents in station 1. Explain whose voices are heard through the documents and why this word would be included in these documents. If appropriate, give students a chance to share their thoughts and feelings on having to read this word in school.

Note: The questions for each station are listed here and are on the CD-ROM in supplementary materials, Items 4.7.A–D.

STATION 1: VOICES OF EX-SLAVES

Students read the recollections of freed slaves on emancipation (4.7.2–4.7.6) and respond to the questions.

- What did freedpeople gain with emancipation?
- What obstacles or hardships did freedpeople face?
- List the range of emotions expressed within these documents and the events or situations that sparked these emotions.
- How would you characterize the language and tone of these documents? What do they reveal to you about the authors?

STATION 2: FORMAL RESPONSES TO FREEDOM

Students read two excerpts from formal presentations to the U.S. government from leaders in the black community (4.7.7 and 4.7.8) and answer the following:

- How did Garrison Frazier define slavery? And freedom?
- List the examples of black community action as described in the document from Richmond, Virginia.

- What were the ways that the black community in Richmond had supported the Union war effort? At what cost?
- What expectations did these black leaders have of the U.S. government after the abolition of slavery? What relationship did they see between what they did during the war and these expectations?
- Who were the people who made these statements? How would you characterize the language and tone of these documents? What do they reveal to you about the authors?

STATION 3: SEARCH FOR FAMILY

Students look at the newspaper advertisements (4.7.9) and the letter to President Johnson (4.7.10) and then answer these questions:

- What were people asking for in these documents? Why weren't their families together in the first place?
- Why do you think that people used these two methods (newspaper advertisements and a letter to President Johnson)?
- What do these documents tell you about the gains and the obstacles that freedom brought blacks?

STATION 4: IMAGES OF EMANCIPATION DRAWN BY WHITE ARTISTS

Students look at the two images of emancipation by white artists with abolitionist sympathies (4.7.11 and 4.7.12) and answer the following questions:

- In Nast's celebration of emancipation, what did "being free" mean? List what he believed freed people gained, including what they were freed from.
- In both images, what did Abraham Lincoln's presence represent? In the eyes of the artists, who was responsible for black freedom?
- Look closely at Nast's "Emancipation." Do you see other suggestions that freedpeople were still dependent on whites? (Notice the posture of the soldier receiving pay and the roles of whites and blacks in the cotton field scene.)
- Look at the depiction of black families in the images. How did these artists believe emancipation had helped black families?

Discussion

Activity 3

- Discuss the answers that students have for each station. Where there are differences, encourage students to refer to the actual documents for evidence to support their answers.
- Compare the language of the documents in stations 1 and 2. What statement can students make about freedpeople's educational level based on this comparison?

- Compare the images of families in the engravings of station 4 with the searches for family in station 3. What connections are there between the attitudes represented in these sympathetic renditions of emancipation and the obstacles facing freedpeople identified in stations 1–3? Think about who the audience was for the engravings.
- What information do we now have which builds our understanding of what being free meant for African Americans in 1865? (Consider the following ideas: emotional responses blacks had to emancipation, the expectations people had of being free, what the reality of freedom was, and the resources within the black community that could help freedpeople face that reality.)
- What is not captured in the documents? (For example, can we hear the jubilation in the songs sung? Can we know the numbers of miles walked and people questioned in search of family members torn apart by slavery? Can we tell how people carried themselves when free as compared to when enslaved?) What else would students like to know? How would they go about finding the information?
- Several of the documents credit Abraham Lincoln with bestowing freedom on the enslaved. Based on what students have learned in this and preceding lessons, is this accurate? How did this belief begin? How and why did it persist?

Activity 4 Creative Extensions

- Based on information in the documents, respond in writing to the following statement: 1865 was a year of celebration for black people, because it was the year that they officially gained their freedom. They were ready to face the future.
- Thinking about Edmonia Lewis' and Thomas Nast's representations of emancipation and what students have learned in the previous documents, how would students express what being free meant for blacks in 1865? They

---

Music Connection

No one can quite imagine how African Americans who had lived their lives in bondage felt when the Thirteenth Amendment to the Constitution was ratified, freeing all enslaved people in the United States. Music selections in Sourcebooks 3 and 4 give a mere hint. In "Ring, Ring the Big Bell" (available on the CD-ROM), freedmen and -women celebrated the end of slavery. The plantation bell would no longer dictate when their workdays would begin and end. They also sang of filling their pockets with money from the plantation coffers—money earned from their labor. Students should listen to the song as well as others that speak to freedom ("Go Down Moses" and "Many Thousand Gone" in Sourcebook 3 and "Before I'd Be a Slave" in Sourcebook 4) to identify common themes.

may use artwork, drama, and/or voice (spoken or sung) to express themselves. Either way, they should explain what their representation means. (Use the descriptions accompanying both the Lewis and Nast pieces as models for describing the representations.)

Further Student and Teacher Resources

Berlin, Ira, Barbara Fields, Steven Miller, Joseph P. Reidy, and Leslie S. Rowland, eds. *Free at Last: A Documentary History of Slavery, Freedom, and the Civil War.* New York: The New Press, 1992.

Berlin, Ira, Marc Favreau, and Steven F. Miller, eds. *Remembering Slavery: African Americans Talk about their Personal Experiences of Slavery and Freedom.* New York: The New Press, 1990.

Botkin, B. A., ed. *Lay My Burden Down: A Folk History of Slavery.* New York: Delta, 1994.

Brink, Dean C. "What Did Freedom Mean? The Aftermath of Slavery as Seen by Former Slaves and Former Masters in Three Societies." *Magazine of History*, Vol IV, No. 1 (Winter 1989): pp. 35–46.

Collier, Christopher, and James Lincoln. *Reconstruction and the Rise of Jim Crow, 1864–1896.* New York: Benchmark, 2000.

Cruden, Robert. *The Negro in Reconstruction.* Englewood Cliffs, NJ: Prentice Hall, 1969.

Friedheim, William et al. eds. *Freedom's Unfinished Revolution: An Inquiry into the Civil War and Reconstruction* (American Social History Project). New York: The New Press, 1996.

Schleichert, Elizabeth. *Thirteenth Amendment: Ending Slavery.* Springfield, NJ: Enslow, 1998.

Smith, John David. *Black Voices from Reconstruction: 1865–1877.* Brookfield, CT: The Millbrook Press, 1996.

Sterling, Dorothy, ed. *We Are Your Sisters: Black Women in the Nineteenth Century.* New York: W. W. Norton & Co., 1984.

Video

Unchained Memories, Readings from the Slave Narratives. New York: HBO Video, 2003.

Website

The Thirteenth Amendment. FindLaw, West Publishing Company
   http://caselaw.lp.findlaw.com/data/constitution/amendment13/
   A detailed look at the Thirteenth Amendment and related documentation and explanations

Contemporary Connection

⇥✳⇤

Slave Narratives

First-person stories are necessarily subjective; those told through an interviewer bear the mark of that person's perspectives. Nevertheless, these stories provide rich sources of information. Used together with other sources, they help us create a deeper and more complete picture of the past. As first-person stories, slave narratives provide a singular way to understand the everyday experience of slavery and its aftermath.

In the 1930s, the Works Progress Administration (WPA), charged with administering public works in order to relieve national unemployment, and other smaller projects organized at both the federal and state levels collected more than 2,000 interviews with former slaves. Boxes of these materials were then shelved during World War II. With a few exceptions, the narratives went relatively untouched until the 1970s. At that time, the Library of Congress began work on the collection, work that will no doubt continue well into the twenty-first century.

Today, thanks to digital technology and the Internet, we all have access to more and more of this important history. See *Born in Slavery: Slave Narratives from the Federal Writers' Project, 1936–38* (*http://memory.loc.gov/ammem/amhome.html*). Students can explore the site, select excerpts from the interviews, and compile their own collection of former slaves' recollections of emancipation and Reconstruction.

Primary Source Materials for Lesson 7

<u>4.7.1</u>

Image of *Forever Free*, sculpture by
Edmonia Lewis, 1867

Born in 1845, Edmonia Lewis is believed to be the first woman sculptor of African American and Native American ancestry. Forever Free, *inspired by the Emancipation Proclamation, is her best known piece. The sculpture is made from marble.*

Howard University
Gallery of Art

4.7.2

Excerpt from interview with former slave
Felix Haywood, age 92, of San Antonio, Texas,
"Like Freedom Was a Place"

The end of the war, it come just like that—like you snap your fingers. . . . How did we know it! Hallelujah broke out—

> Abe Lincoln freed the nigger
> With the gun and the trigger;
> And I ain't going to get whipped any more,
> I got my ticket,
> Leaving the thicket,
> And I'm a-heading for the Golden Shore!

Soldiers, all of a sudden, was everywhere—coming in bunches, crossing and walking and riding. Everyone was a-singing. We was all walking on golden clouds. Hallelujah!

> Union forever,
> Hurrah, boys, hurrah!
> Although I may be poor,
> I'll never be a slave—
> Shouting the battle cry of freedom.

Everybody went wild. We all felt like heroes, and nobody had made us that way but ourselves. We was free. Just like that, we was free. . . .

The full text of Document 4.7.2 is available on the CD-ROM.

4.7.3

Excerpt from interview with former slave
Fred James, age 81, of Newberry, South Carolina,
"When Christmas Came"

I 'member when freedom come, Old Marse said, "You is all free, but you can work on and make this crop of corn and cotton; then I will divide up with you when Christmas comes." They all worked, and when Christmas come, Marse told us we could get on and shuffle for ourselves, and he didn't give us anything. We had to steal corn out of the cob. We prized the ears out between the cracks and took then home and parched them. We would have to eat on these for several days.

4.7.4

Excerpt from interview with former slave Simon Phillips, age 90, of Birmingham, Alabama, "What's Mine is Mine"

One day . . . a few niggers was sticking sticks in the ground when the massa come up.
"What you niggers doing!" he asked.
"We is staking off the land, Massa. The Yankees say half of it is ourn."
The massa never got mad. He just look calm-like.

"Listen, niggers," he says, "what's mine is mine, and what's yours is yours. You are just as free as I and the missus, but don't go fooling around my land. I've tried to be a good master to you. I have never been unfair. Now if you wants to stay, you are welcome to work for me. I'll pay you one-third the crops you raise. But if you wants to go, you sees the gate."

The massa never have no more trouble. Them niggers just stays right there and works. Sometime they loaned the massa money when he was hard pushed. Most of 'em died on the old grounds.

4.7.5

Excerpts from freedpeople's reactions to emancipation from *We Are Your Sisters: Black Women in the Nineteenth Century*, edited by Dorothy Sterling

We done heared dat Lincum gonna turn de niggers free Ole missus say dey warn't nothin' to it Den a Yankee soldier tole someone in Williamsburg dat Marse Lincum done signed de mancipation. Was winter time an' moughty cold dat night, but ev'ybody commence gittin' ready to leave. Didn't care nothin' 'bout Missus—was goin' to Union lines. An' all dat night de niggers danced an' sang right out in de cold. Nex' mornin' at day-break we all started out wid blankets an' clothes an' pots an' pans an' chickens piled on our backs, 'cause Missus said we couldn't take no horses or carts. . . .

The full text of Document 4.7.5 is available on the CD-ROM.

4.7.6

A freedman's description of Norfolk, Virginia, 1865

From the outset, whites thwarted efforts of freedpeople to create new lives.

In many of the more remote districts, individual planters are to be found who still refuse to recognize their negroes as free, forcibly retaining the wives and children of their late escaped slaves; cases have occurred not far from Richmond itself, in which an attempt to leave the plantation has been punished by shooting to death; and finally, there are a number of cases known to ourselves in the immediate vicinity in which a faithfull performance, by colored men, of the duties of labor contracted for, has been met by a contemptuous and violent refusal of the stipulated compensation!

4.7.7

Excerpts from an interview between African American ministers and lay leaders and Secretary of War Edwin M. Stanton and General William T. Sherman, Savannah, Georgia, January 12, 1865

Secretary of War Edwin M. Stanton and General William T. Sherman invited twenty African American leaders to meet with them to discuss the future of thousands of slaves now free as a result of General Sherman's military advances. Garrison Frazier, a Baptist minister, had been born in Granville County, North Carolina and was a slave until 1857, when he bought his freedom. The African Americans present chose him as their spokesman. The interview was reported in a New York newspaper the following month.

Second [Question]—State what you understand by Slavery and the freedom that was to be given by the President's proclamation.
Answer—Slavery is, receiving by *irresistible power* the work of another man, and not by his *consent*. The freedom, as I understand it, promised by the proclamation, is taking us from under the yoke of bondage, and placing us where we could reap the fruit of our own labor, take care of ourselves and assist the Government in maintaining our freedom.

The full text of Document 4.7.7 is available on the CD-ROM.

4.7.8

Excerpts from a Protest Memorial sent to President Andrew Johnson, 1865

On June 10, 1865, more than 3,000 African Americans gathered in the First Baptist Chruch of Richmond, Virginia, to listen as a "protest memorial" that had been sent to President Andrew Johnson on their behalf, was read aloud:

Mr. President,

None of our people are in the alms-house, and when we were slaves the aged and infirm who were turned away from the homes of hard masters, who had been enriched by their toil, our benevolent societies supported while they lived, and buried when they died, and comparatively few of us have found it necessary to ask for Government rations, which have been so bountifully bestowed upon the unrepentant Rebels of Richmond. . . . During the . . . Slaveholders' Rebellion we have been true and loyal to the United States Government; . . . We have given aid and comfort to the soldiers of freedom (for which several of our people, of both sexes, have been severely punished by stripes and imprisonment). We have been their pilots and their scouts, and have safely conducted them through many perilous adventures.

The full text of Document 4.7.8 is available on the CD-ROM.

4.7.9

Advertisements seeking relatives in the *Colored Tennesseean*, Nashville, 1865

Earlier in the nineteenth century, when huge plantations were created in the Deep South, slave owners broke up thousands of African American slave families to fill the need for labor. Once emancipated, freedpeople began to search for sons, daughters, husbands, wives, and parents. African American newspapers frequently carried advertisements such as the ones below.

Saml. Dove wishes to know of the whereabouts of his mother, Areno, his sisters Maria, Neziah, and Peggy, and his brother Edmond, who were owned by Geo. Dove, of Rockingham county, Shenandoah Valley, Va. Sold in Richmond, after which Saml. and Edmond were taken to Nashville, Tenn., by Joe Mick; Areno was left at the Eagle Tavern, Richmond. Respectfully yours, Saml. Dove, Utica, New York!

The full text of Document 4.7.9 is available on the CD-ROM.

4.7.10

Letter from the wife of a Michigan black soldier to the Secretary of War, May 11, 1865

Detroit May 11 1865

    Dear sir I have taken the Liberty to write you afew lines which I am compelled to do I am colored it is true but I have feeling as well as white person and why is it the colored soldiers letters cant pass backward and fowards as well as the white ones Mr Stanton Dear sir I think it very hard We cant get any letters and I wish would please look in this matter and have things arranged so we can hear from our Husband if we cant see them I have not heard from my Husband in three months John Bailey is my husband he was Drum major of the 100th united States Colored Troops he went from Detroit he is the man Senator Howard wrote to you about last summer and tried to get afurlogh for him Then he was sick I have hurd through others he was very sick and since that I have heard he was dead if he is living I wish you would please grant him afurlogh to come home he was promised one when he went away and he has been gone over a year and I do wish you would be so kind as to let him come home if he is living I wish you would look oar your Books and see if he is alive I dont know who to write to only you President Lincoln is gone and he was our best friend and now we look to you and I hope God will wach over and protect you through this war

    Please write me as soon as you get this Direct to Mrs. Lucy Bailey 190 Congress Street 190

4.7.11

"Emancipation," a wood engraving by Thomas Nast, 1865

Drawn by Thomas Nast (1840-1902), the image was published in Harper's Weekly, *January 24, 1863.*

Library of Congress

4.7.12

"Freedom to the Slaves," a print by Currier & Ives

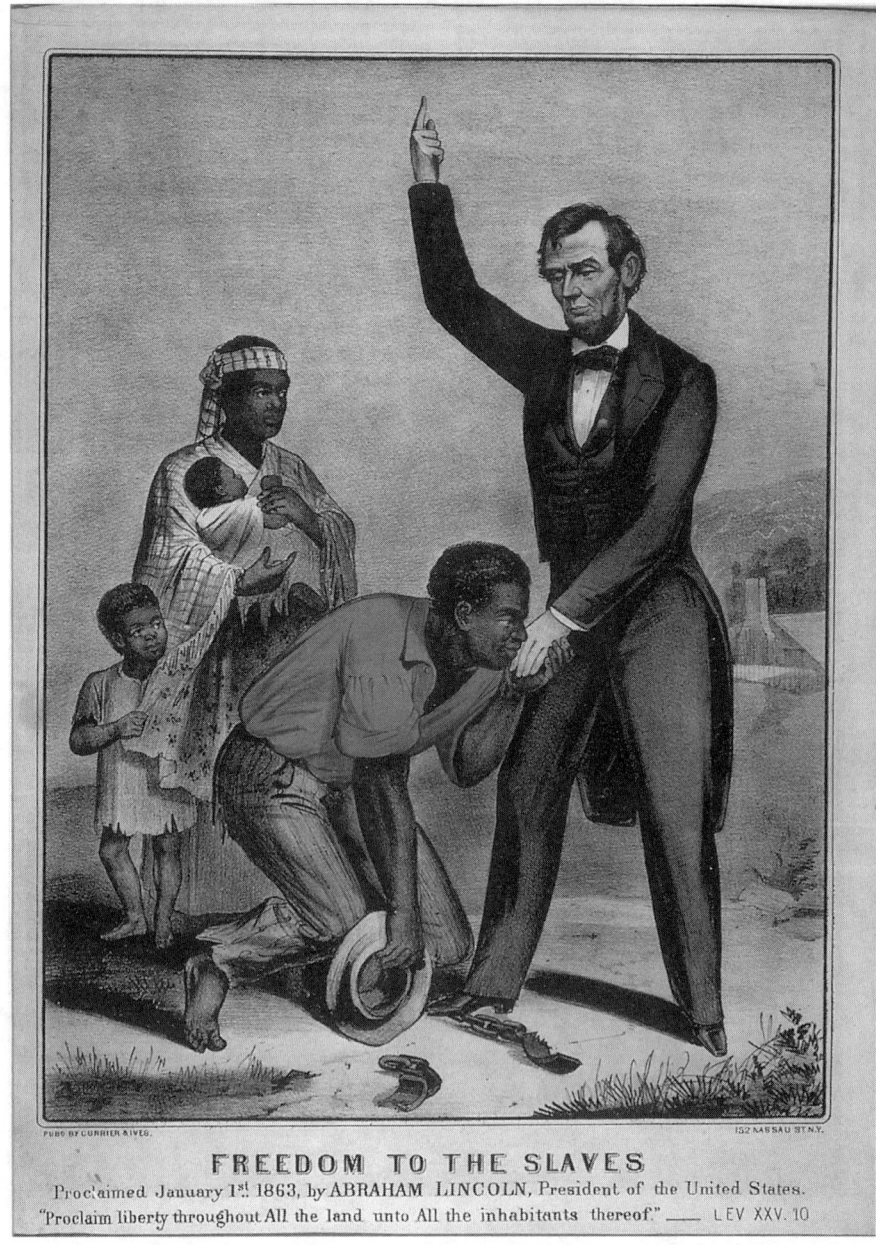

Rare Books and Special Collections Division,
McGill University Libraries, Montreal, Canada

LESSON 8

The Black Codes and Presidential Reconstruction

When Abraham Lincoln was assassinated in April of 1865, the presidency fell to his vice president, Andrew Johnson. Though a long-term veteran of American politics, Johnson lacked the tact and diplomatic skills of the relative political novice Lincoln. Many believed that the new president would impose harsh terms on the defeated South. "Treason must be made odious," the old Tennessee Unionist declared. Johnson surprised everyone, though, when he began pursuing a lenient policy toward former Confederates. An ardent supporter of states' rights, he balked at the idea—championed by some Republicans—that only a strong federal government could secure a just peace. Additionally, Johnson's innate racial prejudice led him to undermine efforts to enfranchise African American men. "White men alone," he said, "must manage the South."

Largely ignoring the will of Congress, Johnson set about to reconstruct the Union on his own terms. First, he granted amnesty to almost all former Confederate officials willing to take an oath of loyalty to the Union and accept the destruction of slavery. Only high officials and large property holders were exempt from this general amnesty, and even they could apply for pardons. Second, he instructed the former Confederate states to call conventions for the purpose of writing new state constitutions. To be readmitted into the Union, the states had only to ratify the Thirteenth Amendment (abolishing slavery) and repudiate secession. Importantly, Johnson said that only those who could vote before the Civil War could vote for delegates to these conventions. Effectively, Johnson had signaled that he had no intention of granting the vote to the freedpeople; he was giving back the southern state governments to those who had supported slavery and the rebellion.

The southern states held elections throughout the summer of 1865, and the constitutional conventions did their work quickly, thus ensuring that the southern states would be able to elect state legislatures and representatives and senators to Congress in November. The new state governments were dominated by white southerners, who had been against secession before the war. It might seem that this was good news for the freedpeople, but it was not. The antisecession whites were mostly nonslaveholders, who had envied the political power of wealthy slaveholders. Now that the slaves were free, these yeomen feared competing with freedmen for jobs and political power. Consequently, they cared little for guaranteeing the civil rights and liberties of newly freed African Americans.

The status of the freedpeople was quite tenuous immediately after the war. All knew that slaves had been freed—by the Confiscation Acts, Emancipation Proclamation, or Thirteenth Amendment. But what exactly was their civil status? Were they citizens? What would their citizenship entail? What rights did they possess? What kind of controls would the states be permitted to exercise over them?

The new state legislatures crafted a set of laws defining the status of the former slaves, which became known as *Black Codes*. These laws, which varied from state to state, granted blacks basic civil rights, such as the right to marry, sign contracts, hold property, and bring suit in court. The Black Codes thus tacitly accepted the freedpeople as legal citizens, endowed with both minimal rights and responsibilities. However, they also sought to reestablish planters' control over the labor of African Americans by replacing the dominance of the slave master with the equally oppressive oversight of the state.

So abusive were the Black Codes that northerners of all political hues stood up to reject them. They had few grounds on which to oppose the laws, however. After all, many northern states continued to withhold the vote from African American men, ban racial intermarriage, and exclude black people from the jury box. What many northerners could not tolerate, however, was the de facto reconstitution of slavery—the sinful institution at the root cause of the bloody Civil War. One incensed northern editor responded as follows to the imposition of Mississippi's onerous Black Code: "The men of the North will convert the State of Mississippi into a frog pond before they will allow such laws to disgrace one foot of the soil in which the bones of our soldiers sleep." To many, the Black Codes seemed to be the recalcitrant South's way of preserving in peace what it could not maintain through war.

The Codes did not remain long in force. The army and the Freedmen's Bureau struck down many of the most racially prescriptive provisions of the Codes. Some southern states, witnessing hostile public reaction to codes such as Mississippi's, wisely toned down their laws. And not too much longer after the Codes were passed in 1866, Republicans used the Military Reconstruction Acts to wrest control of the southern state governments. The new state governments thus created voided the Codes entirely. By 1868, the Black Codes were no longer a force in southern life.

Even though they did not remain long in force, the Black Codes played a critical role in the course of Reconstruction. They illustrated to the nation the commitment of the southern state governments to relegating the freedpeople to subordinate positions as semiservile laborers lacking basic civil rights. This intransigence worked against the interests of southern white supremacists, fueling resistance to presidential Reconstruction and inadvertently uniting the fractured Republican Party. The Republicans responded by pressing for a series of measures designed to guarantee African Americans' civil rights, notably the Civil Rights Act of 1866 and the Fourteenth Amendment.

Had the Black Codes never been passed, it is unlikely that the issue of civil rights for the freedpeople would have emerged so starkly on the agenda of national politics. As it was, the end of the Black Codes marked the waning of Johnson's influence over Reconstruction, and the emergence of Congress as the most crucial shaper of Reconstruction policy. It was clear to Congressional Republicans that, whatever the outcome of the war, the white South could not be trusted to determine the rights of the freedpeople on its own.

Organizing Idea

The Black Codes passed by southern state governments in 1866 sought to enshrine in law the freedpeople's semiservile status after emancipation. They generated Republican resistance and helped lead to the rise of Reconstruction directed by Congress.

Student Objectives

Students will:

- understand the origins and purposes of the Black Codes
- understand the typical features of the Black Codes
- understand reactions to the Black Codes
- understand the place of Black Codes in the politics of Reconstruction

Key Questions

- Who instituted the Black Codes?
- What were the purposes of the Black Codes?
- What kinds of responses greeted the Black Codes?
- What were the political consequences of the Black Codes?

Primary Source Materials

DOCUMENT 4.8.1: "Johnson's Proclamation of Amnesty," 1865

DOCUMENT 4.8.2: Excerpts from Alabama Black Codes, 1865

DOCUMENT 4.8.3: Excerpts from Florida Black Codes, 1865

DOCUMENT 4.8.4: Excerpts from Georgia Black Codes, 1865

DOCUMENT 4.8.5: Excerpts from Louisiana Black Codes, 1865

DOCUMENT 4.8.6: Excerpts from Maryland Black Codes, 1865

DOCUMENT 4.8.7: Excerpts from Mississippi Black Codes, 1865

DOCUMENT 4.8.8: Excerpts from North Carolina Black Codes, 1865

DOCUMENT 4.8.9: Excerpts from South Carolina Black Codes, 1865

DOCUMENT 4.8.10: Excerpts from Tennessee Black Codes, 1865

DOCUMENT 4.8.11: Excerpts from Texas Black Codes, 1865

DOCUMENT 4.8.12: Excerpts from Virginia Black Codes, 1865

DOCUMENT 4.8.13: Excerpts from "What's to Be Done with the Negroes?" by George Fitzhugh, *DeBow's Review* 1:6 (June 1866)

DOCUMENT 4.8.14: Excerpts from "The Rights of the Nation, and the Duty of Congress," by W. M. Grosvenor, *New Englander and Yale Review* 24:93 (October 1865)

DOCUMENT 4.8.15: "Address of the Colored State Convention to the People of the State of South Carolina," 1865

Supplementary Materials

ITEM 4.8.A: Additional vocabulary lists for primary sources

ITEM 4.8.B: Study Sheet on Black Codes

ITEM 4.8.C: Study Sheet—Responses to Black Codes

Vocabulary

affidavit	enfranchise	insurrection	scalawag
amnesty	entice	misdemeanor	vagrant
apprentice	induce	mulatto	warrant
carpetbagger			

Student Activities

Activity 1 **Reading and Analysis of Johnson's Proclamation of Amnesty**

As a class, read through Andrew Johnson's "Proclamation of Amnesty and Pardon" (4.8.1). What does this document reveal about Johnson's approach to Reconstruction? What might it suggest about his willingness to restore the master class to power? His willingness to protect the rights of African Americans?

Activity 2 **Analysis of the Black Codes**

Divide the class into seven groups. Each will work on the Black Codes (4.8.2–4.8.12) of one or two states:

1. Mississippi
2. South Carolina
3. Texas
4. Florida and Tennessee

5. Alabama and North Carolina
6. Maryland and Virginia
7. Louisiana and Georgia

Each group should read through the assigned documents together, completing the "Study Sheet on Black Codes" (Item 4.8.B) provided with this assignment.

Upon completing the study sheet, groups should report back to class on their findings. As a class, discuss:

- ❖ What kinds of strictures did the Black Codes impose on black lives?
- ❖ What were some possible reasons for imposing the Black Codes?

Responses to the Black Codes

Activity 3

Divide the class into three groups, with each one assigned one of three documents: "What's to Be Done with the Negroes?" (4.8.13), "The Rights of the Nation, and the Duty of Congress" (4.8.14), and the "Address of the Colored State Convention to the People of the State of South Carolina" (4.8.15). Each group should complete for its document the "Study Sheet: Responses to Black Codes" (Item 4.8.C). Groups may then report back to the class on what they found.

Creative Extensions

Activity 4

Students should express their thoughts regarding the Black Codes in one of several ways: a letter to the editor, a poem, a poster, or a broadside. Whichever medium students select, they should incorporate phrases and concepts directly from the primary sources.

Further Student and Teacher Resources

Collier, Christopher. *Reconstruction and the Rise of Jim Crow, 1864–1896*. New York: Benchmark Books, 1998.

Freman, David K. *Jim Crow Laws and Racism in American History*. Berkeley Heights, NJ: Enslow, 2000.

Wilson, Theodore Brantner. *The Black Codes of the South*. Montgomery: University of Alabama Press, 1965.

Wormser, Richard. *The Rise and Fall of Jim Crow: The African-American Struggle Against Discrimination, 1865–1954*. New York: Franklin Watts, 1999.

Website

Freedman's Bureau Records. National Archives and Records Administration, Washington, DC
www.archives.gov/publications/prologue/summer_1997_freedmens_bureau_records.html

Contemporary Connection

※

The Case of Affirmative Action

Although the Black Codes were defeated in the South, what followed in the years to come was not much better. Jim Crow laws were in place throughout the South and segregation in public facilities, public transportation, and education was enforced until these laws were overturned as a result of civil rights activism in the 1950s and 1960s. In these early years of the twenty-first century, a new civil rights movement is growing in strength and effectiveness focused now on the struggle for full educational integration and equality and on defeating the challenges to affirmative action programs.

Following a May 2002 victory—the Sixth Circuit Court of Appeals (Michigan) decision to uphold the University of Michigan Law School's affirmative action plan—the activist group BAMN sponsored a conference in Ann Arbor for college and high school students. The conference's purpose was to "organize and mobilize youth, ourselves and at the same time, reinvigorate and direct the establishment civil rights organizations to make the defense of affirmative action their highest priority." Featured speakers included Jesse Jackson, Robert Richardson Jr., an NAACP member and student activist, and Shanta Driver, a BAMN national organizer. The full name of BAMN is the Coalition to Defend Affirmative Action and Integration, and Fight for Equality By Any Means Necessary, thus placing this group of twenty-first-century young people in a direct line of black militants going well back into the eighteenth-century. The case was on its way to the Supreme Court.

Throughout the spring of 2003, the Supreme Court heard arguments from both sides. The case involved three students who challenged the lower court's decision and continued to accuse the University of Michigan and its law school of denying them admittance because they are white. They claimed that affirmative action admission policies are biased against nonminorities and that these policies violate the Constitution. During these hearings, thousands of affirmative action supporters carried signs as they protested outside the Supreme Court. More than 30 years after affirmative action policies were introduced in the 1960s, this issue is once again in the spotlight. In June 2003, the Supreme Court upheld the decision of the lower court to allow the University of Michigan Law School to consider race in its admission policies.

This issue is by no means over. Students can research arguments on both sides of the debate and arrive at their own opinions. How can historic wrongs be corrected with fairness in the present?

Primary Source Materials for Lesson 8

4.8.1

"Johnson's Proclamation of Amnesty," 1865

I, Andrew Johnson, President of the United States, do proclaim and declare that I hereby grant to all persons who have, directly or indirectly, participated in the existing rebellion, except as hereinafter excepted, amnesty and pardon, with restoration of all rights of property, except as to slaves and except in cases where legal proceedings under the laws of the United States providing for the confiscation of property of persons engaged in rebellion have been instituted; but upon the condition, nevertheless, that every such person shall take and subscribe the following oath (or affirmation) and thenceforward keep and maintain said oath inviolate, and which oath shall be registered for permanent preservation and shall be of the tenor and effect following, to wit:

The full text of Document 4.8.1 is available on the CD-ROM.

4.8.2

Excerpts from Alabama Black Codes, 1865

It shall be the duty of the sheriffs, justices of the peace, and other civil officers of the several counties in this State to report to the probate courts all minors under the age of eighteen years, who are orphans, without visible means of support, or whose parent or parents have not the means, or who refuse to provide for and support said minors, and thereupon it shall be the duty of said probate court to apprentice said minor to some suitable and competent person. If said minor be a child of a freedman, the former owner of said minor shall have the preference, when proof shall be made that he or she shall be a suitable person for that purpose.

The full text of Document 4.8.2 is available on the CD-ROM.

4.8.3

Excerpts from Florida Black Codes, 1865

If any negro, mulatto, or other person of color shall intrude himself into any religious or other public assembly of white persons, or into any railroad car or other public vehicle set apart for the exclusive accommodation of white people, he shall be deemed to be guilty of a misdemeanor, and upon conviction shall be sentenced to stand in the pillory for one hour, or be whipped, not exceeding thirty-nine stripes.

The full text of Document 4.8.3 is available on the CD-ROM.

4.8.4

Excerpts from Georgia Black Codes, 1865

Free persons of color shall be competent witnesses in all the courts of this State, in civil cases whereto a free person of color is a party, and in all criminal cases wherein a free person of color is defendant, or wherein the offence charged is a crime or misdemeanor against the person or property of a free person of color.

The full text of Document 4.8.4 is available on the CD-ROM.

4.8.5

Excerpts from Louisiana Black Codes, 1865

Failing to obey reasonable order, neglect of duty, and leaving home without permission will be deemed disobedience; impudence, swearing, or indecent language to, or in the presence of, the employer, his family, or agent, or quarreling and fighting with one another shall be deemed disobedience.

The full text of Document 4.8.5 is available on the CD-ROM.

4.8.6

Excerpts from Maryland Black Codes, 1865

If any free negro intermarry with any white woman, or if any white man shall intermarry with any negro woman, on conviction thereof such negro shall become a slave during life, and such white man or white woman who shall so intermarry shall become servants during the term of seven years.

The full text of Document 4.8.6 is available on the CD-ROM.

4.8.7

Excerpts from Mississippi Black Codes, 1865

Every civil officer shall, and every person may, arrest and carry back to his or her legal employer any freedman, free negro, or mulatto who shall have quit the service of his or her employer before the expiration of his or her term of service without good cause; and said officer and person shall be entitled to receive for arresting and carrying back every deserting employee aforesaid the sum of five dollars, and ten cents per mile from the place of arrest to the place of delivery; and the same shall be paid by the employer, and held as a set off for so much against the wages of said deserting employee.

All freedmen, free negroes and mulattoes in this State, over the age of eighteen years, found on the second Monday in January, 1866, or thereafter, with no lawful employment or business, or found unlawful assembling themselves together, either in the day or night time, and all white persons assembling themselves with freedmen, Free negroes or mulattoes, or usually associating with freedmen, free negroes or mulattoes, on terms of equality, or living in adultery or fornication with a freed woman, freed negro or mulatto, shall be deemed vagrants, and on conviction thereof shall be fined in a sum not exceeding, in the case of a freedman, free negro or mulatto, fifty dollars, and a white man two hundred dollars, and imprisonment at the discretion of the court.

The full text of Document 4.8.7 is available on the CD-ROM.

4.8.8

Excerpts from North Carolina Black Codes, 1865

It shall be the duty of the several courts of pleas and quarter sessions to bind out, as apprentices, all children of free negroes where the parents with whom such children may live do not habitually employ their time in some honest, industrious occupation.

The full text of Document 4.8.8 is available on the CD-ROM.

4.8.9

Excerpts from South Carolina Black Codes, 1865

Persons of color constitute no part of the militia of the State, and no one of them, without permission in writing from the district judge, or a magistrate, shall be allowed to keep a fire-arm, sword, or other military weapon.

Upon view of a misdemeanor committed by a person of color, any person present may arrest the offender and take him before a magistrate to be dealt with as the case may require. In case of a misdemeanor committed by a white person towards a person of color, any person may complain to a magistrate, who shall cause the offender to be arrested.

The full text of Document 4.8.9 is available on the CD-ROM.

4.8.10

Excerpts from Tennessee Black Codes, 1865

The provisions of this act shall not be so construed as to require the education of colored and white children in the same school.

The full text of Document 4.8.10 is available on the CD-ROM.

4.8.11

Excerpts from Texas Black Codes, 1865

Laborers, in the various duties of the household, and in all the domestic duties of the family, shall, at all hours of the day or night, and on all days of the week, promptly answer all calls and obey and execute all lawful orders and commands of the family in whose service they are employed. It is the duty of this class of laborers to be especially civil and polite to their employer, his family, and guests, and they shall receive gentle and kind treatment.

The full text of Document 4.8.11 is available on the CD-ROM.

4.8.12

Excerpts from Virginia Black Codes, 1865

The overseers of the poor are required, on discovering any vagrant within their respective counties, to make information thereof to any justice of the peace. Such justices shall, by warrant, order such vagrant to be employed in labor for any term not exceeding three months, and to be hired out for the best wages that can be procured.

The full text of Document 4.8.12 is available on the CD-ROM.

4.8.13

Excerpts from "What's to Be Done with the Negroes?" by George Fitzhugh, *DeBow's Review* 1:6 (June 1866)

We of the South would not find much difficulty in managing the negroes, at least tolerably well, if left to ourselves, for we would be guided by the lights of experience and the teachings of history, sacred and profane. . . . We should be satisfied to compel them to engage in coarse, common manual labor, and to punish them for dereliction of duty or nonfulfillment of their contracts with sufficient severity, to make the great majority of them useful, productive laborers.

We would take care of, in the most humane and ample manner, those, unable to provide for and take care of themselves; but they should be no charge or burden on the whites. By a tax on the labor of the strong and healthy negroes we would raise a sufficient fund to provide comfortable subsistence for the weak, infirm and aged negroes. We should treat them as mere grown-up children, entitled like children, or apprentices, to the protection of guardians or masters, and bound to obey those put above them, in place of parents, just as children are so bound.

The full text of Document 4.8.13 is available on the CD-ROM.

4.8.14

Excerpts from "The Rights of the Nation, and the Duty of Congress," by W. M. Grosvenor, *New Englander and Yale Review* 24:93 (October 1865)

But the freedom which the nation has solemnly promised is not a mere nominal emancipation. It involves full protection in all rights of person and property—absolute equality before the law. No man will pretend that such protection is possible, after the withdrawal of bureau superintendence [oversight of the Freedmen's Bureau] and military power, unless the testimony of the freedman is received in all the courts, and his rights of contract and property are placed upon the same basis as those of whites. Such provisions do not yet exist in any rebel state. Had the [state constitutional] conventions which have been held incorporated provisions of this nature into the new constitutions, there would have been some security at least, that the rights of the loyal blacks would not be forever at the mercy of every state legislature.

The full text of Document 4.8.14 is available on the CD-ROM.

4.8.15

"Address of the Colored State Convention to the People of the State of South Carolina," 1865

We ask for no special privileges or peculiar favors. We ask only for even-handed Justice, or for the removal of such positive obstructions and disabilities as past, and the recent Legislators have seen fit to throw in our way, and heap upon us.

Without any rational cause or provocation on our part, of which we are conscious, as a people, we, by the action of your Convention and Legislature, have been virtually, and with few exceptions excluded from, first, the rights of citizenship, which you cheerfully accord to strangers, but deny to us who have been born and reared in your midst, who were faithful while your greatest trials were upon you, and have done nothing since to merit your disapprobation.

We are denied the right of giving our testimony in like manner with that of our white fellow-citizens, in the courts of the State, by which our persons and property are subject to every species of violence, insult and fraud without redress.

The full text of Document 4.8.15 is available on the CD-ROM.

The "Misrepresented Bureau"

LESSON 9

During the Civil War and Reconstruction, the federal government intervened in the lives of individual Americans in ways unthinkable before the war. From the personal income tax of wartime to the civil rights acts of the Reconstruction period, the Union toyed with governmental innovations for two reasons: to win the war and to secure a just peace. Of all those experiments, none may be called more revolutionary than the establishment of the Freedmen's Bureau.

The origins of the Freedmen's Bureau lay in the efforts of African Americans themselves to become free. As Union troops slowly penetrated the Confederacy, enslaved African Americans ran to Union lines, requesting relief and offering service. Federal generals and policymakers confronted the dilemma created by their military success: what would happen to the territories conquered by the Union army and to those who had been living on them? The question become particularly urgent as Union success and federal policies of emancipation (Congress's Confiscation Acts and President Lincoln's Emancipation Proclamation) began reaping their rewards in thousands upon thousands of emancipated slaves.

Two sets of institutions took up the initial slack of emancipation: the Union army and northern missionary and benevolent societies. During the war, the Union army pioneered forays into the postemancipation world by administering lands taken from Confederates. Under the command of Union generals whose first desire was the reconstruction of a profitable cotton economy, southern lands were quickly reorganized on the basis of semifree black labor. Under wartime conditions in occupied Louisiana and the Mississippi Valley, freed African Americans became compulsory laborers on army-run cotton plantations. These plantations were neither economically successful nor satisfactory to the freedpeople, who experienced them as little better than enslavement.

The missionary societies—in particular, the American Missionary Association, which had been established in 1839 to aid the captives from the slave ship *Amistad*—proved slightly more benevolent. They focused their attention on relief and education, providing wartime refugees with clothing and rations, and beginning the great Reconstruction-era experiment in mass education. Like the Union army in the Mississippi, they, too, attempted to demonstrate the virtues of free labor by establishing their own plantations, notably in the Sea Islands of South Carolina and Georgia. The experiment foundered on the conflicting desires of freedpeople and northern missionaries. As Eric Foner explains in *Reconstruction: America's Unfinished Revolution*, "As Northern investors understood the term, 'free labor' meant working for wages on plantations; to blacks it mean farming their own land, and living largely independent of the marketplace" (p. 54).

Well before the war was won, then, the federal government recognized the scale of the challenge posed by the prospect of millions of newly freed African Americans. In 1863, the War Department formed the American Freedmen's Inquiry Commission, which was composed of three prominent antebellum abolitionists and reformers. Charged with touring the Union-held parts of the South and making recommendations regarding the fate of the freedpeople, the Commission argued for the creation of a government "Emancipation Bureau," which would oversee the transition to freedom. The Commission also urged the government to grant the freedmen full civil rights, including the right to vote. Finally, it argued that lands confiscated from rebel planters should be distributed to the freedpeople so they could become economically self-sufficient.

Not until March of 1865, with the war nearly won, did Congress establish a government agency of the type the Commission suggested. The new agency was called the Bureau for Freedmen, Refugees, and Abandoned Lands, but it was commonly known as the Freedmen's Bureau. Its first and only commissioner was General Oliver Otis Howard, a graduate of Bowdoin College and wartime Union commander. Howard, though a reformer sympathetic to the plight of the freedpeople (he was known as the "Christian General"), believed fervently that the Bureau was only a temporary expedient with a very limited role. Seeking to quell criticism of the Bureau, he said: "A man who can work has no right to support by government. No really respectable person wishes to be supported by others."

However, it was clear to all and sundry that the South was incapable of reconstructing its economy without the assistance of government. The southern economy was a shambles, its systems of credit and finance ruined. Its labor system—slavery—had been abolished. Nearly everyone believed the freed people were incapable of functioning effectively in a market economy without "instruction." The Freedmen's Bureau was the government's answer.

The first task of the Freedmen's Bureau was one of simple relief. Many thousands, both white and black, were left homeless and destitute by the war. The disruption of agricultural production left others dangerously close to starvation. Bureau officers throughout the South spent a good deal of their time distributing food rations and clothing to displaced southern refugees, both white and black. Through July of 1866, the Bureau issued over 13 million rations, most to African Americans. In addition, it supplied medical care to over half a million patients by 1869.

The second important undertaking of the Bureau was education for the freedpeople. By 1869, the Bureau had coordinated the establishment of more than three thousand free public schools in which 150,000 students enrolled. Chronically understaffed, the Bureau most frequently supplied the buildings for these schools, while northern missionary associations supplied the teachers. Education was the most lasting legacy of the Freedmen's Bureau; Bureau schools led to the creation of normal schools to train teachers as well as the great black colleges of Fisk, Howard, and Hampton.

A final and most important realm of Bureau activity lay in the administration of southern lands. Throughout the South during and shortly after the war, hundreds of thousands of acres of farmland lay vacant, abandoned by masters or destroyed by marching armies. Initially, the freedpeople and their supporters had hoped that some of this land might become their own. Advocates of land distribution argued that land confiscated from former Confederates would secure for the freedpeople a basis for independent living and protection from their former masters. Some early measures—such as General William Tecumseh Sherman's Field Order Number 15, which settled black people on lands abandoned by Georgia planters—seemed to suggest that widespread land distribution might become a reality.

But this was not to be. A lenient program of political amnesty combined with the innate conservatism of American society served to deny the freedpeople their own land. In the White House and halls of Congress, the nation's leaders upheld the sanctity of private property at the cost of the freedpeople's economic independence. Wartime measures to settle black people on abandoned land were rolled back, forcing the freedpeople to seek contracts from whites as tenant laborers or sharecroppers. In its role as mediator between former master and former slave, the Bureau accomplished some of its most important work. Bureau officers, often culled from the ranks of the Union army, oversaw the creation of thousands upon thousands of labor contracts.

Modern audiences may easily criticize the Bureau for its failings—in particular its failure to secure land distribution to the former slaves. Yet during its brief and fragile tenure, the Bureau came under constant attack from the forces of conservatism. If the Bureau failed to do all that it might have to secure a meaningful freedom for the formerly enslaved, it was not because a better vision of freedom did not exist but because the political system failed to put such a vision in place.

Organizing Idea

Charged with easing the transition from an economy rooted in slavery to one based on "free labor," the Freedmen's Bureau represented a remarkable initiative on the part of the Federal government to intervene in the lives of private citizens. It was restrained in its capacity to aid the freedpeople by contemporary economic and social ideology, which stressed the need for the central government to maintain only the most minimal impact on the lives of individuals.

Student Objectives

Students will:

- ❖ understand why the Federal government established the Bureau

- understand the range of functions the Bureau undertook
- understand the conflicts surrounding the Bureau, its work, and its continuation
- develop skills in reading cartoons and images from history
- think about the ways other generations debated events of the past

Key Questions

- Why did the Federal government establish the Bureau?
- Why did the Bureau not become a permanent government agency?
- To what kinds of criticism was the Bureau subject?
- In what ways did the Bureau help the freedpeople?
- Why did the freedpeople and their allies believe the Bureau was necessary?

Primary Source Materials

DOCUMENT 4.9.1: Broadside, "The Freedmen's Bureau!" 1866

DOCUMENT 4.9.2: Illustration, "The Freedmen's Bureau," *Harper's Weekly*, July 25, 1868

DOCUMENT 4.9.3: Excerpts from The First Freedmen's Bureau Act, 1865

DOCUMENT 4.9.4: Excerpts from The Second Freedmen's Bureau Act, 1866

DOCUMENT 4.9.5: Excerpts from "Rules and Regulations for Assistant Commissioners," 1865

DOCUMENT 4.9.6: A Bureau Contract, 1866

DOCUMENT 4.9.7: Excerpts from the testimony before Congress of J. D. B. DeBow, 1866

DOCUMENT 4.9.8: Excerpts from a report by Confederate General Wade Hampton to President Andrew Johnson, 1866

DOCUMENT 4.9.9: Excerpts from the testimony before Congress of Daniel Taylor, an Alabama planter, 1871

DOCUMENT 4.9.10: Excerpts from the testimony before Congress of John Minor Botts, a Unionist from Virginia, 1866

DOCUMENT 4.9.11: Excerpts from a report from General Ulysses S. Grant to President Andrew Johnson, 1865

DOCUMENT 4.9.12: Excerpts from the testimony before Congress of Union General John Tarbell, 1866

DOCUMENT 4.9.13: Excerpt from the report by General Carl Schurz to the United States Senate, 1865

DOCUMENT 4.9.14: Excerpts from the testimony before Congress of T. W. Conway, 1866

DOCUMENT 4.9.15: Excerpt from *The South Since the War*, by Sidney Andrews, 1866

Supplementary Materials

ITEM 4.9.A: Additional vocabulary lists for primary sources

ITEM 4.9.B: Excerpts from *The Tragic Era*, by Claude G. Bowers, 1929

ITEM 4.9.C: Excerpts from "The Freedman's Bureau," by W. E. B. Du Bois, 1901

Vocabulary

| commissioner | insurrectionary | scalawag | veto |
| destitute | reformation | Unionist | |

Student Activities

Analysis of Images of the Freedmen's Bureau

Activity 1

As a class, examine the two images of the Freedmen's Bureau (4.9.1 and 4.9.2). What case does each image make for or against the Bureau? In other words, what in the image suggests that the Bureau is a good or a bad thing? Split up into an even number of groups, with each group responsible for one image.

- What arguments does the opposing image make (list three, noting specific points from the opposing image)? Does your image answer those arguments? If so, how? If not, how would you (as the creator of your image) respond?

- What arguments does your image make (list three, noting specific elements from your image)? Does the opposing image answer those arguments? If so, how? If not, how might the author of the opposing image respond?

- Relying on your answers to the first question, draw a cartoon that directly addresses the opposing cartoon (or describe in words what such a cartoon might contain).

Debate—Should the Freedmen's Bureau Be Extended?

Activity 2

Introduction In this exercise, the class is asked to stage a debate in Congress in 1866 over whether or not the Freedmen's Bureau should be continued for another year. The class should be divided into three main groups: conservatives, moderates, and radicals.

The Briefs   All groups will work with a "common brief" composed of Documents 4.9.3–4.9.6. In addition, each group is responsible for three more documents, which comprise its own group brief.

Conservatives: Documents 4.9.7–4.9.9

Moderates: Documents 4.9.10–4.9.12

Radicals: Documents 4.9.13–4.9.15

(The teacher may wish to further divide each group into three smaller ones, each of which is responsible for a single document.)

Preparation   Students should come to class having read the documents comprising the common brief as well as the documents in their group brief. Students should be prepared to make their case for or against continuing the Freedmen's Bureau. The conservatives must argue against it, the radicals must speak for it, and the moderates may decide on their own which course to pursue. The instructor may wish to require students to come to class with their arguments written out. Arguments should refer to the documents in the briefs.

The Debate   During the class session set aside for the debate, each group is given ten minutes to present its case for or against the Bureau. The conservatives go first and must argue against the Bureau. The radicals go next and must argue in favor of it. The moderates go last and may argue either way. After presenting opening statements, each group is permitted ten minutes to rebut arguments made by other groups. If any class time remains, the groups may discuss the issues freely. At the end of class, a vote will be called for, and the motion to continue or disband the Freedmen's Bureau will be carried by simple majority.

10 minutes: opening statement

10 minutes: rebuttal of other positions

Any time remaining: free discussion

End of class: the vote

Follow Up   In the next class (or for homework), students may be asked to formulate three to five key questions about the Bureau raised in the debate. They may then be asked to formulate a research agenda: What additional sources or kinds of information would be most helpful in addressing the questions raised?

Activity 3   Research Extensions—Views of Freedmen's Bureau

1. Read the two later reflections on the Freedmen's Bureau (Items 4.9.B and 4.9.C) as homework or together in class.

2. Working in groups, identify two claims about the bureau that these authors contest (e.g., that the bureau kept black people idle). Show where the dispute is (i.e., what exactly does Du Bois say, what exactly does Bowers say?). What kind of information would be necessary to settle the dispute? Where could this information be found (what kinds of sources)?

3. Research more background on each author. Given this information, make some conjectures about why these men might have written about the Bureau in the ways they did. (You may wish to bring photocopied entries to class or may assign this task to students as preparation for the assignment.)

4. Finally, as a class, read what your history textbook has to say about the Freedmen's Bureau. As a class, discuss these questions:
   - Which of these authors seems more credible in our day and age?
   - What do you think happened in the last hundred years to make this so?

Further Student and Teacher Resources

Cimbala, Paul A., and Randall M. Miller, eds. *The Freedmen's Bureau and Reconstruction.* New York: Fordham University Press, 1999.

Collier, Christopher. *Reconstruction and the Rise of Jim Crow, 1864–1896.* New York: Benchmark, 2000.

Foner, Eric. *Reconstruction: America's Unfinished Revolution, 1863–1877.* New York: Harper and Row, 1988.

McFeely, William S. *Yankee Stepfather: General O. O. Howard and the Freedmen.* New Haven, Yale University Press, 1968.

Video

Reconstruction: The Second Civil War, 2004, PBS DVD Video, 180 minutes. Available at **www.pbs.org**

Music Connection

In 1866, Fisk University was established in Tennessee by the American Missionary Association with the help of the Freedmen's Bureau. The following year, a group of African American singers, students at the university, held their first public concert. In 1871, the group of eleven singers ventured forth on their first tour, hoping to raise money for a building program at the university. The initial response to the tour was lackluster. Then they added "Jubilee" to their name (from the "year of jubilee," when slavery ended). In 1872, the Fisk Jubilee Singers established their reputation in a concert in Boston, Massachusetts, and went on to tour the country and in Europe. Within seven years, the group raised $150,000 for their university (a huge sum for the time). The Fisk Jubilee Singers' repertoire included a large number of spirituals, including "Wade in the Water" (available on the CD-ROM). After students listen to the spiritual, ask them why they think the Fisk Jubilee Singers met with such success in the United States and abroad. Encourage them to explore the story of the original Fisk Jubilee Singers as well as how the name was adopted by many other "Jubilee" groups who followed them.

Websites

Emancipation and the Freedman's Bureau. University of Virginia, Charlottesville, VA
http://jefferson.village.virginia.edu/seminar/unit6/index.html

The Freedman and Southern Society Project, University of Maryland, College Park, MD
www.history.umd.edu/Freedmen/home.html

Freedmen's Bureau Online. Christine's Genealogy Websites
www.freedmensbureau.com/

Roanoke Island Freedmen's Colony, Patricia Click, University of Virginia, Charlottesville, VA
www.roanokefreedmenscolony.com/

Contemporary Connection

The Penn Center on St. Helena Island

By 1861 the Union had captured the Sea Islands of South Carolina. During the war the islands served as a testing ground for many of the ideas about how to deal with the South after the end of the war. An example of this was the first large-scale government effort to help newly freed black people in the transition from slavery to freedom. More than thirty small independent schools were set up throughout St. Helena Island—funded largely by northern missionary groups. The first of these Freedmen Schools, the Penn School, was established in 1862 with nine adult students. It met in a back room of the Oak Plantation House.

The popularity of the teachers, both black and white, caused the school to relocate to the bigger Brick Baptist Church. Within three years of this move, the Penn School's own building would be completed on the grounds of the church. In the early 1900s the school, following the lead of the Tuskeegee Institute, shifted its curriculum to focus on agricultural and industrial education.

In 1948, when South Carolina began to provide public education for African Americans on the Sea Islands, the school became absorbed into the South Carolina public school system. The building was used as a school until 1953. Since then, the Penn School has become Penn Center, a site for community-development projects and conference groups. In the 1950s and 1960s it was the only facility in all of South Carolina where black and white groups could meet without fear of being harassed. Dr. Martin Luther King Jr. and his staff often met at the school to strategize and plan events such as the 1963 March on Washington, D.C. Today, Penn Center's mission is to promote and preserve the history and culture of the Sea Islands. For current information on Penn Center today, see *www.penncenter.com*. Click on Avery Research Center and then on Avery E-Zine.

Students can research whether, in their communities, there are stories to tell of post–Civil War education for black people. When black families moved west and north, what educational resources were available to them? What information can be discovered in your local historical society?

Primary Source Materials for Lesson 9

4.9.1

Broadside, "The Freedmen's Bureau!" 1866

This broadside was one in a series of racist posters issued during the Pennsylvania gubernatorial election of 1866. Its aim was to attack Radical Republicans on the issue of black suffrage.

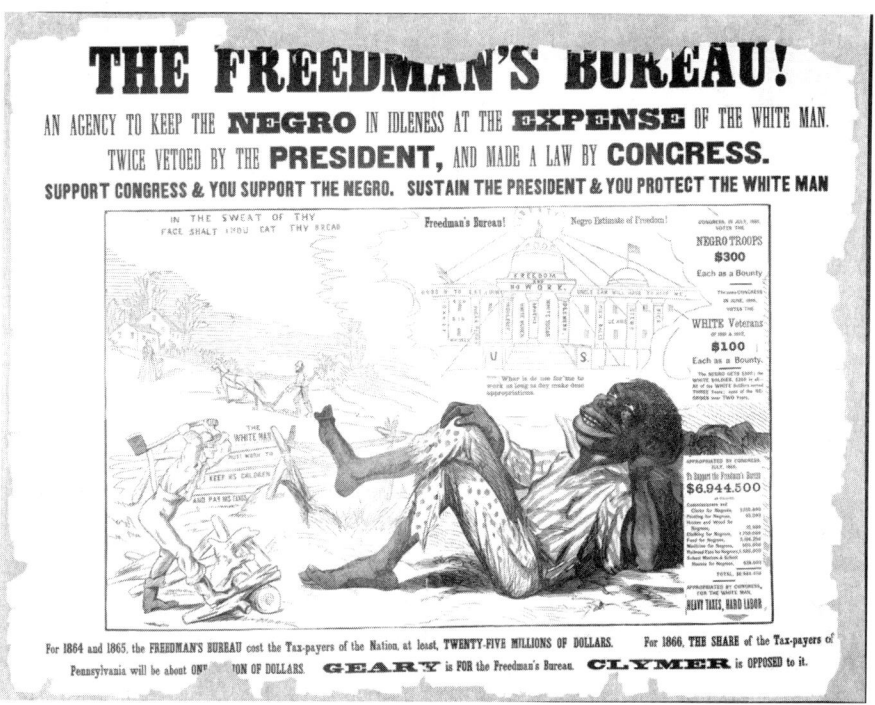

Library of Congress

4.9.2

Illustration, "The Freedmen's Bureau,"
Harper's Weekly, July 25, 1868

A man representing the Freedmen's Bureau stands between armed groups of Euro-Americans and African Americans.

Library of Congress

4.9.3

Excerpts from The First Freedmen's Bureau Act, 1865

The commissioner, under the direction of the President, shall have authority to set apart, for the use of loyal refugees and freedmen, such tracts of land within the insurrectionary states as shall have been abandoned, or to which the United States shall have acquired title by confiscation or sale, or otherwise, and to every male citizen, whether refugee or freedman, as aforesaid, there shall be assigned not more than forty acres of such land, and the person to whom it was so assigned shall be protected in the use and enjoyment of the land for the term of three years. . . . At the end of said term, or at any time during said term, the occupants of any parcels so assigned may purchase the land and receive such title thereto as the United States can convey, upon paying therefor the value of the land, as ascertained and fixed for the purpose of determining the annual rent aforesaid.

The full text of Document 4.9.3 is available on the CD-ROM.

4.9.4

Excerpts from The Second Freedmen's Bureau Act, 1866

The [Freedmen's Bureau] Commissioner shall have power to seize, hold, use, lease, or sell all buildings . . . formerly held under color of title by the late so-called Confederate States, and not heretofore disposed of by the United States, . . . and to use the same or appropriate the proceeds derived therefrom to the education of the freed people. . . .

In every State or district when the ordinary course of judicial proceedings has been interrupted by the rebellion, . . . the right to make and enforce contracts, to sue, be parties, and give evidence, to inherit, purchase, lease, sell, hold, and convey real and personal property, and to have full and equal benefit of all laws and proceedings concerning personal liberty, personal security, and the acquisition, enjoyment, and disposition of estate, real and personal, including the constitutional right to bear arms, shall be secured to and enjoyed by all the citizens of such State or district without respect to race or color, or previous condition of slavery.

The full text of Document 4.9.4 is available on the CD-ROM.

4.9.5

Excerpts from "Rules and Regulations for Assistant Commissioners," 1865

Relief establishments will be discontinued as speedily as the cessation of hostilities and the return of industrial pursuits will permit. Great discrimination will be observed in administering relief, so as to include none that are not absolutely necessitous and destitute. Every effort will be made to render the people self-supporting. Government supplies will only be temporarily issued to enable destitute persons speedily to support themselves. . . .

In all places where there is an interruption of civil war, . . . the control of all subjects relating to refugees and freedmen being committed to this bureau, the Assistant Commissioners will adjudicate . . . all difficulties arising between negroes themselves, or between negroes and whites or Indians. . . .

Negroes must be free to choose their own employers, and be paid for their labor. Agreements should be free, *bona fide* [good faith] acts, approved by proper officers, and their inviolability enforced on both parties. The old system of overseers, tending to compulsory unpaid labor and acts of cruelty and oppression is prohibited.

4.9.6

A Bureau Contract, 1866

This contract represents a typical arrangement between black laborers and a white planter during the early years of Reconstruction. In it, the workers are paid wages, rather than with the proceeds of a share of the crop. The Freedmen's Bureau agent who oversaw the negotiation of this contract likely helped the freedpeople earn more in wages than they would have without his help.

This agreement entered into this the 9th day of January 1866 between Clark Anderson & Co. of the State of Mississippi, County of (blank) of the first part and the Freedmen whose names are annexed of the State and County aforesaid of the second part.

Witnesseth that the said Clark Anderson & Co. agrees to furnish to the Freed Laborers whose names are annexed quarters, fuel and healthey rations. Medical attendance and supplies in case of sickness, and the amount set opposite their respective names per month during the continuation of this contract paying one third of the wages each month, and the amount in full at the end of the year before the final disposal of the crop which is to be raised by them on said Clark Anderson & Co. Plantation in the County of (blank) and State aforesaid. The said Clark Anderson & Co. further agree to give the female laborers one half day in each week to do their washing &c.

The full text of Document 4.9.6 is available on the CD-ROM.

4.9.7

Excerpts from the testimony before Congress of J. D. B. DeBow, 1866

I think if the whole regulation of the negroes, or freedmen, were left to the people of the communities in which they lie, it will be administered for the best interest of the negroes as well as of the white men. I think there is a kindly feeling on the part of the planters towards the freedmen. They are not held at all responsible for anything that has happened. They are looked upon as the innocent cause . . .

The Freedmen's Bureau, or any agency to interfere between the freedman and his former master, is only productive of mischief. There are constant appeals from one to the other and continual annoyances. It has a tendency to create dissatisfaction and disaffection on the part of the laborer, and is in every respect in its result most unfavorable to the system of industry that is now being organized under the new order of things in the South.

The full text of Document 4.9.7 is available on the CD-ROM.

4.9.8

Excerpts from a report by Confederate General Wade Hampton to President Andrew Johnson, 1866

The strong but paternal hand which had controlled him [i.e., "the negro"] through centuries of slavery, having been suddenly and rudely withdrawn, the only hope of rendering him either useful, industrious or harmless, was to elevate him in the scale of civilization, and to make him appreciate not only the blessings, but the duties of freedom. This was the prevalent . . . sentiment of the South. . . .

That much more had not been done to carry this sentiment into effect is due solely to the pernicious and mischievous inference of that most vicious institution, the Freedmen's Bureau. . . . The whole machinery of this bureau has been used by the basest men, for the purpose of swindling the negro, plundering the white man and defrauding the Government.

The full text of Document 4.9.8 is available on the CD-ROM.

4.9.9

Excerpts from the testimony before Congress of Daniel Taylor, an Alabama planter, 1871

The negroes that would go and settle down on plantations and work and stay there always had plenty to eat. The white men who employed them felt bound to keep them in plenty to eat and good clothes to wear when they would stay with them.

But if a man was trying to make a negro work, and talked a little short to the negro, he [the negro] would pick up and go somewhere else. . . . The negroes would quit and go off for this Bureau when they should have had a dependence in the country. They depended upon the Bureau for their rations. . . .

The negroes cheated the farmers out of their labor. . . . The negroes were to pay for their provisions out of their part of the crop and they did not go on making their crop, so that their part of the crop was not sufficient to pay the owner the amount that was due him for the land and stock and the advance.

4.9.10

Excerpts from the testimony before Congress of John Minor Botts, a Unionist from Virginia, 1866

I think that one of the great difficulties in Virginia, in regard to the colored people, arises from the organization of the Freedmen's Bureau—not that the Freedmen's Bureau is not in itself proper, and perhaps in some localities an indispensable institution, but that it stands very greatly in need or reformation. . . .

I have heard of a great many difficulties and outrages which have proceeded . . . from the ignorance and fanaticism of persons connected with the Freedmen's Bureau, who do not understand anything of the true relation of the original masters to the slave, and who have, in many instances, held out promises and inducements which can never be realized to the negroes, which have made them entirely indifferent to work, and sometimes ill behaved.

On the other hand, there are many persons connected with the Freedmen's Bureau who have conducted themselves with great propriety; and where that has been so there has been no trouble between the whites and blacks that I know of.

4.9.11

Excerpts from a report from General Ulysses S. Grant to President Andrew Johnson, 1865

Many, perhaps a majority, of the agents of the Freedmen's Bureau advise the freedmen that by their own industry they must expect to live. To this end they endeavor to secure employment for them, and to see that both contracting parties comply with their engagements. In some instances, I am sorry to say, the freedman's mind does not seem to be disabused of the idea that a freedman has the right to live without care or provision for the future. . . .

It cannot be expected that the opinions held by men at the South for years can be changed in a day; and therefore the freedmen require for a few years not only laws to protect them, but the fostering care of those who will give them good counsel, and in whom they can rely.

The full text of Document 4.9.11 is available on the CD-ROM.

4.9.12

Excerpts from the testimony before Congress of Union General John Tarbell, 1866

I think they [the planters] have well grounded complaints against the Freedmen's Bureau; and I do not think their criticism upon that bureau are in every instance dictated by motives of disloyalty. I do not mean to say what proportion of the officers of that bureau are incompetent or corrupt, but that there are many such I have no doubt. In such districts there has been a good deal of complaint, and to a casual observer their comments might be ascribed, perhaps, to motives of disloyalty; but a more careful attention to the subject satisfied me that their complaints were well grounded in a great many cases, for in districts where they had upright, intelligent, and impartial officers of the bureau, the people expressed entire satisfaction. They stated to me that where they had such officers, and where they had soldiers who were under good discipline, they were entirely welcome, and indeed they were glad to have their presence—in some cases approving the action of the bureau officers in punishing white men for the ill treatment of colored people, saying that the officers were perfectly right.

The full text of Document 4.9.12 is available on the CD-ROM.

4.9.13

Excerpt from the report by General Carl Schurz to the United States Senate, 1865

While the southern people are always ready to expatiate upon the shortcomings of the Freedmen's Bureau, they are not so ready to recognize the services it has rendered. I feel warranted in saying that not one-half of the labor that has been done in the south this year, or will be done there next year, would have been or would be done but for the exertions of the Freedmen's Bureau. The confusion and disorder of the transition period would have been infinitely greater had not an agency interfered which possessed the confidence of the emancipated slaves; which could disabuse them of any extravagant notions and expectations and be trusted; which could administer to them good advice and be voluntarily obeyed.

The full text of Document 4.9.13 is available on the CD-ROM.

4.9.14

Excerpts from the testimony before Congress of T. W. Conway, 1866

I should expect in Louisiana, as in the whole southern country, that the withdrawal of the Freedmen's Bureau would be followed by a condition of anarchy and bloodshed . . . I am pained at the conviction that I have in my own mind that if the Freedmen's Bureau is withdrawn the result will be fearful in the extreme.

What it has already done and is now doing in shielding these people, only incites the bitterness of their foes. They will be murdered by wholesale, and they in their turn will defend themselves. It will not be persecution merely; it will be slaughter; and I doubt whether the world has ever known the like.

These southern rebels, when the power is once in their hands, will stop at nothing short of extermination. Governor Wells himself told me that he expected in ten years to see the whole colored race exterminated, and that conviction is shared very largely among the white people of the south. It has been threatened by leading men there that they would exterminate the freedmen. . . . The wicked work has already commenced, and it could be shown that the policy pursued by the government is construed by the rebels as not being opposed to it.

4.9.15

Excerpt from *The South Since the War*, by Sidney Andrews, 1866

Of the thousand things that the bureau has done no balance sheet can ever be made. How it helped the ministers of the church, saved the blacks from robbery and persecution, enforced respect for the negro's rights, instructed all the people in the meaning of the law, . . . brought about amicable relations between employer and employed, corrected bad habits among white and blacks, restored order, sustained contracts for work, compelled attention to the statute books, . . . furthered local educational movements, . . . dignified labor, . . . rooted out old prejudices, . . . assisted the freemen to become land-owners, . . . set idlers at work, . . . carried the light of the North into the dark places of the South, steadied the negro in his struggle with novel ideas, . . . checked the passion of the whites and blacks, . . . assisted in creating a sentiment of nationality—how it did all this and a hundred-fold more, who shall ever tell? What pen shall ever record?. . .

The full text of Document 4.9.15 is available on the CD-ROM.

LESSON 10

Occupations and Obstacles

African Americans and their white allies recognized the importance of economic independence if freedpeople were to truly become equal participants in society. Conversely, former slave owners understood the necessity of maintaining their former slaves in economic servitude if they were to retain their hold on power. The history of African American labor during Reconstruction reflects the struggle of these conflicting tensions.

The white planters gained the initial edge with the passage of Black Codes throughout the South in 1865. However, this blatant attempt to undermine the more lofty ideals of the Civil War outraged Radical Republicans in the North and led to three acts designed to cut the legs out from underneath the Black Codes: the extension of the Freedman's Bureau (1865), the Civil Rights Act (1866), and the Fourteenth Amendment (ratified in 1868). These acts extended federal oversight in the South and allowed African Americans more opportunity to explore some of the promises of freedom.

However, the obstacles to economic independence continued to be enormous. After the war, as before, African American labor provided the lifeblood for southern agriculture, which was the backbone of the southern economy. Freedpeople's hopes for ownership of land had been raised by General Sherman's Field Order Number Fifteen (January 16, 1865), which gave almost half a million acres of land to freedpeople, and by the Freedman's Bureau's promise of "40 acres and a mule." Throughout the South, African Americans worked on land confiscated from former plantations, assuming that after several years of farming they would have the cash needed to buy the land outright, as implied by the aforementioned promises. Sharing this vision, Thaddeus Stevens, leader of the Radical Republicans in the House of Representatives, introduced a bill for widespread confiscation of former Confederate land to be redistributed to former slaves, arguing that:

> Nothing is so likely to make a man a good citizen as to make him a freeholder [landholder]. Nothing will so multiply the production of the South as to divide it into small farms. Nothing will make men so industrious and moral as to let them

feel that they are above want and are the owners of the soil which they till. . . . No people will ever be republican in spirit and practice where a few own immense manors and the masses are landless. Small and independent landholders are the support and guardians of republican liberty.

Yet even Radical Republicans balked at the precedent that would be set by such an act. "[Land confiscation] is a question not of humanity, not of loyalty, but of fundamental relation of industry to capital; and sooner or later, if begun in the South, it will find its way into the cities of the North," claimed the *New York Times* on July 9, 1867. The bill eventually foundered in the House. President Johnson's efforts to pardon former rebels in 1865–1866, coupled with a general reluctance to dramatically interfere with the rights of property owners and an ongoing undercurrent of racism and terror that even the government's best efforts were powerless to quell, dashed most freedpeople's chances of landholding. Most ended up in some form of tenant farming, or sharecropping. Although sharecropping initially constituted a step forward for African American farmers by allowing them to benefit from their own labor, the social and political climate soon reduced it to an economically oppressive structure little better than slavery.

Throughout the United States, African Americans worked in all professions and trades, not just in agriculture. Yet, as in agriculture, they struggled for equality of opportunity. In the industrializing North, the 1860s and 1870s were already a time of growing tension between labor and bosses. Labor unions were growing in numbers, power, and militancy. Through them, workers sought better conditions and wages. The question was, where did African American workers, whose numbers had swelled with the abolition of slavery, fit in? Were they to be welcomed into the fight as fellow workers or shunned as inferiors and potential scabs? Like their white counterparts, African American workers used strikes to protest unfair conditions. However, it quickly became clear that the vast majority of white workers wanted nothing to do with their African American counterparts. African Americans were actively excluded from unions; in response, they formed their own labor organizations. The first convention of the Colored National Labor Union (CNLU) in Washington, D.C., was held on December 6, 1869, and led by Isaac Myers. Phillip Foner writes in *The Black Worker* that the convention "demonstrated that, by 1869, northern and southern black leaders had reached the conclusion that blacks could achieve equal employment opportunities and better pay only through independent organization" (p. 10).

The CNLU met for the last time in 1871. Conditions for African American workers had deteriorated with the demise of the Radical Republicans and the rise of terrorism in the South. Some workers continued to work for equality through black unions; others opted to leave the South altogether. A minority managed to find economic success in the South despite all the obstacles they faced, but the vast majority struggled to support themselves and their families. Although voices for equality and justice never ceased, the late 1870s marks the beginning of a nadir in African American labor history.

Organizing Idea

The history of African American labor during Reconstruction reflects the tension between freedpeople, seeking to be equal participants in society, and former slave owners, who wanted to retain their power. In the increasingly industrialized North, black workers were actively excluded from labor unions and, as in the South, they struggled for economic justice.

Student Objectives

Students will:

- learn about the range of professions African Americans undertook
- recognize the obstacles faced by African American workers across the nation and strategies they used to combat these obstacles
- understand what options African Americans saw available for themselves at the time

Key Questions

- What professions did African Americans enter after the war?
- What obstacles did African Americans face in these professions? To what extent did the obstacles exist because of race?
- What options did African Americans have for overcoming these obstacles? What strategies did they use?

Primary Source Materials

DOCUMENT 4.10.1: Contract for Agricultural Laborers, Alabama, 1874

DOCUMENT 4.10.2: A broadside nailed to the door of freedpeople's houses in Robertson and Sumner counties in Tennessee by a "regulator" group, precursor to the Ku Klux Klan, January 1867

DOCUMENT 4.10.3: Excerpts from Testimony taken by the Joint Select Committee to Inquire into the Condition of Affairs in the Late Insurrectionary States, Spartanburgh, South Carolina, July 6 and 7, 1871

DOCUMENT 4.10.4: "Colored Trouble at Stretcher's Neck," *New York World,* April 20, 1873

DOCUMENT 4.10.5: "Strike at Saw Mills," *Jacksonville Republican,* Florida, June 3, 1873

DOCUMENT 4.10.6: "What Does it Mean?" *Advertiser and Mail*, Montgomery, Alabama, November 4, 1873

DOCUMENT 4.10.7: "Robert Small on the Combahee Strike," *Savannah Tribune,* Georgia, September 2, 1876

PART FIVE: LABOR

DOCUMENT 4.10.8: "Petition of the Colored Washerwomen," published in *Jackson Daily Clarion,* Mississippi, June 24, 1866

DOCUMENT 4.10.9: Convention of Bricklayers National Union, 1871

DOCUMENT 4.10.10: "A Call for the Colored National Labor Union Convention," 1869

DOCUMENT 4.10.11: Excerpts from "Resolution Adopted by Negro Convention," Montgomery, Alabama, December 1, 1874

DOCUMENT 4.10.12: "150,000 Exiles Enrolled for Liberia," November 1877

Supplementary Materials

ITEM 4.10.A: Additional vocabulary lists for primary sources

Student Activities

Activity 1 — Analysis of and Response to Restrictions

Students should examine Documents 4.10.1–4.10.3 and address the following points:

- What contractual restrictions were placed on African American workers?
- Which specific phrases lent themselves to loose interpretation?
- What tactics were used to "keep African Americans in their place"?
- Define "terror tactics."
- List the activities black people were warned against in the broadside, and then list the warnings to white people. How do they differ? How are they the same?
- How were these warnings enforced?

Activity 2 — Creative Extensions

Students can choose to write a letter to the editor, create a poster, or prepare a short speech where they respond to the Labor Contract (4.10.1), "I am a Committee" broadside (4.10.2), or Ku Klux Klan investigation (4.10.3).

Activity 3 — Extracting Facts from Documents

Using Documents 4.10.1–4.10.9, students should prepare a list of the following:

- the professions that African Americans engaged in
- the obstacles that African American workers faced
- the strategies that they used to combat these obstacles

There are a large number of documents listed in this lesson. Many of them are short, but they are of varying reading levels. Teachers have several options for using them, depending on class reading levels and time constraints. Students might read all the documents with a partner over the course of a class, to finish for homework, compiling individual lists for the three categories mentioned here. Students could then compare their lists in a large group the next day. Students could also be divided into "expert groups," with each group being responsible for understanding one document. Each expert group would then report to the class and together the class could compile the lists. Finally, the teacher could choose several of the documents and go over them as a class, making the lists together. Whatever the format, it is important to emphasize that students must point to the exact words or phrases in the documents that gave them the information.

After looking at the lists, students should discuss or respond in writing to the following questions:

- Are the lists complete?
- If they are complete based on the documents we looked at, does that mean they are comprehensive historically?
- Based on what you know of history, what else could you add to these lists?
- What sources would you look for to come up with more comprehensive lists?
- Look at each list again. How much of what is on them is determined by race? In other words, is there anything on the lists that is there because the people involved are African American? Are there things on the list that would be there on a list of all workers, regardless of race? Explain. Is there anything to be gained in our understanding of history and society from asking these questions?

Debate—How Do We Address the Problems? *Activity 4*

By reading Documents 4.10.10–4.10.12, students will be exposed to some of the far-reaching options African Americans were pursuing in the face of the dimming economic reality. Students can then engage in a debate concerning what constitutes the "best" choice. Once students are clear on what options the documents represent, then they can make their choices and defend them. The teacher should encourage students to use concrete information from the previous documents as well as their knowledge of history in support of their opinions. One approach is to have students physically stand in a particular part of the room, depending on their choice. Having to take a literal position forces students to choose. Students could be given a fifth place to stand, representing an option not covered in the documents but one that they think would have been viable in history. Students should also be encouraged to move to a new location if their opinion changes; if they do this, they should state the reason that convinced them to move.

Activity 5   **Reflection on Using Primary Sources**

After looking at all the documents, students should reflect on the process of using documents to gather information and form a picture of history. Guiding questions could include these:

- Which documents did you find most interesting? Why?
- Which, if any, of the documents did you find more objective in the history they conveyed? Explain.
- Which, if any, of the documents, in your opinion, gave a more subjective, or limited, perspective on the time period? Explain.
- In addition to the lists we made, was there anything else that you learned or that you found important as you read these documents?
- What questions do these documents raise that could be used to guide you in further research to better understand this time period and these issues? Where might you go to find those answers?

Activity 6   **Essay Writing—The Best Option(s)**

For a more formal assessment, students could write their opinion on the most viable option for African Americans given the economic reality of the late 1870s, supporting their conclusion with at least three concrete pieces of information. The writing could be either a formal essay or a letter to the editor as a person in the 1870s.

Further Student and Teacher Resources

Edwards, Cheryl, ed. *Reconstruction: Binding the Wounds*. Carlisle, MA: Discovery Enterprises, 1995.

Foner, Eric. *Reconstruction: America's Unfinished Revolution, 1863–1877*. New York: Harper and Row, 1988.

Foner, Philip Sheldon, and Ronald L. Lewis, eds. *The Black Worker: A Documentary History from Colonial Times to 1869*, Vol. 1–7. Philadelphia, PA: Temple University Press, 1978.

Foner, Philip Sheldon. *Organized Labor and the Black Worker, 1619–1973*. New York: Praeger, 1974.

Harris, William. *The Harder We Run: Black Workers Since the Civil War*. New York: Oxford University Press. 1982.

Kronewetter, Michael. *United They Hate: White Supremacist Groups in America*. New York: Walker and Company, 1992.

Naden, Corinne J., and Rose Blue. *Civil War Ends: Assassination, Reconstruction, and the Aftermath*. Austin, TX: Raintree Steck-Vaughn, 2000.

Websites

Freedmen's Bureau Online. Christine's Genealogy Websites
 www.freedmensbureau.com/
 A comprehensive site that covers all aspects of the Freedmen's Bureau, including information on the Freedmen's Bureau Preservation Act of 2000

Oliver Otis Howard Papers. Bowdoin College, George J. Mitchell Dept. of Special Collections and Archives, Brunswick, ME
 http://library.bowdoin.edu/arch/mss/oohsd.shtml#003

Contemporary Connection

Black Labor Unions

"The white and black workers... cannot be organized separately as the fingers on my hand. They must be organized all together, as the fingers on my hand when they are doubled up in the form of a fist. If they are organized separately, they will not understand each other. They will fight each other, and if they fight each other, they will hate each other. And the employing class will profit from that condition."

—A. Philip Randolph

Economic independence in this country has always been an indicator of power, position, and prestige. The ability to earn a livelihood and provide for family and the opportunity to ascend up the ladder of success are of vast importance. Because of the immense emphasis placed on economic and financial stability in this country, it is no wonder that equality in the work force has been an issue of utmost significance for black Americans.

In the late nineteenth century, black people were often hired to work in mines or on railroads in the southern states when white workers would strike. Assailed as "union-busters," these black workers were often the targets of brutality and torment from disgruntled union members. Only 41,000 of the 2.1 million union workers in the U.S. during the early 1900s were black.

It was not until 1925 that an ambitious worker from Florida named A. Philip Randolph organized the very first black labor union, the Brotherhood of Sleeping Car Porters. (See Sourcebook 5, Lesson 12.) Randolph spent most of his life advocating equal rights and opportunities for minorities in labor unions. He was a key influence in the 1941 signing of Roosevelt's executive order banning job discrimination and was elected the first African American vice president of the AFL-CIO in 1955. In the 1960s, labor unions and black organizations worked side by side to develop federally funded programs. During the 1980s and 1990s, the shift towards deindustrialization, a growing workplace dependence on technology, and the movement of production to foreign countries together dealt a swift blow to the steel, textile, and auto industries—all of which employ large numbers of black workers. The ability of the unions to protect jobs continues to erode in the twenty-first century. (This information was obtained from *http://africana.com, www.now.org,* and *www.afscme.org/about/afram link.htm.*)

Questions for students to research: Which unions are active in your community? Are the unions integrated? How do they work to protect jobs?

Primary Source Materials for Lesson 10

4.10.1

Contract for Agricultural Laborers, Alabama, 1874

He will be required to be ready for work by sunrise in mornings, then repair to same and render good and faithful service until noon, when he will be allowed for dinner one hour, during winter and spring and one hour and a half during the summer months. Then to perform faithful labor until sun down. Then feed stock or perform any other necessary duty demanded of him by his employer or agent.

All time lost to be deducted from the wages of the laborer, to be assessed by his employer.

Bad or unfaithful labor, careless breakage or loss of tools, willful destruction of property or abuse of stock will be charged for, and deducted out of the wages of the laborer.

The laborer binds himself to be obedient to his employer or agent. To obey all orders willingly and cheerfully of either employer or agent, and to render good and faithful service at all times. . . .

The full text of Document 4.10.1 is available on the CD-ROM.

4.10.2

A broadside nailed to the door of freedpeople's houses in Robertson and Sumner counties in Tennessee by a "regulator" group, precursor to the Ku Klux Klan, January 1867

In many instances, former slave owners acted on the belief that they were entitled to freedpeople's labor. In extreme cases, "regulator" groups, which preceded the Ku Klux Klan, threatened African Americans with violence and acted on these threats.

I AM COMMITTEE

1st. No man shall squat negroes on his place unless they are all under his employ male and female.

2d. Negro women shall be employed by white persons

3d. All children shall be hired out for something.

4th. Negroes found in cabins to themselves shall suffer the penalty.

5th. Negroes shall not be allowed to hire negroes.

6th. Idle men, women or children, shall suffer the penalty.

7th. All white men found with negroes in secret places shall be dealt with and those that hire negroes must pay promptly and act with good faith to the negro. I will make the negro do his part, and the white must too.

8th. For the first offence is one hundred lashes—the second is looking up a sap lin.

9th. This I do for the benefit of all young or old, high and tall, black and white. Any one that may not like these rules can try their luck, and see whether or not I will be found doing my duty.

10th. Negroes found stealing from any one or taking from their employers to other negroes, death is the first penalty.

11th. Running about late of nights shall be strictly dealt with.

12th. White man and negro, I am everywhere. I have friends in every place, do your duty and I will have but little to do.

4.10.3

Excerpts from Testimony taken by the Joint Select Committee to Inquire into the Condition of Affairs in the Late Insurrectionary States, Spartanburgh, South Carolina, July 6 and 7, 1871

Q. Where did you come from?
A. From Union County, in this State.

Q. Are you a native of this State?
A. Yes, sir. I was born and raised in Union County.

Q. Have you suffered any violence at the hands of any person in this county?
A. From persons in this county or some others, I have.

Q. Go on and tell in what manner it was inflicted upon you, and when it was.
A. I had two attacks; the first was on the 4th of March last, on Saturday night; the second was on that night two weeks, which would make it the 18th of March.

Q. Go on and tell what occurred each time.
A. On the 4th of March there came a body of men to my house. They were all around my house before I knew they were there, and were hallooing and beating and thumping the house. I was nearly asleep, and as quick as I awoke I jumped up. They told me to open the door. I told them I would do so. They told me to strike a light before I opened the door. I lighted a lamp and set it on a desk by the side of the house. I opened the door. These men were standing in front of the door with pistols drawn. They were knocking at the other door also. I said, "Gentlemen, somebody is knocking at the other door; let me open it." They let me turn around and open it. There were five men there. While I was opening that door more men came through the other door and into the room where I was. To the best of my mind, there were twelve men in all in my house. My wife thinks there were more, but I did not see them. They asked me to take a walk. I told them I would. I asked them to let me put on my clothes and shoes. They told me to put on my shoes, but not my clothes. They took me out and tied my hands together and hit me a few strokes and sent me back to the house. . . .

The full text of Document 4.10.3 is available on the CD-ROM.

4.10.4

"Colored Trouble at Stretcher's Neck," *New York World,* April 20, 1873

The strikers were augmented in strength as they proceeded, and when they arrived at Kanawha Falls last night there was a very large force of them. They have continually shown a very hostile and mutinous feeling towards the railroad company and its officers. At the Hawk's Nest, about twelve miles east of Kanawha Falls, on New River, the negroes took possession of the station, and among other acts of violence broke and turned a switch so that a train going east a short time afterwards collided with a construction train upon the switch. The collision resulted in the wrecking of an engine and slight injury of several persons on board the train. At about the same time a very large rock and two or three stumps were rolled down the steep mountain next above the Hawk's Nest upon the track, and the probabilities are undoubted that the strikers were the perpetrators of the acts. . . .

The full text of Document 4.10.4 is available on the CD-ROM.

4.10.5

"Strike at Saw Mills," *Jacksonville Republican,* Florida, June 3, 1873

The mill owners having refused to allow the reduction of a day's work to ten hours, in compliance with the demand of the Labor League, the colored laborers, with pre-concerted action, refused to go to work yesterday morning before 7 o'clock. The owners of the mills, determined not to yield, told them that they must continue to work as heretofore, or find other employment. Both parties stood firm. . . .

The full text of Document 4.10.5 is available on the CD-ROM.

4.10.6

"What Does it Mean?" *Advertiser and Mail,* Montgomery, Alabama, November 4, 1873

Whereas, We, the laborers, hold that we are in no way responsible for the failure of the crops, and that we have worked as faithful during the present year as we have any year since emancipation, but in consequence of a bad season, wet weather and rain, followed up by the ravages of cotton worms, &c., came the present calamity.—Therefore be it

Resolved, That we consider it nothing but humane and just that the white planters should take our poverty and distresses under advisement, as well as their own, we being the bone and sinew of the beat, and in times past while seasons were favorable rendered them valuable service at their own prices. Be it further resolved, That we desire to cultivate a friendly relation with the white planters of this beat, but cannot do so, if they insist upon discriminating against us by framing to deprive us of our rightful privilege to have a voice in settling the price of our labor, and the hours in which we shall work. . . .

The full text of Document 4.10.6 is available on the CD-ROM.

4.10.7

"Robert Small on the Combahee Strike,"
Savannah Tribune, Georgia, September 2, 1876

I did not find a single colored striker with any kind of deadly weapon about him, and found that they were peaceably inclined with no other object in view than to be paid in good money for honest labor; this they are determined to have or not to work.

The rice planters have been in the habit of using checks instead of money, which are not good at any but the Planters stores for the reason that they are payable in 1878 and 1880, and that when these checks are used in purchasing goods at these stores they become checks as change instead of money thus making it impossible for the laborers to purchase medicines, or employ physicians or obtain any thing except through the agency of the planter.

So far as violence on the part of the strikers is concerned there were warrants issued by Trial Justice Puller, for whipping one of their own number who had gone to work contrary to the agreement they had made in their own clubs, not to work for checks. These men upon being requested to give themselves up, walked out of the crowd and came into Beaufort without the Sheriff or even a guard, and were waiting in town hours before the arrival of the Sheriff. . . .

The full text of Document 4.10.7 is available on the CD-ROM.

4.10.8

"Petition of the Colored Washerwomen," published in *Jackson Daily Clarion,* Mississippi, June 24, 1866

Mayor Barrows—Dear Sir: —At a meeting of the colored Washerwomen of this city, on the evening of the 18th of June, the subject of raising the wages was considered, and owing to many circumstances, the following preamble and resolution were unanimously adopted:

Whereas, under the influence of the present high prices of all the necessaries of life, and the attendant high rates of rent, while our wages remain very much reduced, we, the washerwomen of the city of Jackson, State of Mississippi, thinking it impossible to live uprightly and honestly in laboring for the present daily and monthly recompense, and hoping to meet with the support of all good citizens, join in adopting unanimously the following resolution:

Be it resolved by the washerwomen of this city and county, That on and after the foregoing date, we join in charging a uniform rate for our labor, that rate being an advance over the original price by the month or day the statement of said price to be made public by printing the same, and anyone belonging to the class of washerwomen, violating this, shall be liable to a fine *regulated by the class.* . . .

The full text of Document 4.10.8 is available on the CD-ROM.

4.10.9

Convention of Bricklayers National Union, 1871

The subject of the admission of negroes to the rights and privileges of the union was introduced, and provoked a lively discussion, in which many members engaged.

Among others, Mr. A. Martin, of No. 2, Kentucky, gave a history of affairs in his vicinity. He said that in Lexington, Cynthiana, and Paris, the negroes were standing up for regular prices, and he was in favor of organizing colored unions.

Josiah Bradley, of No. 1, Kentucky, followed, and said that his union would never admit a nigger into their fellowship. As an instance showing the feeling of bricklayers toward colored men, he told a story in regard to the erection of the Galt house in Louisville. A large number of men were engaged on the job, and one negro was put to work, but, as soon as he put in an appearance, all hands quit, and would not go to work until the negro was discharged. . . .

The full text of Document 4.10.9 is available on the CD-ROM.

4.10.10

"A Call for the Colored National Labor Union Convention," 1869

Fellow Citizens:—At a State Labor Convention of the Colored Men of Maryland, held July 20th, 1869, it was unanimously resolved that a National Labor Convention be called to meet in the Union League Hall, City of Washington, D.C., on the 1st Monday in December, 1869, at 12 M., to consider:

1st. The Present Status of Colored Labor in the United State, and its relationship to American Industry.

2nd. To adopt such rules and devise such means as will systematically and effectually organize all the departments of said labor, and make it the more productive in its new Political relationship to Capital, and consolidate the Colored Workingmen of the several States, to act in co-operation with our White Fellow-Workingmen in every State and Territory in the Union, who are opposed to Distinction in the Apprenticeship Laws on account of Color, and to so act cooperatively until the necessity for separate organization shall be deemed unnecessary. . . .

The full text of Document 4.10.10 is available on the CD-ROM.

4.10.11

Excerpts from "Resolution Adopted by Negro Convention," Montgomery, Alabama, December 1, 1874

An experience of nine years convinces us that it is to the interest of our people. . . to leave this state for some other state or territory more favorable to their material, social and intellectual advancement.

We have labored faithfully since our emancipation for the landed class of Alabama, without receiving adequate compensation, or without the possibility of ever receiving any reasonable remuneration. . . . And consequently, instead of advancing our material interests . . . our condition is becoming worse . . . and many of our people are on the verge of starvation. And inasmuch as there is no prospect of our opportunities being any better . . . we recommend the formation of an association to be called the "Emigration Association of Alabama."

4.10.12

"150,000 Exiles Enrolled for Liberia," November 1877

>Rooms of The Liberia
>Joint Stock Steamship Company
>Charleston, S.C.
>November 6th, 1877

To the President of the Republic of Liberia,

Dear Sir,—This will inform you that the colored people of America and especially of the Southern State, desire to return to their fatherland.

We wish to come bringing our wives and little ones with what wealth and education, arts, and refinement we have been able to acquire in the land of our exile and in the house of bondage. We come pleading in the name of our common Father that our beloved brethren and sisters of the Republic which you have the high and distinguished honor of presiding over, will grant unto us a home with you and yours in the land of our Fathers. We would have addressed you before on this subject, but we have waited to see what would come of the sudden up-heaval of this movement. We are now in position to say, if you will grant us a home in your Republic where we can live and aid in building up a nationality of Africans, we will come, and in coming we will be prepared to take care of ourselves and not be burdensome to the Government. By our present plan of operations, we will be able to furnish food, medicine and clothing to last us for from six months to a year.

We desire to ask you the question, can we come? Will you be able to furnish us with a receptacle, where we could spend the first few weeks of our arrival, or will it be necessary for us to build our own? Would it be convenient for us to settle on the St. Paul's river? We hope to hear your decision at your earliest convenience.

>Yours, for and in behalf of 150,000 exiles enrolled for Liberia.
>Benj. F. Porter
>Pres. Liberia J. S. S. S. Co.

LESSON 11

The Rise of Sharecropping

At the end of the Civil War in April 1865, a great many Americans agreed that the biggest challenge confronting the South was the reconstruction of southern agriculture. Union politicians, army leaders, southern planters, and foreign observers all agreed—for the South to become productive again, it must resume the production of cotton. Before the war, cotton had been "king" in the South, fetching high prices from foreign manufacturers who used it to weave cloth. After the war, few asked whether it should be grown again. Instead, they wondered who would grow it and under what terms.

All believed that the freedpeople must be the basis of a new southern agricultural system. Whites were too few and often too unwilling to give up traditional stations of social privilege, which had exempted them from arduous field work. Attempts to attract European immigrants to the Reconstruction South largely failed. The source of labor being clear, the question turned on labor arrangements. *How* would the freedpeople work? Obviously, because they were now freed, they could not be compelled to work solely through the threat of violence. But it was unclear what else "free labor" might mean.

A variety of arrangements had been experimented with during the war itself, in places like the Sea Islands of South Carolina, where abolitionists had sought to create models of free labor, or in places like Northern Louisiana, where the U.S. Army had sought to reconstruct the cotton economy in Union-occupied territory during the war. To African Americans, most of these arrangements looked too much like slavery. They sometimes entailed wages, but because cash was so rare in the southern economy after the war, often wages were not paid in a timely fashion. With increasing frequency, the new labor contracts stipulated that African Americans working for the crop would share the profits of a small portion of the proceeds—say, one-tenth or one-fifth of the final cotton production. More disheartening, the freedpeople were frequently organized in gangs, as they often had been under slavery, and placed in the fields under the oversight of field managers, who looked to them suspiciously like the hated drivers of the slavery days.

Operating independently, the freedpeople generally rejected these arrangements, forcing throughout the South a complex set of ad hoc negotiations between the freedpeople and white landowners, with government agents of the Freedmen's Bureau often looking on. It would be terribly wrong to portray African Americans as equal partners in these negotiations. Freed with virtually nothing, they possessed no capital, little social status, and so little leverage. In contrast, those with whom they negotiated owned most of the land of the South and had the sympathetic ear of a national government eager to quickly reestablish southern agriculture.

But the freedpeople did possess one hugely important asset: their labor. No longer forced to work under the threat of the whip, they chose not to. Economic historians estimate that the actual number of hours worked by African Americans fell between 28 and 37 percent after emancipation. In the immediate postwar years, planters complained incessantly that they lacked the labor necessary to grow their crops; they complained even more of the "uppity" former slaves who refused to accept labor contracts on terms they found unfavorable.

The withdrawal of freedpeople from the labor force—and particularly of freedwomen, who began taking up traditional roles in the home—forced the planters to the bargaining table. In hundreds of thousands of separate instances, planters and freedpeople hammered out agreements in which each side gave and gained. The net result of these negotiations was the sharecropping contract. In a sharecropping arrangement, the landowner rented out a parcel of land to a family. But instead of paying him rent, the family owed him half of the profits of the cotton and corn grown on that land. This was the landlord's "share," and sharecropping families operating under this arrangement were known to be "working on halves." Other arrangements were entered into. Sometimes the family would owe the landowner less (perhaps a third of the crop) but would not receive the use of the landowner's livestock or farm tools.

White landowners liked sharecropping for several reasons. Most importantly, it solved their labor crisis. Also, it required of them no capital outlay—they merely locked up their land for a season. Furthermore, because the sharecropping family shared in the risk of growing the crop, landowners believed they had a greater stake in bringing in a profitable crop. Finally, this approach relied on legal contracts in a system wherein the legal machinery lay largely within their control. African American families liked sharecropping for different reasons: They were able to live and work as families, rather than in the enforced communality of the plantation. In addition, relative to slavery or the early gang systems of the postwar period, they could manage their own time and work independently.

Eventually, sharecropping became associated with an economically oppressive system that maintained its victims in a system of virtual servitude, or *debt peonage*. It is important to remember that the sharecropping contract was only one mechanism by which southern black people were kept from equal participation in the economy. Sharecropping contracts were often unfair because they were prepared by planters instead of workers and because they sought to exploit the freedpeople's widespread lack of literacy. But still more mechanisms were necessary to transform the promise of the free market into the nightmare of economic dependency.

The crop-lien system evolved in the years after the Civil War, not according to a centralized plan, but as an ad hoc response to the lack of finance capital available in the South after the war. Before the war, a sophisticated network of banks and cotton agents (or "factors") had supplied southern plantations with the funds they needed to buy cotton seed, upgrade capital equipment, effect needed repairs, and provision their workers for the year. This complex system of credit broke down during the war. After the war, it was replaced by large numbers of local furnishing merchants—small tradesmen who operated general stores in the countryside and who supplied basic goods and provisions on credit to farmers.

The postwar breakup of the plantation into scattered family farms multiplied the number of transactions between farmers and their creditors. Now, instead of one plantation drawing on the resources of a single large cotton factor, many sharecropping families drew individual contracts with many local furnishing merchants. This created multiple opportunities for furnishing merchants to defraud the freedpeople and minimized former slaves' capacity to act collectively. Worse yet, the furnishing merchants colluded to space themselves apart throughout the South. This reduced competition between them, ensuring them a monopoly over the local market and helping to keep prices artificially high.

The local furnishing merchant, as much as the white planter who owned the land freedpeople sharecropped, controlled the economic life of the sharecropper. The freedpeople had been freed into a competitive capitalist economy with no capital—they needed food and clothing simply to live. Although they would have preferred to grow food products for their own consumption, they were not given that option. The landowners and the furnishing merchants, who were out to make a profit, demanded that they grow cotton. In exchange, they would "advance" the sharecropping family food, clothing, and provisions until they could be paid for later with profits expected from the crop. The terms of the arrangement were rarely spelled out clearly and could be very unfair. The lack of competition between credit providers made for exploitative interest rates, often reaching effective rates of 60, 70, 80, and even 90 percent for provisions.

When the sharecropper's cotton crop was harvested, he often lacked the means to repay the debt he had incurred at the start of the farming season. The terms of the original transaction had been unfavorable, and there were no guarantees that the furnishing merchant would even honor them. Often, when the cotton crop came in, landowners and furnishing merchants colluded to defraud the sharecropping family (by, for example, underweighing the sharecropper's portion of the cotton or by adding the weights incorrectly). Even the shrewdest sharecroppers feared to challenge the figures of men who could call upon the law to (justly or unjustly) enforce their claim. Black families often ended the growing season having not made enough, in the reckoning of the furnishing merchant, to cover their previous debts, let alone clear a profit for next season. They would be compelled to take out an even larger loan for the next season, perhaps at still more unfavorable terms, just to get by. And year after the year the cycle continued.

Under such circumstances, the crop-lien system (so called because the cotton crop was used as a guarantee, or "lien," for a previously incurred debt) became a system of debt peonage, in which the freedpeople seemed to perpetually owe local landowners and furnishing merchants. Through such mechanisms, those who had lost the use of enslaved labor found a new source of inexpensive, docile, and immobile labor. They continued to reap the profits of the cotton and corn harvests while the freedpeople generally failed to become prosperous and independent farmers.

Organizing Idea

The system of sharecropping developed out of a complex negotiation between the freedpeople and southern landowners and sometimes representatives of the federal government. Only later did sharecropping lead to debt peonage.

Student Objectives

Students will:

- understand the interests of the various parties involved in the postwar labor settlement
- understand how the agency of African Americans themselves contributed to the eventual outcome
- become familiar with the various alternatives to wage labor experimented with in the Reconstruction South
- understand the evolution of sharecropping into a system of debt peonage

Key Questions

- At the end of the Civil War, what advantages and disadvantages did the freedpeople possess as agricultural laborers?
- Regarding southern agriculture, what were the goals and interests of the freedpeople, southern landowners, and the federal government at the end of the Civil War?
- What different kinds of labor arrangements were attempted in the South during and shortly after the Civil War?
- How did sharecropping develop from these experiments?
- How did sharecropping become an economically oppressive institution to the freedpeople?

Primary Source Materials

DOCUMENT 4.11.1: Letter from a white planter in Georgia to a local Freedmen's Bureau agent, April 17, 1866

DOCUMENT 4.11.2: Excerpt from an interview with former slave Anne Ulrich Evans

DOCUMENT 4.11.3: Excerpt from "Bureau Major's Business and Pleasures," by John William De Forest. *Harper's New Monthly Magazine,* November 1868

DOCUMENT 4.11.4: Excerpt from the slave narrative of a freedman who identified himself as "Charlie X," Tennessee

DOCUMENT 4.11.5: Sharecropping contract from North Carolina, 1882

DOCUMENT 4.11.6A AND B: Illustration, A Georgia Plantation before and after the Civil War, *Scribner's Monthly* 21:5 (March 1881)

Supplementary Materials

ITEM 4.11.A: Additional vocabulary lists for primary sources.

ITEM 4.11.B: Study guide—"Alternatives to the wage-labor system developed during Reconstruction"

Vocabulary

crop-lien system	local furnishing	sharecropping
debt peonage	merchant	

Student Activities

Activity 1 — Preparation—Reading Firsthand Accounts

The sharecropping simulation is the central activity for this lesson and consumes a good bit of time. Prepare for the simulation ahead of time by preassigning students to the character roles in the simulation and providing a document to each.

- White planter: Letter from a white planter in Georgia to a local Freedmen's Bureau agent, 1866 (4.11.1)
- Freedwoman: Excerpt from an interview with former slave Anne Ulrich Evans (4.11.2)
- Freedmen's Bureau officer: Excerpt from "Bureau Major's Business and Pleasures" (4.11.3)
- Freeman: Excerpt from the slave narrative of a freedman (4.11.4)

Prior to class, students should have read their documents and be prepared to report to the class on the following questions:

- When was the document written and by whom?
- What was the author's motive or purpose in preparing the document?
- What is the most important thing the document tells us about land and labor during Reconstruction?

Sharecropping Simulation

Activity 2

The instructions and materials for the sharecropping simulation are included with this lesson (Item 4.11.B). The teacher should read through the materials thoroughly (beginning with the instructions for the teacher). Students will assume the roles of freedmen and women, white planters, or government agents and then will participate in negotiations such as those occurring constantly during the Reconstruction years. Consult these sheets:

- Land and Labor Simulation: Introduction
- Land and Labor Simulation: Instructions for the teacher
- Land and Labor Simulation: Instructions for the student
- Land and Labor Simulation: Character role sheet and point schedules
- Land and Labor Simulation: Point schedules for all characters (teacher only)
- Land and Labor Simulation: Tally sheets (overhead)

Review and Synthesize—Sharecropping Contract

Activity 3

Examine the sharecropping contract from 1882 included with this assignment (4.11.5). Read the contract paragraph by paragraph, as a class, discussing the ways that it reflects elements of the simulated labor negotiation.

Students should also examine the image of the Georgia plantation (4.11.6a and b). What differences between the plantation in 1860 and in 1881 suggest the changes that occurred between those two times?

Further Student and Teacher Resources

Mann, Susan L. "Slavery, Sharecropping, and Sexual Inequality." *Signs* 14 (1989): 774–98.

Mays, Osceola. *Osceola: Memories of a Sharecropper's Daughter.* New York: Hyperion Books for Children, 2000.

Ransom, Roger L., and Richard Sutch. *One Kind of Freedom: The Economic Consequences of Emancipation.* Cambridge, UK: Cambridge University Press, 1977.

Roark, James L. *Masters Without Slaves: Southern Planters in the Civil War And Reconstruction.* New York: Norton, 1977.

Website

U.S. History: Reconstruction. Best of History Websites
   www.besthistorysites.net/USHistory_Reconstruction.shtml
   A portal with links to several useful sites for information on the aftermath of the Civil War

Contemporary Connection

⸎

Equal Employment Opportunity

Following World War I, the price of cotton collapsed, leading many white farmers to minimize their losses by cheating their African American sharecroppers of their due income. In response, a group of African Americans founded the Progressive Farmers and Householders Union to prevent exploitation and "advanc[e] the intellectual, material, moral, spiritual, and financial interests of the Negro race." This union was destroyed in the "Elaine Massacre" of 1919 in Phillips County, Arkansas, when law enforcement officials and vigilantes from neighboring counties and states attacked the union leaders and members. Upwards of one hundred African Americans were killed in this slaughter.

In 1930 only 50,000 of the 1,500,000 African American workers engaged in transportation, extraction of minerals, or manufacturing were members of any trade union. In 1935, the Committee for Industrial Organization (later renamed the Congress of Industrial Organizations) broke from the American Federation of Labor and actively recruited and organized industrial workers regardless of race or ethnic background. This led to the large-scale unionization of African American workers. However, even with these steps forward, African Americans continued to be excluded from many unions until the passage of Title VII, Equal Employment Opportunity, part of the Civil Rights Act of 1964, which prohibits discrimination in employment because of race, color, religion, sex, or national origin.

Looking at the kinds of jobs available in their own communities, students can research how employees in these jobs are protected against discrimination. Are there labor unions in the local industries? Who insists that employers obey the Civil Rights Act of 1964? See *www.nara.gov/publications/prologue/cassedy.html*.

Primary Source Materials for Lesson 11

4.11.1

Letter from a white planter in Georgia to a local Freedmen's Bureau agent, April 17, 1866

Most of the freedwomen who have husbands are not at work, never having made any contract at all. Their husbands are at work while they are as nearly idle as it is possible for them to be, pretending to spin, knit, or something that really amounts to nothing. Now these women have always been used to working out and it would be far better for them to go to work for reasonable wages and their rations. Their labor is a very important percent of the entire labor of the South, and if not made available must affect to some extent the present crop. I have several that are working well, while others and generally younger ones who have husbands and children are idle—indeed refuse to work and say their husbands must support them. I beg you will not consider this matter lightly, for it is a very great evil, and one that the Bureau ought to correct.

4.11.2

Excerpt from an interview with former slave Anne Ulrich Evans

When freedom came I asked my old owner to please let me stay on with them; I didn't have nowhere to go nohow. He said, "Anne, you can stay here if you want to, but I ain't going to give you nothing but your victuals and clothes enough to cover your hide. Not a penny in money do no nigger get from me." He cursed me to all the low names he could think of and drove me out like a dog. I was barefooted, so I asked Moses Evans to please buy me some shoes. My feet was so sore and I didn't have no money nor no home neither. So he said for me to wait till Saturday night and he'd buy me some shoes. Sure enough, when Saturday night come he buyed me some shoes and handkerchiefs and a pretty string of beads and got an old man neighbor named Rochel to let me stay at his house. Then in a few weeks me and him got married, and I was mighty glad to marry him to get a place to stay—yes, I was. Hard times as I was having, if I seed a man walking with two sticks and he wanted me for a wife I'd marry him to get a place to stay.

4.11.3

Excerpt from "Bureau Major's Business and Pleasures," by John William De Forest. *Harper's New Monthly Magazine,* November 1868

For nothing were the Negroes more eager than for transportation. They had a passion, not so much for wandering as for getting together. Every mother's son among them seemed to be in search of his mother; every mother in search of her children. In their eyes the work of emancipation was incomplete until the families which had been dispersed by slavery were reunited. In short, transportation was a nuisance. I believed in it less than I believed in the distribution of rations and in modes of charity generally. It was necessary, I thought, to convince the Negroes of the fact that the object of the government was not to do them favors, but justice; and of the still greater fact that there is very little to get in this world without work.

4.11.4

Excerpt from the slave narrative of a freedman who identified himself as "Charlie X," Tennessee

We had some pretty hard times after we first married. I had to go about mighty to provide for my children and my old lady. I moved on a farm owned by old Robert Bishop and stayed on and sharecropped, giving him one-third. One day he came by my little shack in his buggy and said, "Charlie, I want your woman to come up to the big house and do some work for my wife." I said, "What woman?" He said, "Sarah, your wife, of course." I said, "I tell you, Bishop, when I married my wife I married her to wait on me and she has got all she can do right here for me and my children." He got awful mad and said, "Well, Charlie, I keep this house for people who can do what I want done. It is the custom for whoever lives here to let his wife help around the big house, and if you can't let your wife do it, I need my house." He tried to make me move right away, but I went to court and they made him let me stay on.

LESSON 11: THE RISE OF SHARECROPPING

4.11.5

Sharecropping contract from North Carolina, 1882

No cropper to work off the plantation when there is any work to be done on the land he has rented, or when his work is needed by me or other croppers. Trees to be cut down on Orchard, House field & Evanson fences, leaving such as I may designate.

Road field to be planted from the *very edge of the ditch to the fence*, and all the land to be planted close up to the ditches and fences. *No stock of any kind* belonging to croppers to run in the plantation after crops are gathered.

If the fence should be blown down, or if trees should fall on the fence outside of the land planted by any of the croppers, any one or all that I may call upon must put it up and repair it. Every cropper must feed, or have fed, the team he works, Saturday nights, Sundays, and every morning before going to work, beginning to feed his team (morning, noon, and night *every day* in the week) on the day he rents and feeding it to and including the 31st day of December. . . .

The full text of Document 4.11.5 is available on the CD-ROM.

4.11.6A AND B

Illustration, A Georgia Plantation before and after the Civil War, *Scribner's Monthly* 21:5 (March 1881)

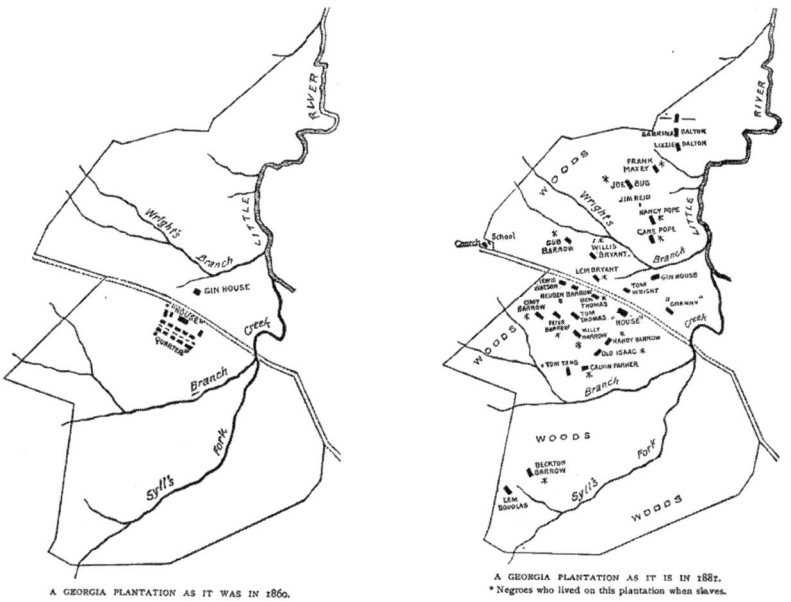

A GEORGIA PLANTATION AS IT WAS IN 1860.

A GEORGIA PLANTATION AS IT IS IN 1881.
* Negroes who lived on this plantation when slaves.

Cornell University Library, Making of America Digital Collection

LESSON 12

Reuniting and Protecting Family

One of the most emotionally wrenching challenges facing freedpeople at the war's end was how to reunite and protect their families. Former slaves faced a double-edged sword in slavery's legacy. Not only had their families been torn apart for economic gain by cruel or unfeeling masters, but white society used the very disarray of slave families—a tragedy that slaveowners had created—to fuel a stereotype of African Americans as caring little for family ties. This stereotype inhibited any careful and systemic attention on how to foster family reunification of freedpeople. Poor, lacking formal education, unheeded by those in power, freedpeople nonetheless did whatever was in their power to find and support not just immediate family, but extended family as well. They traveled hundreds of miles, wrote advertisements seeking lost relatives, and petitioned government agencies for assistance. Although success was not universal, some families did manage to find each other and build new lives together.

Emancipation also changed freedpeople's expectation of the government's role in their family lives. As citizens, they expected the government to meet their needs. In vast numbers, they sought legal sanctification of marriage, long forbidden under slavery. Marriages recognized by the law brought not only respectability, but also rights over property and children. Women and men alike also sought protection from irresponsible or abusive spouses, using government agencies to forge a new understanding of the responsibilities that came with relationships entered under free will.

Although postwar government offered routes to greater family unity and responsibility, it was just as often an obstacle to black families. The Freedmen's Bureau, ostensibly an agency for improving the condition of freedpeople, often supported the apprenticing of orphaned black children to former owners rather than releasing them to the custody of extended relations.

African American soldiers faced particular frustrations. Many had enlisted under promises by the government to protect and support their families in the South. Yet the federal government, eager to lessen its wartime expenditures, quickly withdrew what support they had provided when the war ended. Black soldiers were enraged at the violence and poverty to which this betrayal exposed their families.

Moreover, they were helpless to leave the army to help their families. The Union discharged soldiers in the order that they had enlisted. Because black soldiers were late in being allowed to enlist, they were among the last to be mustered out. They watched helplessly while white soldiers returned to their families, unable to respond to reports from their families of retaliation by their former owners. To make matters worse, the federal government sent many African American regiments into Texas to protect against French aggression in Mexico instead of including black regiments in the occupying forces in the South—where the soldiers would at least have been closer to their families.

As was true with every promise freedom carried, the realities of family reunification often fell short of the ideals for which freedpeople had longed and fought.

Organizing Idea

Freed African Americans worked hard against many odds to reunite families torn apart by slavery. In some cases they were supported in their efforts by the federal government; in others the government itself was part of the obstacle.

Student Objectives

Students will:

- identify and reflect upon strategies used by freedpeople to support family structures
- identify obstacles facing freedpeople trying to reunite their families
- explore reasons for these obstacles
- practice problem-solving skills by trying to envision structures or actions the government could have taken to better support black families
- practice critical thinking skills by reflecting on the feasibility of government solutions proposed by their classmates

Key Questions

- What strategies did freedpeople use to reunite families torn apart by slavery?
- What obstacles did they face in their efforts?
- What do the documents reveal about the ways in which the government both helped and hindered family reunification? What do they suggest about how the government's role might have been more actively supportive?

Primary Source Materials

DOCUMENT 4.12.1: Report from army chaplain A. B. Randall, attached to a regiment of black soldiers in Little Rock, Arkansas, 1865

DOCUMENT 4.12.2: Excerpts from requests for intervention sent to the Freedmen's Bureau, June 1865

DOCUMENT 4.12.3: Excerpt from a report by George W. Cole of mutiny by his black brigade, June 1865

DOCUMENT 4.12.4: Freedwoman's letter to her husband, who had been seeking her, April 7, 1866

DOCUMENT 4.12.5: A grandmother's letter to the chief agent of the Freedmen's Bureau seeking aid in gaining the custody of her grandson, along with the endorsement letter of an agent of the Bureau, January 1867

DOCUMENT 4.12.6: Image of article "Finding His Family," *Cleveland Gazette*, April 27, 1889

Supplementary Materials

ITEM 4.12.A: Additional vocabulary lists for primary sources

ITEM 4.12.B: Note-taking guide for Congressional commission

ITEM 4.12.C: Study sheets for primary sources

Student Activities

Activity 1 **Engaging the Students—How Does Government Support Families?**

Ask students, individually or in groups, to identify the ways that the government today supports their family specifically and/or families in general. How much and what kinds of support should the government give families? Are there any groups to whom the government owes particular support? Explain.

Activity 2 **Working with Documents—Simulating a Congressional Commission**

Divide students into six groups. Each group will become "experts" on one of the documents. They will then choose one person to be their "voice." That person in the group will join other voices as part of a panel reporting to a Congressional commission investigating the status of freedpeople's families in the South during Reconstruction. That "commission" will be the rest of the class.

Each person on the panel will make a prepared statement to present his or her experiences; the statements will be prepared in their small groups. The "commission" may ask questions for clarification. Students then will break into new groups to reflect on what they have heard and propose one or more government actions to address the needs that they heard expressed. (*Note:* It would be ideal to have these new groups composed of one person from each of the original small groups to allow for a mixing of experts.) The groups then report their ideas to the class and receive feedback on strengths and weaknesses of their proposals.

To begin, hand each group a copy of their document (4.12.1–4.12.6) and the accompanying worksheet (Item 4.12.B). Students should also refer to the advertisements freedpeople placed in newspapers, seeking lost relatives (4.7.9). Ask them to read through the document aloud as a group, helping each other with vocabulary. Then they should complete the worksheet.

Panel Presentation to Congressional Commission

Have one representative from each expert group sit in a semicircle at the front of the room. Representatives should bring their prepared statements and documents with them for reference. The rest of the class should sit in a larger semicircle facing them. Either the teacher or a student can moderate the proceedings.

First, remind the class of the objectives. Have each panel member present the prepared statement from their group. The commission (the rest of the class) should be encouraged to ask clarifying questions and should take notes on the form provided.

After hearing from each panel member, the class will work in their small groups to make proposals for government programs or actions to address freedpeople's needs, as expressed in the commission hearings.

Generating Government Proposals for Supporting Families

Students break into new groups to make their proposals. One member of each group should record the proposals. Students should keep in mind the following questions as they prepare their proposals:

- Do the proposals seem to address the needs expressed by the panelists? Will the effects of the proposals be long term or short term?
- Do the proposals miss any needs? Which ones?
- How feasible are the proposals? In other words, what would it take to implement them? Based on your knowledge of the period, does the government have the resources to do this?

Reporting on Proposals

A student from each group should report on the group's proposals. This should be a different student than the one who recorded. The rest of the class should give feedback on the proposal, using the preceding questions as criteria. As a class, discuss hypotheses students have as to why these types of proposals did not happen during Reconstruction.

Writing Extensions

Activity 3

Have students write their own opinions, based on the documents they read or heard presented, about the value placed on family by freedpeople. They can express their thoughts in a standard essay, a letter to a congressman or the editor of a newspaper, or by writing a poem.

Activity 4 **Creative Extensions**

Students can create an advertisement seeking lost relatives. They also need to create a plan for distributing the advertisement. Where would they have sent it in 1865? What newspapers existed in the area? Alternatively, students can choose to design a broadside (a printed sign that could be widely distributed). Where would they have placed it immediately following the Civil War?

Further Student and Teacher Resources

Blassingame, John W., ed. *Slave Testimony: Two Centuries of Letters, Speeches, Interviews, and Autobiographies*. Baton Rouge: Louisiana State University Press, 1977.

Fradin, Dennis Brindell. *My Family Shall Be Free: The Life of Peter Still*. New York: HarperCollins, 2001.

Frazier, Edward Franklin. *The Negro Family in the United States*. Chicago, IL: University of Chicago Press, 1969, 1939.

Gutnam, Herbert. *The Black Family in Slavery and Freedom, 1750–1925*. New York: Pantheon Books, 1976.

Jones, Jacqueline. *Labor of Love, Labor of Sorrow: Black Women, Work, and the Family from Slavery to the Present*. New York: Vintage Books, 1986, 1985.

Websites

First Person Narratives of the American South 1860–1920. Library of Congress, Washington. DC
http://memory.loc.gov/ammem/award97/ncuhtml/fpnashome.html

Freedmen's Bureau Online. Christine's Genealogy Websites
http://freedmensbureau.com/
Links to several other sites with specific family records and other primary documents

Harper's Weekly: Reconstruction I: 1866–1871. HarpWeek
www.harpweek.com/04Products/products-recon1.htm
Articles that appeared in the weekly journal covering all the events surrounding the Reconstruction era

Contemporary Connection

Black Families—Technology, Economics, and Education

In the twenty-first century, there are many resources for black families, almost all initiated and organized by African Americans. *Black Family Today* is a bimonthly publication published by Sentinel Communications in Florida. One recent issue focused entirely on education. In March of 2002, Hampton University in Virginia sponsored their twenty-fourth annual conference on the black family. The topic in 2002 was *Pushing Boundaries: The Impact of Technology on the Black Family*. Topics included careers in math and science and the importance of technology. Another organization interested in technology and the black family is The Black Family Network, which offers conferences, publications, and other resources to end the "digital divide" between black and white families in the United States. Other initiatives are encouraging young people to engage in the political process and community organizing against black-on-black crime. Although issues, challenges, and resources have changed dramatically over the past century, black families today, as in the past, are concerned about economics, their children, and education. Institutions in the black community support programs to address these concerns.

This lesson offers the opportunity for students to discover existing support services for families within their own communities. Economic and educational issues are important to all families everywhere. Some communities have more resources than others. Students can survey their community and perhaps make recommendations to their local town or city government.

Primary Source Materials for Lesson 12

4.12.1

Report from army chaplain A. B. Randall, attached to a regiment of black soldiers in Little Rock, Arkansas, 1865

Weddings, just now, are very popular, and abundant among the Colored People. They have just learned of the Special Order No. 15 of Gen. Thomas by which, they may not only be lawfully married, but have their Marriage Certificates *Recorded*; in *a book furnished by the Government.* This is most desirable; and the order, was very opportune as these people were constantly losing their certificates. Those who were captured from the "Chepewa" at Ivy's Ford on the 17th of January, by Col. Brooks, had their Marriage Certificates taken from them and destroyed; and then were roundly cursed for having such papers in their possession. I have married, during the month at this Post; Twenty five couples, mostly those who have families and have been living together for years. I try to dissuade single men who are soldiers from marrying until their time of enlistment is out, as that course seems to me to be most judicious.

The Colored People here, generally consider, this war not only; their *exodus,* from bondage; but the road, to Responsibility; Competency; and honorable Citizenship—God grant that their hopes and expectations may be fully realized. Most Respectfully

A. B. Randall

4.12.2

Excerpts from requests for interventions sent to the Freedmen's Bureau, June 1865

There are many who are sick and disabled whose ration has been cut off, and these instances are not isolated, but oft recurring and numerous. It is a daily occurrence to see scores of women and children crying for bread, whose husbands, sons and fathers are in the army today, and because these things are fully known, and understood by those whose duty it is to attend to, and remedy them and disregarded by them. we appeal to a Source more remote and out of the ordinary channel. . . .

The full text of Document 4.12.2 is available on the CD-ROM.

4.12.3

Excerpt from a report by George W. Cole of mutiny by his black brigade, June 1865

During the excitement, some (20) twenty Men deserted and left with their families, but in a few hours order was restored and the leaders of the Mutiny I took from the Boat—placed in irons, and have them in custody.

All the men appearing contented before seeing their families, and even afterward promptly obeyed all orders in arresting their comrades, but were enraged at the threat of using white troops to coerce them, as was offered by Major Dollard 2nd USC[olored] C[avalry].—

I found the same feeling of discontent and insubordination in the 1st Regiment USC[olored] Cavalry. Many were wishing to see their families and being unable to make any provision for their support from not having been paid and rations having been stopped to soldiers and their wives.—

The full text of Document 4.12.3 is available on the CD-ROM.

4.12.4

Freedwoman's letter to her husband, who had been seeking her, April 7, 1866

Dear Husband,
You wish me to come to Virginia. I had much rather that you would come after me but if you cannot make it convenient you will have to make some arrangements for

me and the family. I have 3 little fatherless girls. My husband went off under Burbridges command and was killed at Richmond, VA. If you can pay my passage through there I will come the first of May. I have nothing much to sell as I have had my things all burnt so you know that what I would sell would not bring much. You must not think my family too large and get out of heart for if you love me you will love my children and you will have to promise me that you will provide for them all as well as if they were your own. I heard that you spoke of coming for Maria but was not coming for me. I know that I have lived with you and loved you then and I love you still. Every time I hear from you my love grows stronger. I was very low spirited when I heard that you was not coming for me. My heart sank within me in an instant. . . .

The full text of Document 4.12.4 is available on the CD-ROM.

4.12.5

A grandmother's letter to the chief agent of the Freedmen's Bureau seeking aid in gaining the custody of her grandson, along with the endorsement letter of an agent of the Bureau, January 1867

I am the mother of a woman Dina who is now dead. My Daughter Dina had a child boy by the name of Porter. I am a Colored Woman former slave of a Mr. Sandy Spears of the parish of East Feliciana La. Said Porter is now about Eleven years of age. Mr. Spears has had the little boy Porter bound over to him so I am told by the agent of the Freedmen in this parish. . . .

We do not think Mr. Spears a suitable person to control this boy. Mr. Spears is very old and infirm. He is and has been for many years addicted to the use of ardent spirits. This fact I do not like to mention but truth requires me to speak. Now is there no chance to get my little boy. The agent of this place will not listen to me, and I am required to call on you or I must let my Grand Child go which greatly grieves me. . . .

The full text of Document 4.12.5 is available on the CD-ROM.

4.12.6

Image of article "Finding His Family," *Cleveland Gazette*, April 27, 1889

FINDING HIS FAMILY.

Twenty-Three Years' Search of an Old Man—Partially Successful.

ST. LOUIS, Mo.—One of the most remarkable family reunions on record occurred at Dennison, Texas. At the outbreak of the civil war a family by name of Lindsey, consisting of man and wife and three children, a girl and two boys, were sold into slavery at Independence, Mo. The entire family were separated. At the close of the war the father made up his mind that he would devote the balance of his life to discovering the whereabouts of his family. For the past twenty-three years he had that sole object in view. He has traveled and worked, bearing innumerable hardships to accomplish his purpose. In Missouri a few weeks ago the old man obtained the first clew to his son Allen, who was reported to be at Paris, Tex. The old man worked his way to Paris, and there met his son Allen. He was so beside himself with joy that he embraced and kissed his son and wept like a child. Through Allen he learned that the other son, named Jim, had been a porter on the Missouri & Kansas railway for a number of years, and the only remaining child, Amanda, was married and living in the country within five miles of Dennison. The old man left Paris and came to Dennison, where he met his son, Jim, and made himself known. For a few moments Jim was loth to believe that it was his father, from whom he had been separated for over twenty-three years. Leaving Jim, the old man started for the country on foot, where he met his daughter Amanda, with whom he is spending a few days. The dearest object of all his wanderings, the wife, is yet to be found, and the old man declares he will devote the remaining years of his life in finding her out.

Library of Congress

LESSON 13

Knowledge Is Power

Nearly every northern visitor to the South after the Civil War noted the freedpeople's remarkable thirst for education. A white teacher in North Carolina reported that the freedpeople "will endure almost any penance rather than be deprived of this privilege." In Mississippi in 1865, one Freedmen's Bureau officer reported the reaction of former slaves told that schooling would be provided for them: "Their joy knew no bounds. They fairly jumped and shouted in gladness."

The freedpeople did not generally wait for white people to help them out. One of the first things newly freed African Americans did was to establish systems of schooling for themselves and their children. Some moved to towns and cities where schools were plentiful. More often, they created their own schools, right where they were. When they could, they demanded support for schooling as part of their labor contracts. Many willingly taxed themselves in order to pay for the expense of a teacher. Others volunteered their time and expertise to construct and maintain school buildings. All freedpeople had to contend with the hostility of local white people to the experiment in education. Potential educators were threatened with hanging or public floggings. Arson reduced some black schoolhouses to ashes; more were never opened because of threats.

Often, freedpeople elevated the most literate among them to the role of schoolmaster. Before the Civil War, in every state except for Tennessee, it had been illegal to teach the enslaved to read and write. Some intrepid few had gained these skills nonetheless (see Sourcebook 3, Lesson 8), and their numbers were supplemented by antebellum free blacks who volunteered their services after the war. Yet everywhere throughout the South, experienced and trained black educators were hard to come by.

Into this breach stepped the federal government and northern benevolent societies. The federal government supported efforts to educate the freedpeople through the Bureau of Freedmen, Refugees, and Abandoned Lands (BFRAL). Education quickly became one of the most important tasks of the Freedmen's Bureau. The Bureau lacked the funds to pay teachers; instead, it provided the buildings for schools, and northern benevolent societies supplied educators. Recruiting largely from the considerable pool of abolitionists in their home states of New England, the societies used public donations to send ardent young men and women south to teach the freedpeople.

The Reconstruction experiment in education thus brought together two very different groups. On the one hand were the freedpeople themselves, who may have lacked formal education but who shared a rich cultural education in the values and mores of the slave community. The educators, on the other hand, were primarily white Protestants, who went to the South during and after the Civil War to teach those they saw as needy freedpeople. Motivated by sincere enthusiasm and missionary zeal, these "Yankee" teachers often considered themselves "friends of the negro." For them, freedom meant little without basic literacy and numeracy, and the experiment in free labor would not be vindicated unless the freedpeople rose in what they called "the scale of civilization."

Yet those in this northern contingent, like most Americans of their day, harbored a chauvinism for the values of their own culture. They had been raised in the North, often in the system of free public education pioneered by people such as Massachusetts educator Horace Mann. Mann and those like him had stressed not simply basic reading and writing skills, but also civic and moral education. The purpose of schooling, thought Mann and those of his ilk, was to protect the self-governing republic by fostering virtue in its people and to mold citizens who could function in an expanding market economy.

And so the "Yankee schoolmarms" who went to the South to educate the freedpeople sought to teach them far more than basic literacy. Success in freedom, they thought, depended utterly on the freedpeople's capacity to learn and internalize a veritable litany of Yankee virtues: thrift, industry, economy, perseverance, pluck, determination, independence, sobriety, punctuality, etc. They saw their duty as teaching the freedpeople how to adapt to a new world of free labor and free trade—one that claimed to reward civic virtue with the blessings of democracy, and moral virtue with elevated social status.

Steeped deeply in these values, the northern teachers not surprisingly looked on their southern charges as wanting—not just in basic skills, but also in the habits demanded by free society. Many northern teachers saw the adult freedmen and -women as hopelessly lacking in the self-control demanded of middle-class society. Approaching the freedpeople as essentially devoid of culture, they quickly began imposing the kind of discipline they thought had been lacking in slavery, where the only incentive to work had been the lash. For them, the Reconstruction South was a vast field on which might play out all the principles of antebellum reform. One white missionary teacher in North Carolina captured the general mood, exclaiming "We can make them all that we desire them to be."

This view conflicted sharply with the values of the freedpeople. The freedpeople were not blank slates upon which new values could quickly be written. They had rich traditions and values of their own. They adhered to the preindustrial work regime of agricultural labor and had long refined the art of day-to-day resistance to masters' authority through work slowdowns and feigned ignorance. At first, the freedpeople took to the new learning eagerly, understanding the great significance of literacy in their new world. Over time, however, they sometimes found the rigid requirements of the New England schoolroom pointlessly constraining. Classes often took second priority to opportunities to share community culture. Children past a certain age often withdrew from school to earn money for their families.

The northern teachers responded with dismay to freedpeople who seemed not to appreciate them. They complained of children who attended school irregularly or who never appeared on time. They grew frustrated when their students failed to enact the values they so earnestly sought to instill in them. But what they viewed as innate laziness or lack of ambition was often a cover for the freedpeople's deep understanding of the forces arrayed against them. The Yankee values, which may have served middle-class folks in the market society of northern cities, offered little to working-class black people in the rural South. The middle-class ideology the teachers brought to the South presumed that a level playing field existed for all so that personal initiative would yield success. In the South, however, blacks had long known that the level playing field did not exist. Even after freedom, whites colluded—often with the complicity of the federal government—to deny blacks the rewards of hard work.

Sensing this, many freedpeople soured of lessons that offered little practical use. Sometimes, they effectively struck in silent protest against an education they found patronizing or lacking in relevance to their daily experience. When they could, they demanded that blacks teach them rather than whites, arguing that "we must take into our own hands the education of our race." Such calls went beyond calls for black teachers, often extending into requests for control of school funds—funds raised largely from the freedpeople themselves. In contrast, the white philanthropists in charge of the freedmen's schools found local black teachers wanting, not simply in education, but in the middle-class ethos deemed such an important part of public education. Although they grudgingly conceded the appointment of some black teachers as necessary, they steadfastly fought for control of vital funds and school buildings.

Still, the Reconstruction experiment in education accomplished great feats. Through it, despite the cultural clash between freedpeople and the northern white teachers, innumerable African Americans gained basic literacy skills. The greatest educational legacy of the era was a system of institutions that survives to this day. With the rise of the Republican Party in the South in 1868, many states enacted the first-ever systems of free and compulsory public education in that region. Even when the Republican governments failed in the 1870s, they left a legacy of institutions for black education—from normal schools, which prepared future black teachers, to colleges and universities, which have trained generations of black professionals.

Alas, most of these institutions were segregated. Many African Americans publicly denounced this policy, arguing that segregated schools, like segregated public accommodations in general, stamped blacks with the stigma of inferiority. More, however, capitulated to the white South's incredibly vociferous defense of racial privilege, acknowledging that notwithstanding the justice of integrated schools, they were unlikely to become a widespread reality for some time. While blacks' calls for social equality and equal access to public accommodations grew as Reconstruction advanced, integrating public schooling was commonly thought to be among the most radical of all Reconstruction plans. Given their thirst for learning, few African Americans failed to relish the opportunity for education on their own terms, even if segregated.

Organizing Idea

Reconstruction saw a blossoming of educational opportunities for freedpeople, which they seized in huge numbers and with great determination. Still, obtaining a quality education was not an easy achievement, and freedpeople faced multiple obstacles. Nonetheless, Reconstruction did see a vast increase in black literacy and the laying of a strong foundation of public education upon which later efforts during the Civil Rights Movement could be built.

Student Objectives

Students will:

- explore questions around education for freedpeople during Reconstruction
- develop research skills by using the documents to identify questions that might guide further study
- reflect upon the underlying values and priorities that in many cases determined the type of education freedpeople received
- use their study of education during Reconstruction to reflect more broadly on the idea of what educational policies and realities can reveal about a society

Key Questions

- What obstacles did freedpeople face in trying to secure a quality education?
- What arguments did men give in support of integrated schools?
- To what types of schools did freedpeople have access? What were they taught?
- What actions and policies did African Americans pursue in order to improve their educational opportunities?

Primary Source Materials

DOCUMENT 4.13.1: Photograph of black soldiers from the Port Hudson, Louisiana, "Corps D'Afrique" posing with textbooks in front of their school

DOCUMENT 4.13.2: "Zion" School for Colored Children, Charleston, South Carolina, an 1866 engraving showing one of the many schools organized and run by freedpeople

DOCUMENT 4.13.3: Excerpt from "Life on the Sea Islands," by Charlotte Forten in *Atlantic Monthly*, March 1864

DOCUMENT 4.13.4: Excerpt from testimony before Congress from Sydney Andrews, 1866

DOCUMENT 4.13.5: Letter from George Wells to a class of white Sunday School children in the North, Athens, Alabama, February 15, 1868

DOCUMENT 4.13.6: Letter to the editor from Susan Paul Vashon, *The New National Era*, June 20, 1872

DOCUMENT 4.13.7: A page from *The Freedman's Second Reader,* 1865

DOCUMENT 4.13.8: Excerpt from an essay by Faith Lichen for *The New National Era*, January 25, 1872

DOCUMENT 4.13.9: Excerpt from an interview by congressional investigators with two teachers in Georgia, 1872

DOCUMENT 4.13.10: Letter to the editor from Jonathon C. Gibbs, school superintendent in Tallahassee, Florida, *The New National Era*, October 19, 1871

DOCUMENT 4.13.11: Letter to the Freedmen's Bureau on July 22, 1867

DOCUMENT 4.13.12: Summary of the state of education by *The New National Era*, December 8, 1870

DOCUMENT 4.13.13: Letter to the editor from W. V. Tunstall, president, Board of School Directors, *The New National Era*, November 29, 1871

DOCUMENT 4.13.14: Quote from Douglass Wilson, a black Civil War veteran living in New Orleans, 1866

DOCUMENT 4.13.15: Excerpt from a letter by Georgian freedman Richard Reese, printed in *The New Era*, February 17, 1870

DOCUMENT 4.13.16: Statement by Congressman Joseph H. Rainey of South Carolina, quoted in "Education," *The New National Era,* February 15, 1872

DOCUMENT 4.13.17: Editorial in The New Orleans *Tribune*, May 9, 1867, arguing for integration of schools

DOCUMENT 4.13.18: Report by Thomas W. Conway, superintendent of education, printed in *The New National Era,* June 4, 1874

Supplementary Materials

ITEM 4.13.A: Additional vocabulary lists for primary sources

ITEM 4.13.B: Study sheet for documents

Student Activities

Activity 1 **Engaging the Students—Education Today**

To engage students with the notion of what can be gained from reflecting on education policies and realities, put the following questions on the board and ask them to reflect on them in writing:

- Who can go to public school in our education system? Why do they go?
- What do students learn in school? Who decides what is taught?
- What obstacles are there to receiving a good education?
- If you were going to make public education more successful, what would you do, and why?

Discuss students' responses. Encourage them to explore the "free" and "compulsory" concepts in our education system. Also encourage them to explore the notion of power by identifying where individuals have control over the quality of their education and where the system has more control. Then discuss what one can get out of considering these questions. What can their exploration tell us about our values, as individuals and as a society? Tell students that they will be looking at these same questions with regard to the education of African Americans during Reconstruction.

Reading and Discussion—Education for Freedpeople

Activity 2

This lesson includes many short primary sources, grouped in four sets. Students will work in teams of two or three. For each set of documents, students have guiding questions.

Set 1: Documents 4.13.1–4.13.5

- Who in the African American community wanted to go to school immediately before and during Reconstruction?
- Why did they want to go?

Set 2: Documents 4.13.6–4.13.10

- What did African American students learn in Freedmen's schools?
- What do you think about what they were taught?

Set 3: Documents 4.13.11–4.13.15

- What obstacles did African Americans face in their pursuit of a quality education?
- What do you think was the source of these obstacles?

Set 4: Documents 4.13.16–4.13.18

- If you had the power to create policies to improve the quality of education for African Americans in the post–Civil War South, what would you suggest?

For each document, students will be asked to respond on a record sheet (Item 4.13.B) to the following points:

- Complete a quick description of the primary source (e.g., date, type of document, originator, topic, etc.)

❖ What do you learn from this source that can help you answer the question?
❖ What questions does the source raise?

Teachers may opt to divide the class into four groups, where each group will become experts on its set of documents and then report findings to the class. Or, teachers may give all the students the opportunity to examine all the primary sources. Either way, students should be sure to read the guiding questions before analyzing the documents.

After completing the first two sets, discuss as a class what students have found out during their exploration of the documents. Ask them what generalizations they can make and what questions the documents raised for them. Be sure that students ground their comments with concrete references to the documents themselves. (Because not everyone may have had a chance to look at every document, it can be helpful to have copies of the documents on overheads.) This is the chance for everyone to learn from documents that he or she might not have personally explored. Generalizations that one person makes may be challenged by someone who looked at a different document. Such challenges can help students see that understanding the past is an ongoing journey—there is always some other piece of evidence to be explored. Discuss with students *when* they (or any historian) think they have enough evidence to be able to make a safe generalization.

When students complete the final set of documents, have them individually complete the final question on the document record sheet. Encourage them to refer to information from all four sets of documents as they answer this question.

Place students into groups of four to six. Ask each individual to read his or her answer of the central questions to the group. (This stage is important because it again gives everyone a chance to be heard as a "historian.") Have students discuss the similarities and differences in their answers. Then ask each group to report to the class. Have them discuss the likelihood of any of their suggestions occurring.

Ask students what they learned about education in the South during Reconstruction. What questions do the documents raise for them? If they were going to go on to further explore this time period and this topic, what would they like to learn more about? Where might they find answers to their questions? After looking at education for African Americans during Reconstruction, has their perspective on their own education changed at all?

Further Student and Teacher Resources

Anderson, James. *The Education of Blacks in the South, 1860-1935.* Chapel Hill, NC: University of North Carolina Press, 1988.

Ballard, Allan. *The Education of Black Folk: The Afro-American Struggle for Knowledge In White America.* New York: Harper & Row, 1973.

Cornelius, Janet. *When I Can Read My Title Clear: Literacy, Slavery, and Religion in the Antebellum South.* Columbus, SC: University of South Carolina Press, 1991.

Jones, Jacqueline. *Soldiers of Light and Love: Northern Teachers and Georgia Blacks, 1865–1873.* Chapel Hill, NC: University of North Carolina Press, 1981.

Morris, Robert Charles. *Reading, Writing and Reconstruction.* Chicago: University of Chicago Press, 1981.

Smith, John David. *Black Voices from Reconstruction, 1865–1877.* Brookfield, CT: The Millbrook Press, 1996.

Website

First-Person Narratives of the American South. University of North Carolina, Chapel Hill, NC
http://docsouth.unc.edu/fpn/fpn.html

Contemporary Connection

Restoring the Brainerd Institute and the Story of Education for Freed Slaves

The Brainerd Institute in Chester County, South Carolina, opened its doors in 1866 to offer a high school education to the children of freed slaves. The school remained open as the only high school in the county for black students until the 1920s. All that remains today is a boarded-up brick building that once served as a dormitory. But if Vivian Ayers Allen of Mt. Vernon, New York, a member of the last graduating class in 1928, has her way, the building will be restored. The restoration would not only preserve the history of the school but also help to commemorate the long struggle of African Americans to provide their children with a good education.

Ms. Ayers has allies in her two daughters, Phylicia Rashad, an actress (TV wife of Bill Cosby on *The Cosby Show*), and Debbie Allen, choreographer and director. Ms. Rashad purchased the property and turned it over to her mother, and the sisters have performed at benefit events to raise money for restoration of the building.

In 2002, the Brainerd Memorial Project was dedicated in a ceremony that drew a number of people who shared their personal memories of the school. Although the project will cost two or three million dollars to complete, its true value lies in the preservation of the story of a people. To follow the progress, see *www.chesterchamber.com/history_of_the_brainerd_institut.htm*

Most communities have old houses or public structures that commemorate an important time, event, or person from the past. Ask students to identify one or more such sites in their community and link its story to the larger narrative of U.S. history.

Primary Source Materials for Lesson 13

4.13.1

Photograph of black soldiers from the Port Hudson, Louisiana, "Corps D'Afrique" posing with textbooks in front of their school

"The first schoolhouse built for the instruction of freed men."

The Chicago Historical Society

4.13.2

"Zion" School for Colored Children, Charleston, South Carolina, an 1866 engraving showing one of the many schools organized and run by freedpeople

The engraving was published in Harper's Weekly, *December 15, 1866, with a caption that read, "It is a peculiarity of this school that it is entirely under the superintendence of colored teachers."*

Library of Congress

4.13.3

Excerpt from "Life on the Sea Islands," by Charlotte Forten in *Atlantic Monthly*, March 1864

I never before saw children so eager to learn, although I had several years' experience in New-England schools. Coming to school is a constant delight and recreation to them. They come here as other children go to play. The older ones, during the summer, work in the fields from early in the morning until eleven or twelve o'clock and then come to school, after their hard toil in the hot sun, as bright and anxious to learn as ever. . . .

The majority learn with wonderful rapidity. Many of the grown people are desirous of learning to read. It is wonderful how people who have been so long crushed to earth . . . can have so great a desire for knowledge, and such a capacity for attaining it . . .

4.13.4

Excerpt from testimony before Congress from Sydney Andrews, 1866

Many of the negroes....common plantation negroes, and day laborers in the towns and villages, were supporting little schools themselves. Everywhere I found among them a disposition to get their children into schools, if possible. I had occasion very frequently to notice that porters in stores and laboring men in warehouses, and cart drivers on the streets, had spelling books with them, and were studying them during the time they were not occupied with their work. Go into the outskirts of any large town and walk among the negro inhabitants, and you will see children and in many instances grown negroes, sitting in the sun alongside their cabins studying.

4.13.5

Letter from George Wells to a class of white Sunday School children in the North, Athens, Alabama, February 15, 1868

Dear Children:

I have read through the First and Second Reader and now I am in the Third Reader. I have very nice clothes with pockets in them; I eat with a fork. I used to sit on the floor and eat with my fingers, and get grease and molasses all over myself. I didn't have any manners nor anything to eat hardly. Now I have everything nice and I try very hard, I am a temperance boy. I don't drink any rum and I never will. . . .

The full text of Document 4.13.5 is available on the CD-ROM.

4.13.6

Letter to the editor from Susan Paul Vashon, *The New National Era*, June 20, 1872

To the Editor:

I have been so fortunate as to attend several of the [Washington, D.C.] schools during their examinations. I cannot forbear to record my gratification with the closing exercises of the preparatory high school. The reading was especially fine. The original essays showed thought and research. It was, however, in Latin grammar and algebra that the most perfect triumphs were achieved. The recitations, consisting of parsing and translations, were nearly perfect, there being scarcely a hesitation, and no failures. In algebra, too, alike satisfactory result was attained. Problems involving one, two and three unknown quantities were stated with an ease which prophesied a successful elucidation.

Susan Paul Vashon

4.13.7

A page from *The Freedman's Second Reader*, 1865

Library of Congress

4.13.8

Excerpt from an essay by Faith Lichen for *The New National Era*, January 25, 1872

Have you ever studied Smith's Geography with that very worst type of Negro presented in painful contrast to the most perfect of the Caucasian on the opposite page? Have the words "superior to all others," referring to the latter, ever stuck in your throat and defiant pride made you "go down" while some other boy, no more ambitious but less sensitive, "went up"?

Have you ever tasted the sweet revenge of sticking pins into the eyes of the soul-driver in the picture of a cotton field at the head of the lesson on Georgia? No! Then you don't know what a jolly experience belongs to nine-tenths of the colored men in this land of liberty.

The full text of Document 4.13.8 is available on the CD-ROM.

4.13.9

Excerpt from an interview by congressional investigators with two teachers in Georgia, 1872

Columbus Jeter: I and my wife generally taught night-school at home until 9 o'clock at night. The neighbors would come into the school and I would give them lessons as far as I knew how. I did not charge them for it.

Aury Jeter: I was teaching a day-school and he had a night-school for those who could not come in the day-time, for the old settled men in the country.

Q—How much education have you and he?
A—I have studied geography, arithmetic, and grammar, and reading and spelling. In slave times we had a colored man who knew how to spell a little, and unbeknown to the others I learned my letters. I went to school in Knoxville, and awhile in Memphis and two months here since I was free.

Q—How much education had your husband?
A—He can just read and can spell pretty well. I taught him what little he knows. I can write some, not much. The hardest thing I have tried to learn has been writing. I can make the letters, but I cannot write a letter very well, for it takes me so long.

Condition of Affairs
(Washington, 1872)

4.13.10

Letter to the editor from Jonathon C. Gibbs, school superintendent in Tallahassee, Florida, *The New National Era*, October 19, 1871

To the Editor:

I have been writing a number of sketches of distinguished colored men for the newspapers of Florida and they have been widely copied. My object was to incite the colored youth of this state to acquire knowledge and fit themselves for the higher walks of usefulness. Among the sketches was one of Benjamin Banneker. A gentleman in this State sent the sketch into Kentucky and it is fiercely denied that any such man as Banneker existed and I am charged with inventing the sketch for sensational purposes. . . .

The full text of Document 4.13.10 is available on the CD-ROM.

4.13.11

Letter to the Freedmen's Bureau on July 22, 1867

Dear Sir,

I write to inform you of the most Cowardly outrage that took place last Saturday night. Our teacher whom we have employed here was shot down by a crowd of Rebel Ruffians for no other cause than teaching School.

General, this is the second teacher that has been assaulted. The Rebels make their brags to kill every Yankee teacher that they find. We do not know what we may do if the military does not assist us. The Freedmen are much excited at such an outrage.

George H. Clower, William Wilkes &c, Freedmen

4.13.12

Summary of the state of education by *The New National Era*, December 8, 1870

We copy from a report made to the National Teachers Association which will show how little attention has been paid in the South to Common schools:

- Delaware without school supervisors and no provision for the blacks.
- Maryland only educating colored children in Baltimore.

- Virginia just putting a free school law on her statute book.
- Kentucky just enacting a new school law, but giving no opportunity to colored youth.
- Tennessee, by Conservative Democratic triumph, delaying the whole Republican school system.
- North Carolina at the close of the last year, not a school in the country districts under state law. . . .

The full text of Document 4.13.12 is available on the CD-ROM.

4.13.13

Letter to the editor from W. V. Tunstall, president, Board of School Directors, *The New National Era*, November 29, 1871

To the Editor:

We need immediately five hundred teachers for colored schools in Texas. The colored people in this State cannot supply the demand. There are but few white Republicans who can engage in the profession of teaching and rebels will not teach them. Therefore our only prospect is to get teachers among the educated colored people of the North or Christian white people who are willing to endure privations among the heartless whites of the "sunny South." The late elections have opened the South, I trust, for the introduction of civilization. Send us teachers.

W.V. Tunstall, President, Board of School Directors, Houston County

4.13.14

Quote from Douglass Wilson, a black Civil War veteran living in New Orleans, 1866

We had no idea that we should see them return home alive in the evening. Big white boys and half-grown men used to pelt them with stones and run them down with open knives, both to and from school. Some times they came home bruised, stabbed, beaten half to death, and some times quite dead. My own son was often thus beaten. He has on his forehead to-day a scar over his right eye which sadly tells the story of his trying experience in those days in his efforts to get an education. I was wounded in the war, trying to get my freedom, and he over the eye, trying to get an education.

4.13.15

Excerpt from a letter by Georgian freedman Richard Reese, printed in *The New Era*, February 17, 1870

Last spring we built a schoolhouse and hired a white lady to teach. Friday night, February 5, our schoolhouse was burned up. We have a deed of one and a half acres but there is no timber on it and the owners of the land around have put up paper forbidding us to cut a stick on theirs. See how tight they have got us. We want the Government or somebody to help us build. We could burn their churches and schoolhouses but we don't want to break the law or harm anybody. All we want is to live under the law.

4.13.16

Statement by Congressman Joseph H. Rainey of South Carolina, quoted in "Education," *The New National Era*, February 15, 1872

Now, since he is no longer a slave, one would suppose him a leper, to hear the objections expressed against his equality before the law. Sir, this is the remnant of the old pro-slavery spirit, which must eventually give place to more humane and elevating ideas. Schools have been mixed in Massachusetts, Rhode Island, and other States, and no detriment has occurred. Why this fear of competition with the negro? All they ask for is an equal chance in life, with equal advantages, and they will prove themselves to be worthy American citizens.

4.13.17

Editorial in The New Orleans *Tribune*, May 9, 1867, arguing for integration of schools

We do not see why the city should go to the expense of organizing twenty or thirty new schools when she already has a sufficient number. Discrimination among children on account of religion and language would certainly be better justified than a distinction based on their complexions. The idea of having schools over the doors of which will be inscribed the words "for children of fair complexion only" or "for children with blue eyes only" and of other schools set apart "for children of dark complexion" is of itself ridiculous, and brings a smile on the lips of every reader, outside the Southern States.

Even a distinction based on the occupation of parents would be better justified than a distinction on color. Yet nobody thinks of setting apart in schools children of merchants and of mechanics, of tradesmen and of laborers. It is not proposed to separate bad children from good ones. Why? Because such distinctions are against the democratic principle of American society.

The next step, therefore is to do away with the distinction of race in the public schools.

4.13.18

Report by Thomas W. Conway, superintendent of education, printed in *The New National Era*, June 4, 1874

All the newspapers in the city, except the *Republican*, advised the white people not to send their children to the public schools. The white pupils all left and the schoolhouse was virtually in the hands of the colored pupils. This was the picture one day. In a few days I went back to see how the school was progressing and, to my surprise, found nearly all the former pupils returned to their places; and that school, like all the schools in the city, reported at the close of the year a larger attendance than at any time since the close of the war. A year ago I visited the same school and saw therein about as many colored children as whites, with not a single indication of ill-feeling.

The full text of Document 4.13.18 is available on the CD-ROM.

LESSON 14

The Role of the Church

Dr. Martin Luther King Jr. proclaiming the triumph of the Montgomery Bus Boycott from the pulpit; African Americans and white supporters filling the air around the Washington Monument with hymns of faith and strength; people bowed in prayer against the fire hoses of Mississippi State Troopers. Images abound that illustrate the central role of the church in the Civil Rights Movement of the 1960s. Yet churches were not newcomers to this fight. Throughout this nation's history, African Americans have gathered in religious communities to gain strength and to work together for equality, openly when allowed and secretly when not. By the time of the Civil War, they had a long established rich and varied religious life, both through churches and loosely organized services, often deeply rooted in African traditions.

The end of the Civil War, however, marked a new period of agency for African American churches. It gave free black religious organizations in the North the chance to unite with their newly freed brethren in the South. The African Methodist Episcopal Church (A.M.E.) was in the vanguard of this movement, sending missionaries into regions in the South as soon as they had been secured by Union army victories. (The A.M.E. was formed in 1816 in Philadelphia by a group of free blacks led by Richard Allen, after a racial dispute with the Methodist Episcopal Church. See Sourcebook 2, Lesson 8)

During the war, A.M.E. clergymen were outspoken critics of Union reluctance to end slavery and later challenged the hypocrisy of enlisting blacks to fight in an army with unequal pay for a society plagued by racial inequality. A.M.E. had been banned in the South for thirty years before the war's end, but as the Union army marched south, the church's missionaries followed. The A.M.E. leaders believed passionately in their obligation to freedpeople. Their missionaries brought thousands of new souls into the church. In his book, *A Rock in a Weary Land*, historian Clarence Earl Walker notes that in 1866, the church's membership was 70,000; by 1876 it was over 300,000. By contrast, black membership in the Methodist Episcopal Church, South (a white-dominated church) dropped from 200,000 in 1861 to 70,000 in 1867 (p. 50).

Why such a swelling of membership? R. H. Cain, the A.M.E. superintendent in South Carolina, believed that, "The blacks recognize in our organization the idea of nationality of manhood. They feel the time has come for the black man to take his place as a free man" (quoted by Walker, p. 63). Yet the numbers also have to do with emancipation. Freedom meant the ability to choose one's own religious institution, and African Americans did so eagerly.

The A.M.E. leaders took their mission seriously. There was a literacy requirement for ministers so that they would be better able to serve their congregations. The A.M.E. organized Union Leagues and voting efforts and kept up pressure on the federal government to support black equality. Events in Norfolk, Virginia, on May 25, 1865, provide one example of their success. One thousand African Americans met in the Bute Street African Methodist Church to mobilize a "freedom ballot." Hundreds of black men voted, surprising a government expecting only white men to vote. The ballots were contested, but they sparked activism throughout the state, culminating in a meeting with President Johnson himself. A few months later African American leaders secured the right to vote for black men in Virginia.

The A.M.E.'s presence in the South during Reconstruction was not an unmitigated success. There were struggles between the A.M.E. and existing churches and independent ministers, as well as differences within the church itself over strategies and priorities. Nor was it by any means the only significant religious activity in the South. African Americans, regardless of their religious affiliation, seized the opportunity to practice religion as they chose, often in ebullient ways, which disconcerted white and even some black missionaries and churchgoers. And churches of all denominations served as the organizers of countless self-help organizations, from relief services to orphanages to schools. Released from the fetters of slavery, religious communities exploded as active agents in the fight for black equality, a role that has continued to this day.

Organizing Idea

The black church took an active part in organizing for civil rights and education for African Americans after the Civil War ended.

Student Objectives

Students will:

- understand the role of black churches in supporting efforts for equality
- identify goals ministers had and activities they participated in to achieve these goals
- identify tensions between black and white communities as well as those within the black community itself
- understand the role of the black churches in promoting education

Key Questions

- What were the roles of the black church during Reconstruction?
- What were some of the characteristics of the newly founded churches?

❖ What church-related tensions existed between black and white communities as well as within the black community itself?

Primary Source Materials

DOCUMENT 4.14.1: Illustration by W. L. Sheppard, "The First African Church, Richmond, Virginia," *Harper's Weekly*, June 24, 1874

DOCUMENT 4.14.2: Comments made by a freedwoman at a religious meeting in 1865

DOCUMENT 4.14.3: Excerpts from *Proceedings of the Colored People's Convention of the State of South Carolina*, 1865

DOCUMENT 4.14.4: Excerpt from a speech by Henry McNeal Turner, 1871

DOCUMENT 4.14.5: Excerpts from "Citizenship, its rights and duties," a lecture delivered by D. Augustus Straker at the Israel A.M.E. Church and before the Pioneer Lyceum at Hillsdale, Washington, D.C., April 13 & 14, 1874

DOCUMENT 4.14.6: Excerpts from "Education in the South," Chapter XXVI in *African Methodism in the South*, by Wesley J. Gaines, 1890

Supplementary Materials

ITEM 4.14.A: Additional vocabulary lists for primary sources

Student Activities

Engaging the Students—Inside an African American Church After the Civil War

Activity 1

What are people looking for when they go to religious institutions, such as a church, temple, or mosque? What is talked about there? Give contemporary examples of a religious organization being actively involved in an issue or event.

Have students look at Documents 4.14.1 and 4.14.2. Identify the sources. What are they struck by in the image? In the quotation? What statements can they make about the characteristics of newly founded black churches from these two documents? What do they think ministers in these churches might have talked about?

Reading—Church Agency

Activity 2

In pairs or small groups, students should examine Documents 4.14.3–4.14.5 and respond to the following questions.

Document 4.14.3

❖ Give the context for this document (e.g., the who, what, where, when, and why).

- What was the author's political agenda? In other words, for what is he or she asking?
- List all the ways that the authors felt blacks were being obstructed by whites in attaining these goals.

Document 4.14.4

- Based on the introduction, list the different experiences that Henry Turner had that you think helped to shape his ideas and attitudes.
- Look at the quote of Turner's after he was removed from Georgia's legislature. List all the action words that he says describe what he is *not* doing. List the words that describe what he *is* doing. What do these word choices tell us about this man?
- List the different activities in which Turner engaged to fight for black rights.
- List the obstacles he encountered while fighting for his goals.

Document 4.14.5

- Where and when was this lecture presented?
- What does the speaker believe are the duties of citizenship?
- Explain in your own words Starker's beliefs regarding "labor."
- What does Starker ask of white Americans?

Note: The full title of this lecture was "Citizenship, its rights and duties—woman suffrage." To read Starker's thoughts on suffrage for women, students can access the full text at *http://memory.loc.gov* in the African American Pamphlet Collection, 1824–1909.

Activity 3   Reading and Analysis—The Church and Education

Document 4.14.6 summarizes the role churches had in promoting education. Students should read the excerpts and then as a class address the following questions:

- Who was involved in creating schools for freedpeople?
- List some of the schools the A.M.E. church founded. What types of schools were they originally?
- Why did the A.M.E. church and so many African Americans place such emphasis on the need for education?
- What did you learn from this document? What would you like to learn more about, and where can you find the answers?

Use the websites in the resources list to research the history and mission of several of the schools established by the A.M.E church.

Discussion—The Role of the Church

Activity 4

- Using students' answers, list on the board the goals that ministers had for their community. Then list the activities that the ministers involved themselves in trying to achieve these goals.

- What conflicts do these documents reveal as existing between the black religious communities and white southern society?

- Ask students to look at the list of goals and activities they came up with. What do these have to do with religion? What do their lists suggest about the churches' idea of their mission? Look at the words within the documents themselves. What do they reveal about the emotions of those who wrote them? What do these word choices suggest about the commitment of ministers to their cause?

- Have students explore what the limits are to the conclusions they can draw about the role of the churches from these documents alone. What else would they like to know about the churches? Where would they find this information? Is there anything that they think they could not really know, for which there might not be any lasting evidence?

Essay Writing—Is It Better That We Know?

Activity 5

In his history, the Rev. Gaines writes, "Thank God, our children and our children's children can never know the ways through which their fathers and mothers have passed." In a well-planned essay, respond to his statement. Consider also: Can we ever know what enslaved men and women "passed through"?

Further Student and Teacher Resources

Cooper, Michael L. *Slave Spirituals and the Jubilee Singers*. New York: Clarion Books, 2001.

Cornelius, Janet. *When I Can Read My Title Clear: Literacy, Slavery, and Religion in the Antebellum South*. Columbus, SC: University of South Carolina Press, 1991.

Gilkes, Cheryl Townsend. *If It Wasn't For the Women: Black Women's Experience and Womanist Culture in Church and Community*. Maryknoll, NY: Orbis Books, 2001.

Higginbotham, Evelyn Brooks. *Righteous Discontent: The Women's Movement in the Black Baptist Church, 1880–1920*. Cambridge: Harvard University Press, 1993.

Lincoln, C. Eric, and Lawrence H. Mamiya. *The Black Church in the American Experience*. England: Oxford University Press, 1980.

Lutz, Norma Jean. *The History of the Black Church*. Philadelphia: Chelsea House Publishers, 2001. (juvenile literature)

Raboteau, Albert J. *Slave Religion: The Invisible Institution in the Antebellum South*. North Carolina: Duke University Press, 1990.

Smith, John David. *Freedom's Unfinished Revolution: An Inquiry Into the Civil War and Reconstruction 1865–1877*. Brookfield, CT: The Millbrook Press, 1996.

Walker, Clarence Earl. *A Rock in a Weary Land: The African Methodist Episcopal Church During the Civil War and Reconstruction.* Baton Rouge: Louisiana State University Press, 1982.

Websites

African American American Sheet Music: 1850–1920. American Memory, Library of Congress, Washington, DC
http://memory.loc.gov/ammem/award97/rpbhtml/aasmhome.html

The Church in the Southern Black Community. Documenting the American South. University of North Carolina, Chapel Hill, NC
http://docsouth.unc.edu/church/index.html

Partial list of colleges established by A.M.E church

www.allenuniversity.edu
www.wilberforce.edu
www.MorrisBrown.edu
www.ewc.edu (Edward Waters College)
www.pqc.edu (Paul Quinn College)

Contemporary Connection

The Black Church

Historically, black churches have provided a focal point for African American communities. In the twentieth century, urbanization and modernization put additional pressure on the church to be involved with political and social welfare issues as well as with spiritual concerns.

During the Civil Rights era, organizations such as the Negro Improvement Association and the NAACP received much of their financial support from local ministries and churches. Martin Luther King Jr. and Jesse Jackson, both key figures in the Civil Rights Movement, are well known for their affiliation with the black church and Baptist faith. This was a time period during which the organizational power of the black church was truly revealed.

Today, groups such as the Congress of National Black Churches (CNBC) are proving to be influential. The CNBC initiated national programs focused on several community upliftment areas, such as Child and Family Development, Health and Wholeness, and Theological Leadership and Development. They have also launched a "Combined Federal Campaign" to solicit more funding from the U.S. Government for underdeveloped black communities. Organizations like the CNBC are keeping the activist tradition of black churches alive and well in the twenty-first century. (This information is from: Lincoln, C. Eric, and Lawrence H. Mamiya, *The Black Church in the American Experience* and Raboteau, Albert J., *Slave Religion: The Invisible Institution in the Antebellum South.*)

Question for students: If you were a member of the CNBC task force dedicated to the important cause of obtaining more federal funding for underdeveloped communities, how would you present your case to a representative from Americans for Separation of Church and State? In their presentations, students should incorporate their understanding of the historic role of black churches in addressing discrimination.

Primary Source Materials for Lesson 14

4.14.1

Illustration by W. L. Sheppard, "The First African Church, Richmond, Virginia," *Harper's Weekly,* June 24, 1874

The Granger Collection

4.14.2

Comments made by a freedwoman at a religious meeting in 1865

Northern white visitors reported the African American woman's comments.

I go to some churches, and I see all the folks sitting they don't know what the Holy Spirit is. But I find in my Bible, that when a man or a woman gets full of the Holy Spirit, if they should hold their peace, the stones would cry out; and if the power of God can make the stones cry out, how can it help making us poor creatures cry out, who feel to praise Him for His mercy. Not make noise!

Why we make a noise about everything else; but they tell us we must not make noise to praise the Lord. I don't want such religion as that. I want to go to Heaven in the good old way. And my brothers and sisters, I want you all to pray for me, that when I get to Heaven I won't never come back again.

4.14.3

Excerpts from *Proceedings of the Colored People's Convention of the State of South Carolina*, 1865

We are also . . . not only denied the right of citizenship, the inestimable right of voting for those who rule over us in the land of our birth, but by the so-called Black Code we are deprived . . . the right to engage in any legitimate business free from any restraints . . .

You have by your Legislative actions placed barriers in the ways of our educational and mechanical improvement; you have given us little or no encouragement to pursue agricultural pursuits, by refusing to sell us lands, but . . . bring foreigners to your country and thrust us out or reduce us to a serfdom, intolerable to men born amid the progress of American genius and national development.

The full text of Document 4.14.3 is available on the CD-ROM.

4.14.4

Excerpt of a speech by Henry McNeal Turner, 1871

I first organized the Republican party in this State, and have worked for its maintenance and perpetuity as no other man in the State has. I have put more men in the field, made more speeches, organized more Union Leagues, Political Associations, Clubs, and have written more campaign documents that received larger circulation than any other man in the state . . . And . . .these labors have not been performed amid sunshine and prosperity. I have been the constant target of Democratic abuse and venom, and white Republican jealousy. The newspapers have teemed with all kinds of slander, accusing me of every crime . . . I have even been arrested and tried on some of the wildest charges, and most groundless accusations ever distilled from the laboratory of hell. Witnesses have been paid as high as four thousand dollars to swear me in the penitentiary; white preachers have sworn that I tried to get up insurrection, . . a crime punishable with death, and all such deviltry has been resorted to for the purpose of breaking me down—and with it all they have not hurt a hair of my head, . . . I neither replied to their slanders nor sought revenge . . . I invariably let them say their say, and do their do; while they were studying against me I was studying for the interest of the Church, and working for the success of my party, . . . So that up to this time my trials have been a succession of triumphs, I have enemies, as is natural, but at this time their tongues are silent, and their missles are chaff, while my friends can be counted by hundreds of thousands.

4.14.5

Excerpts from "Citizenship, its rights and duties,"
a lecture delivered by D. Augustus Straker at
the Israel A.M.E. Church and before the
Pioneer Lyceum at Hillsdale, Washington, D.C.,
April 13 & 14, 1874

Another public duty and civil obligation is the exercise of our suffrage as voters. Evasion or omission of this duty is recreancy to our trust as suffragists as well as infidelity to a sacred privilege. One vote may save a city, or State, or nation, from ruin. Who, by his neglect, would like to bear the stigma of criminal in this respect? . . .

But I cannot leave this subject without admonishing the white race in this country not to throw itself across the path of a struggling class of citizens—a part of the body politic with themselves. It is suicidal. The elevation of the colored race in this common country, and its con-association in all legitimate business with the white race is necessary to the safety, permanence, and prosperity of the Government. This may appear extravagant; but, as the whole is made up of all its parts, so the whole is imperfect, unsafe, unsteady, and weak, without all its parts; and the man who would debar his fellow-citizen from any opportunity to rise in the scale of industry and education, is more a traitor than a patriot.

The full text of Document 4.14.5 is available on the CD-ROM.

4.14.6

Excerpts from "Education in the South," Chapter XXVI, in African *Methodism in the South*, by Wesley J. Gaines, 1890

For years our people had toiled in rice swamps and cotton fields as servants in every menial capacity, as tried and trusty friends as well as during the days of bloodshed and battle where men's souls were tried to the utmost. But they knew of something better and higher than the slave life they led then. There were summits to which many an aspiring mind would climb were but the slightest opportunity given. Yea, more, these would climb without the opportunity—rather, would make the opportunity. . . .

But while friends [teachers from the North] have worked, the negro himself has not been idle, and the A. M. E. Church has taken upon herself the great work of education in the South with a most creditable showing. Wilberforce University, the mother school in our Church, was founded in 1856, passing into our hands in 1863. . . .

Southward, in Columbia, S. C., is situated Allen University, named after the first Bishop of our Church. It is located in a beautiful spot, a mile and a half from the center of the city, and once the home of a wealthy family of the Southern aristocracy who little thought one day their home would be one of the centers of education for the slaves they had once owned. There are four acres of land and five buildings, with four departments in working order. It promises well for the future. It first opened its doors in 1881, and has thus seen hardly a decade, but its progress has been onward with instructors from Howard University, Hampton, Boston and Wilberforce. . . .

The most reliable statistics concerning the education of the race are those from the last census, and out of that we find that the negro race in the United States has 17,822 schools, with 16,865 teachers. There has been great increase since then, as the census of the present year will show.

There is to be a day of deliverance from ignorance; the outlook is grand, and our hopes the brightest. . . . No man or community of men, can elevate another. Elevation must always come from within. What the North and the South, however, can do is to cease their injustice, direct and indirect, and allow the negro to elevate himself.

The full text of Document 4.14.6 is available on CD-ROM.

Voting and Representation

LESSON 15

Before the Civil War began in 1861 few Americans—even die-hard abolitionists and black activists—imagined that within the next decade all African American men would possess the legal right to vote. Such were the travails of war and Reconstruction, however, that this would come to pass—even to the extent of amending the Constitution so as to prohibit the denial of the elective franchise on the basis of race (the Fifteenth Amendment).

The key to these transformations lay in the conflict between Republicans in Congress and the legislatures of the former Confederate states. The issue over which they battled was one on the lips of every American after the war: What shall be done with the freedpeople? The freedpeople themselves argued vociferously that they were entitled to all the rights of free citizens in a democracy. In a series of meetings held in the southern states shortly after the war, they asserted their full rights as citizens.

The Republicans, who as the party of Union and Lincoln now controlled Congress, were not so farsighted and could have imagined a postwar settlement in which all African American men did not have the right to vote. Some moderate Republicans, for example, believed that only those African Americans who had fought for the Union cause should enjoy the elective franchise. More progressive Radical Republicans, some of whom had strong abolitionist leanings before the war, argued for a more liberal franchise for blackmen. But the Radicals did not reflect popular racial sentiments; their hold on Congress was tenuous, and their early efforts to grant blacks the vote failed.

What really tipped the scales in favor of black manhood suffrage was the behavior of the first southern state governments put in place after the war. When Andrew Johnson, the vice president during Abraham Lincoln's second term of office, succeeded to the presidency after Lincoln was assassinated in April of 1865, he began to direct the path of Reconstruction without consulting Congress. Johnson was both conservative and bullheaded. He permitted the former Confederate states to reenter the Union under lenient provisions. The states had to hold conventions to write new state constitutions, and these new constitutions had to abolish slavery and repudiate secession. As far as the rights of the freedpeople went, Johnson had little patience for them. Believing that "white men alone must manage the South," he made no provision for black suffrage in the former Confederate states.

Johnson's plan for Reconstruction dealt a terrible blow to black rights. Emboldened by his leniency, former Confederates returned to office, and southern state governments began openly repudiating federal authority. The first elections held under the newly reconstructed state governments returned to office a slew of officials who had once served in the rebel government, including nine former Confederate congressmen. Worse yet, the reconstructed state governments of 1865–1866 drafted a series of Black Codes, which severely limited the civil rights of the freedpeople, denying them the right to serve on juries, limiting their access to the courts, and strictly controlling the terms of their labor (see Lesson 8).

Even moderate Republicans in Congress began to worry about these developments. Several members of Congress began to wonder: If the vulnerable freedpeople were not to be protected in their civil rights—if their contracts were not to be respected and they had no way to sue for denied wages—then of what value was the Thirteenth Amendment abolishing slavery? Didn't the freedpeople remain slaves in all but name? To many in Congress, the Confederates seemed to be winning in peace what they had lost in war. Republicans joined forces with African Americans and reluctantly took measures to ensure black men's right to vote. (Women, black and white, gained the right to vote when the Nineteenth Amendment was ratified in 1920.)

The most important measures the Republican-controlled Congress took up were the Military Reconstruction Acts of 1867. Under these acts, the former Confederate states (except for Tennessee) were to be taken out of the Union and placed under the temporary rule of military governors. New state constitutional conventions were to be called in each of the ten states. Adult black men had to be able to vote for representatives at the new conventions. The new conventions had to create new state governments that abolished slavery, ratify the Fourteenth Amendment guaranteeing blacks citizenship rights, and provide for the enfranchisement of black men.

The new state governments thus created constituted the nation's first meaningful experiment in biracial democracy. African Americans were represented in them not only through their votes (which tended to go to the Republican Party) but also through themselves, because for the first time African Americans began to hold office in number. In 1869, shortly after the new governments were formed, Congress began moving the Fifteenth Amendment to the Constitution, which consolidated these gains by prohibiting the denial of suffrage on the basis of race and which was ratified in March of 1870.

Unfortunately, the Republican state governments in the South did not last long. Former Confederates and white supremacists attacked them immediately, derisively labeling the Northern Republicans among them "carpetbaggers" and the southern whites who supported them traitorous "scalawags." African Americans came in for particular mistreatment. Southern Democrats and their supporters claimed that the presence of "ignorant" former slaves in the voting populace led to a "tragic era" of corruption and misrule. Such stereotypes long haunted popular and historians' views of this era and were not overturned until the Civil Rights Movement of a century later.

Organizing Idea

Voting rights for black men came about as the product of *both* African Americans themselves arguing for their constitutional rights and of the political tensions between those who sought to resubjugate African Americans (the southern Democrats) and those who sought to secure a meaningful equality for the freedpeople (the Republicans).

Student Objectives

Students will:

- understand why and how African American men were guaranteed the right to vote
- learn to closely read historical documents for meaning
- think critically about historical images

Key Questions

- Why did the Republicans support African American men's right to vote?
- What actions did the Republicans in Congress take to guarantee African American men's right to vote?
- How did the forces of white supremacy respond to African Americans' attempt to vote and hold office?

Primary Source Materials

DOCUMENT 4.15.1: Excerpt from "Reconstruction," by Frederick Douglass, *Atlantic Monthly*, 1866

DOCUMENT 4.15.2: Excerpts from Carl Schurz's letter to President Andrew Johnson, 1865

DOCUMENT 4.15.3: Illustration by Thomas Nast, "Pardon," *Harper's Weekly*, August 5, 1865

DOCUMENT 4.15.4: Illustration by Thomas Nast, "Franchise," *Harper's Weekly*, August 5, 1865

DOCUMENT 4.15.5: Illustration by Alfred Waud, "The First Vote," *Harper's Weekly*, November 16, 1867

DOCUMENT 4.15.6: Illustration by Thomas Nast, "Time Works Wonders," *Harper's Weekly*, April 9, 1870

DOCUMENT 4.15.7: Cartoon by Albert James Wales, "Everything Points to a Democratic Victory This Fall," *Harper's Weekly*, October 31, 1874

DOCUMENT 4.15.8: Illustration and text, "Electioneering in the South," *Harper's Weekly*, July 25, 1868

DOCUMENT 4.15.9: Cartoon by Thomas Nast, "Colored Rule in a Reconstructed (?) State," *Harper's Weekly*, March 14, 1874

DOCUMENT 4.15.10: Color lithograph, "The First Colored Senator and Representatives, in the 41st and 42nd Congress of the United States," 1872

DOCUMENT 4.15.11: Photograph, "Radical Members of the First Legislature after the War, South Carolina," 1878

DOCUMENT 4.15.12: Excerpts from *The Prostrate State* by James Shepherd Pike, 1874

Supplementary Materials

ITEM 4.15.A: Additional vocabulary lists for primary sources

ITEM 4.15.B: Study guide, "African American Officeholders in the Reconstruction South"

Vocabulary

| enfranchisement | Radical | ratify | suffrage |
| legislature | Republicans | servile | |

Student Activities

Activity 1 **Engaging Students—Who Votes?**

Many Americans do not realize that in the early years of their democracy, many people could not vote. At various times in American history, slaves and free blacks, women, Native Americans, East Asians, and non–property-holding whites could not vote. Children, noncitizens, and many convicted felons still cannot vote. Discuss this with students. Who should be permitted to vote in a democracy, and why? Why might some people have been prohibited from voting? What qualifications, if any, should there be to vote? Indeed, why is it important to be able to vote at all?

Activity 2 **Reading and Discussion—How to Protect Freedpeople**

As a class, read Frederick Douglass' "Reconstruction," (4.15.1). Because it is a difficult document, it may be best to have a different student read each paragraph aloud to the class and then clarify its meaning. After reading the article, answer these questions:

- What is the overall purpose of this article?
- Why, according to Douglass, is the federal government unable to secure a meaningful peace for African Americans and those loyal to the Union in the South?
- What is the firm principle of government that Douglass says is "deeply rooted in the minds of men of all sections of the country"?
- Why does this principle make it difficult to ensure the rights of Union loyalists in the southern states?
- Why does Douglass believe that "all the laws of the federal government" are insufficient to guarantee blacks people's civil rights?
- Why does Douglass believe that it is important to enfranchise African American men?

Essay Writing—Role of Government

Activity 3

Follow up the class discussion by having the students write an essay in which they address the following points:

- What is the acceptable role of the federal government in American society? In what ways do we permit the national government access to local affairs and private life?
- How have popular attitudes about the acceptable limits of federal intervention into American life changed since the time of Reconstruction?
- On the basis of this document, how did ideas about the acceptable role of government influence the development of black voting rights during Reconstruction?

Comparison and Contrast—Douglass and Schurz

Activity 4

Students should read Carl Schurz's letter to President Andrew Johnson (4.15.2). On what points do Schurz and Douglass agree? Where do they differ?

Image Analysis—Black Voting Rights

Activity 5

Divide students into four groups. Assign to each group the analysis of image(s) "Pardon" (4.15.3) and "Franchise" (4.15.4), viewed together; "The First Vote" (4.15.5); "Time Works Wonders" (4.15.6); and "Everything Points to a Democratic

Victory This Fall" (4.15.7). Have each group consider the following questions while the instructor circulates from group to group to assist.

- What is the name of the print you are working on?
- When was this print produced? At what point in the process of Reconstruction did it appear?
- What is the central event or phenomenon depicted in the print?
- What does the text in the print (if any) tell about its subject matter?
- Oftentimes, political cartoons use symbols to help express their meaning. What symbols do you identify in the print, and what do you think they mean?
- What do you think the artist who made the print, thought about the central event or phenomenon depicted in the print? Was he for it or against it? What specific elements of the print leads you to this conclusion?
- What point about black electoral politics during Reconstruction does the print make?

Upon completing the questions, each group should report to the class on the print it analyzed. (It is suggested that the prints should be reported on in their chronological order.) After reporting on all the prints, the class should attempt to outline the story of black voting rights during Reconstruction as told through the prints.

Activity 6   **Image Analysis—Conflicting Interpretations of African American Involvement in Politics**

Students should examine several images that depict aspects of black participation in the electoral process: "Electioneering in the South" (4.15.8), "Colored Rule in a Reconstructed (?) State" (4.15.9), "The First Colored Senator and Representatives in the 41st and 42nd Congress of the United States" (4.15.10), and "Radical Members of the First Legislature after the War, South Carolina" (4.15.11). Address the following questions:

Document 4.15.8: "Electioneering in the South"

- What in the image and text suggests to you that the authors are in favor of African Americans voting and holding office?
- What suggests to you that the authors hold negative attitudes?

Document 4.15.9: "Colored Rule in a Reconstructed (?) State"

- What in the image suggests the attitude of the cartoon's creator toward black state legislators?
- How does this image differ from 4.15.8?

- What might account for the apparent change in attitude towards African Americans and the electoral process between 1868 and 1874 in *Harper's Weekly*?

Documents 4.15.10: "The First Colored Senator and Representatives" and 4.15.11: "Radical Members"

- What do these images suggest about the African Americans depicted in them?
- How does the idea of African American officeholders in these images differ from their image in 4.15.9?
- Which of these images seems to contain the most positive portrayal of African American officeholders? Why?

The White Response

Activity 7

Read excerpts from James Shepherd Pike's, *The Prostrate State* (4.15.12). Discuss with the class:

- How did this supporter of white rule portray African Americans who held office?
- Does his view of black participation in politics favor the position of "Electioneering at the South" (4.15.8) or "Colored Rule in a Reconstructed (?) State" (4.15.9)?

Now examine "African American Officeholders in the Reconstruction South" (Item 4.15.B). As a class formulate several general statements supported by the data and note them on the board. Compare the data on African American officeholders during Reconstruction to Pike's account of the South Carolina state legislature. Do the data support or undermine Pike's statements?

Writing Extension—The South Carolina Legislature

Activity 8

Write a letter to James Shepherd Pike, responding to his description of the South Carolina legislature. Use data from the chart to support the points you make.

Further Student and Teacher Resources

Foner, Eric. *Freedom's Lawmakers: A Directory of Black Officeholders during Reconstruction.* New York: Oxford University Press, 1993.

Holt, Thomas. *Black over White: Negro Political Leadership in South Carolina During Reconstruction.* Urbana: University of Illinois Press, 1979.

Kolchin, Peter. "Scalawags, Carpetbaggers, and Reconstruction: A Quantitative Look at Southern Congressional Politics, 1868–1872." *Journal of Southern History* 45:1 (February 1979): 63–76.

Contemporary Connection

※

African Americans in Public Office

Even to this day, the fight for equal representation for African Americans continues. According to CNN, blacks make up only 1.7 percent of all elected officials, whereas in the 2000 census they comprised 12 percent of the U.S. population. "African American representation in the United States Congress comes as the result of centuries of struggle, pressure, compromise, and unswerving devotion to the principle of enfranchisement. More than any other experience in American history, the African American toil to participate in the democratic process defines the paradox of promise and pain that is our country." (This information is from the essay "Narrative of the Fight for Freedom, Enfranchisement, and the Seating of the First Blacks in Congress," found on *www.house.gov/ebjohnson/cbchistoryprerevels. htm.*)

In 1971, the Congressional Black Caucus (CBC) was formed by thirteen black members of the House of Representatives, who were all "determined to give legitimate representation to the underrepresented millions of blacks residing in most of the other 422 congressional districts. In the process, the Caucus became, and remains today, the most viable vehicle for confronting conditions that deny rights to minorities, and dealing with issues to improve the quality of life for all poor people and other powerless minorities" (from *www.house.gov/ebjohnson/cbcbirth.htm*). The CBC remains strong and active today. In 2003, with thirty-eight members, the mission remains the same: to make every vote count with high black representation at the polls, to improve access to health care, technology, and affordable housing, and to continue to push for the representation and consideration of all underrepresented and marginalized groups through universal civil and human rights. Students might use this lesson to discover who represents them at the state and federal levels. What do their elected officials stand for? Are there any members of the CBC from their district? If the students could vote, whom would they elect to public office? For more information on the Congressional Black Caucus, see *www.cbcfonline. org/History.html* and *www.house.gov/ebjohnson/cbc main.htm.*

Video

Reconstruction: The Second Civil War, 2004, PBS DVD Video, 180 minutes. Available at www.pbs.org

Websites

African American World: Building Democracy, 1866–1953. PBS Online, Alexandria, VA
www.pbs.org/wnet/aaworld/timeline/building_01.html

Harper's Weekly: Presidential Elections Cartoons, 1860–1884. HarpWeek
http://elections.harpweek.com/

Primary Source Materials for Lesson 15

4.15.1

Excerpt from "Reconstruction," by Frederick Douglass, *Atlantic Monthly*, 1866

While there remains such an idea as the right of each State to control its own local affairs—an idea, by the way, more deeply rooted in the minds of men of all sections of the country than perhaps any one other political idea—no general assertion of human rights can be of any practical value. To change the character of the government at this point is neither possible nor desirable. All that is necessary to be done is to make the government consistent with itself, and render the rights of the States compatible with the sacred rights of human nature.

The arm of the Federal government is long, but it is far too short to protect the rights of individuals in the interior of distant States. They must have the power to protect themselves, or they will go unprotected, spite of all the laws the Federal government can put upon the national statute-book. . . .

The full text of Document 4.15.1 is available on the CD-ROM.

4.15.2

Excerpts from Carl Schurz's letter to President Andrew Johnson, 1865

The interference of the national authority in the home concerns of the southern States would be rendered less necessary, and the whole problem of political and social reconstruction be much simplified, if, while the masses lately arrayed against the government are permitted to vote, the large majority of those who were always loyal . . . were not excluded from all influence upon legislation. . . . In the right to vote we would find the best permanent protection against oppressive class-legislation, as well as against individual persecution. . . . It is a notorious fact that the rights of a man of some political power are far less exposed to violation than those of one who is, in matter of public interest, completely subject to the will of others. . . . The effect of the extension of the franchise to the colored people upon the development of free labor and upon the security of human rights in the south being the principal object in view, the objections raised on the ground of the ignorance of the freedmen become unimportant.

4.15.3 AND 4.15.4

Illustrations by Thomas Nast, "Pardon" and "Franchise," *Harper's Weekly*, August 5, 1865

Thomas Nast drew "Pardon" and "Franchise" to advocate for voting rights for black men. He contrasted former prominent Confederates in "Pardon" with a Union army black veteran who lost his leg in service to his country. "Columbia," representing the United States, asks, "Shall I trust these men, and not this man?"

Columbia. - "Shall I trust these men, And Not This Man?"

Library of Congress

4.15.5

Illustration by Alfred Waud, "The First Vote," *Harper's Weekly*, November 16, 1867

Alfred Waud's engraving appeared on the first page of Harper's Weekly *accompanied by the following text: "The good sense and discretion, and above all the modesty, which the freedmen have displayed in the exercise, for the first time, of the great privilege [to vote] which has been bestowed upon them, and the vast power which accompanies the privilege, have been most noticeable. Admiration of their commendable conduct has suggested the admirable engraving which we give on the first page of this issue. The freedmen are represented marching to the ballot-box to deposit their first vote, not with expressions of exultation or of defiance of their old masters and present opponents depicted on their countenances, but looking serious and solemn and determined. The picture is one which should interest every colored loyalist in the country."*

Library of Congress

IAGO (Jeff Davis) "For that I do suspect the lusty moor hath leap'd into my seat: the thought whereof doth like a poisonous mineral gnaw my inwards." — Othello

4.15.6

Illustration by Thomas Nast, "Time Works Wonders," *Harper's Weekly*, April 9, 1870

Hiram Revels, an African American, won the Senate seat once held by Jefferson Davis, who served as president of the Confederate states. In the Thomas Nast cartoon, Senators Henry Wilson and Charles Sumner of Massachusetts, Oliver Morton of Indiana, and Carl Schurz of Missouri welcome Revels to the Senate chamber. Nast often used Shakespearian references in his work. In this illustration, he shows Davis as the scheming Iago, from Othello. Hiram Revels is depicted as Othello, the Moor.

EVERYTHING POINTS TO A DEMOCRATIC VICTORY THIS FALL

4.15.7

Cartoon by Albert James Wales, "Everything Points to a Democratic Victory This Fall," *Harper's Weekly*, October 31, 1874

By 1874, black men who attempted to vote risked their lives. Wales shows members of the Louisiana "White League" at the polls, intimidating and discriminating against African Americans.

Documents 4.15.6 and 4.15.7: Library of Congress

4.15.8

Illustration and text, "Electioneering in the South," *Harper's Weekly,* July 25, 1868

The image in Harper's Weekly *included the following text, "The illustration . . . shows the newly-enfranchised citizens of the United States engaged in the discussion of political questions upon which they are to vote. . . The scene is wholly characteristic. The eager attention of the listeners, and the evidently glib tongue of the speaker, reveal that remarkable adaptability and readiness so observable in the colored race. They take naturally to peaceful and lawful forms; they are naturally eloquent; and instead of scoffing loftily at them as incompetent, their white brethren will find it necessary to bestir themselves, or the "incompetent" class will be the better educated and more successful. Does any man seriously doubt whether it is better for this vast population to be sinking deeper and deeper in ignorance and servility, or rising into general intelligence and self-respect? They can not be pariahs; they can not be peons; they must be slaves or citizens. The policy of enslaving them has produced such results as we have seen; and we are now to see that liberty is truly conservative, and that honesty is the best policy."*

Library of Congress

4.15.9

Cartoon by Thomas Nast, "Colored Rule in a Reconstructed (?) State," *Harper's Weekly*, March 14, 1874

Even Thomas Nast, who championed civil rights for African Americans for years, was not immune to the commonly held belief that Reconstruction governments were corrupt. He drew an imaginary scene of the South Carolina legislature and resorted to stereotypical depictions of black legislators. The accompanying newspaper text noted, however, that the corruption was probably no worse than other instances of political graft.

Library of Congress

4.15.10

Color lithograph, "The First Colored Senator and Representatives, in the 41st and 42nd Congress of the United States," 1872

The Fifteenth Amendment to the U.S. Constitution gave the vote to all male citizens regardless of color or previous condition of servitude. African Americans were elected to office at the local, state, and national levels. Pictured here are Senator Hiram R. Revels and Representatives Benjamin S. Turner, Josiah T. Walls, Joseph H. Rainer, Robert Brown Elliot, Robert D. De Large, and Jefferson H. Long.

Library of Congress

4.15.11

Photograph, "Radical Members of the First Legislature after the War, South Carolina," 1878

Library of Congress

4.15.12

Excerpts from *The Prostrate State* by James Shepherd Pike, 1874

Yesterday, about 4 P.M., the assembled wisdom of the State . . . issued forth from the State-House. About three-quarters of the crowd belonged to the African race. They were of every hue, from the light octoroon to the deep black. . . .

Let us approach nearer and take a closer view. We will enter the [South Carolina] House of Representatives. . . . The Speaker is black, the Clerk is black, the chairman of the Ways and Means is black, and the chaplain is coal-black. At some of the desks sit colored men whose types it would be hard to find outside of Congo; whose costume, visages, attitudes, and expression, only befit the forecastle of a buccaneer. It must be remembered, also, that these men, with not more than half a dozen exceptions, have been themselves slaves, and that their ancestors were slaves for generations. . . .

The full text of Document 4.15.12 is available on the CD-ROM.

LESSON 16

The Undoing of Radical Reconstruction

By the end of 1877, the Republican Party, which had hesitatingly championed the rights of the freedpeople since the Civil War, had lost political control of the former Confederate states. Under the banner of the Democratic Party, those who sought a return to the prewar racial order surged back into power, spelling disaster for the rights of southern blacks.

The undoing of Radical Reconstruction was the result of multiple factors. Within the Republican Party in the southern states, tensions arose between various party constituencies. Individuals derisively referred to by some southern whites as "scalawags" argued with "carpetbaggers" over who should lead the party; African American politicians often felt neglected and voiced their concerns when they could. These tensions weakened the party. In states where the party had never gained a foothold—such as Virginia, Texas, and Georgia—the Democratic Party took advantage of the Republicans' weaknesses and returned the states to "home rule" by 1873.

But the ultimate cause of Reconstruction's failure throughout the South was an unbridled campaign of illegal fraud, terror, and intimidation on the part of some southern whites who refused to accept the outcome of the Civil War and Reconstruction. Under the auspices of secret organizations such as the Ku Klux Klan or the White League in the late 1860s and early 1870s or under the title of the Democratic Party itself in the mid-1870s, white supremacists refused to permit the electoral process to function. By intimidating, beating, and even murdering prominent Republican politicos and those who voted for them, the Democrats circumvented the electoral process to put an end to so-called "negro rule."

The federal government and the national Republican Party, under the leadership first of the moderate Ulysses S. Grant (1868–1876) and then the conservative Rutherford Hayes (1876–1880), gradually conceded the South to the Democrats. Grant had been willing to use federal troops in limited ways to ensure the integrity of the electoral process, but Hayes was not. In exchange for receiving the electoral votes of key southern states in the hotly contested presidential election of 1876, he promised that the Republican Party would no longer meddle in the affairs of the southern states.

Why was it possible for Hayes to make such a bargain? Why did the Congress and the president finally cease their efforts to guarantee African Americans' right to exercise the franchise? It is impossible to understand the national government's neglect of the Reconstruction effort without reference to popular thought at the time about the acceptable role of the federal government in state affairs. Many Americans believed strongly that in a democracy liberty was best maintained by permitting state and local government, rather than the federal government, the lion's share of the power. This would prevent a tyrannical government from forming. After all, Americans said, they had originally rebelled against England because its strong centralized monarchy was violating their rights.

Reconstruction demonstrated that only a strong national government could secure the rights of the freedpeople at the state and local level. For example, had the Congress not acted strongly in passing the Military Reconstruction Acts in 1867, the Black Codes of 1865 might well have remained in the statute books. But to continue to guarantee black rights against the wishes of intransigent white supremacists in the South required a continual exercise of federal power—often in the form of the army. In a political system so deeply suspicious of the power of central authority, it became ever more difficult to justify federal military intervention into state and local affairs.

By continually requiring this kind of federal presence in the South through their violent acts, those who would subjugate African Americans won the battle of Reconstruction. The northern public became less and less enamored of federal intervention into southern affairs, and the Republicans in Congress and the White House found it harder and harder to justify it. In order to maintain their own political viability, the Republicans sacrificed the federal commitment to black rights on the altar of political expediency.

African Americans lost much that had been won through their own efforts. By resisting slavery during the Civil War, they had put pressure on the federal government to develop a policy of universal emancipation. By resisting the Black Codes and calling for their full rights of citizenship during Presidential Reconstruction, they had precipitated the Civil Rights Act of 1865 and the Fourteenth Amendment of 1867. By refusing to surrender their civil rights in the face of an unbridled campaign of terror, they had compelled the federal government to guarantee the right to vote with the Fifteenth Amendment. In supporting the Civil Rights Act of 1875 they helped secure key measures of social equality—in public transportation, housing, and public accommodation.

By 1877, all these hard-won rights were threatened. In the 1880s and 1890s, the Supreme Court struck down key civil rights provisions of the Reconstruction era. Even when it let laws stand, it interpreted them in ways which did little to protect black rights. And, if Reconstruction demonstrated anything, it was that laws on paper—no matter how strongly they defended black rights—were only as good as the government's will to enforce them. By 1877, that will had failed.

PART SEVEN: POLITICS AND THE END OF RECONSTRUCTION

Organizing Idea

Reconstruction promoted by Radical Republicans ended, and with it African Americans' hopes for economic and political equality, as the result of a widespread campaign to circumvent the electoral process and reestablish white supremacy.

Student Objectives

Students will:

- understand the range of popular opinion on the issue of federal intervention into southern state affairs during Reconstruction
- develop explanations for the federal government's disavowal of the civil rights of the freedpeople
- understand some of the tactics southern white supremacists used to disenfranchise African Americans
- understand that the history of Reconstruction has been deeply contested by historians over the years

Key Questions

- How did the advocates of white supremacy act to take control of the southern state governments from the Republican Party?
- Why did the federal government relinquish its support for Radical Reconstruction?
- What are some of the different ways historians have understood Reconstruction and its end?

Primary Source Materials

DOCUMENT 4.16.1: Cartoon by Thomas Nast, "Worse Than Slavery," *Harper's Weekly*, October 24, 1874

DOCUMENT 4.16.2: Illustration and text, "Visit of the Ku Klux," *Harper's Weekly*, February 24, 1872

DOCUMENT 4.16.3: Testimony taken by the Joint Select Committee to inquire into the condition of affairs in the late insurrectionary states, Atlanta, Georgia, October 21, 1871

DOCUMENT 4.16.4: Excerpts from "The Freedman and His Future: A Rejoinder," by George Fitzhugh, *Lippincott's Magazine*, February 1870

DOCUMENT 4.16.5: Excerpts from a speech by U.S. Senator from Missouri Carl Schurz, July 22, 1872

DOCUMENT 4.16.6: Excerpts from editorial, "The Mississippi Plan in Action," *Aberdeen Examiner* (Mississippi), October 7, 1875

DOCUMENT 4.16.7: Excerpts from a speech by Frances E. W. Harper, "The Great Problem to Be Solved," given during the centennial anniversary of the Pennsylvania Society for Promoting the Abolition of Slavery, April 1875

DOCUMENT 4.16.8: Excerpts from a speech by Daniel Chamberlain, "On Hayes's Southern Policy," 1877

DOCUMENT 4.16.9: Excerpts from "The Result in South Carolina," *The Atlantic Monthly*, January 1878

DOCUMENT 4.16.10: Excerpts from Pinkney Benton Stewart Pinchback's address given during the Presidential campaign of 1880

Supplementary Materials

ITEM 4.16.A: Additional vocabulary lists for primary sources

ITEM 4.16.B: Study guide: "Efforts to secure civil rights for freedpeople, with responses"

ITEM 4.16.C: Excerpts from *The American Pageant: A History of the Republic,* a history textbook from 1956

ITEM 4.16.D: Study Sheet 1

ITEM 4.16.E: Study Sheet 2

Vocabulary

carpetbagger	enfranchisement	scalawags
corruption	Radical	suffrage
disenfranchisement	Reconstruction	

Student Activities

Engaging Students—The Power of the Federal Government

Activity 1

Although the federal government in the present age is empowered to behave in many ways that connect with the lives of individual citizens, this was not always the case. What does the class think are the permissible limits of government intervention in the lives of everyday Americans?

- Should, for example, the United States government be able to regulate prices in consumers' interest? What about taxing individual incomes?
- Should agents of the government (such as the police) be able to search citizens merely because they suspect illegal activity?
- What are the potential problems of a government so empowered?
- What safeguards against the misuse of government authority does the law provide?

❖ If a state refuses to comply with federal law, should federal troops be sent in?

Activity 2   **Image and Testimony Analysis—KKK**

As a class, briefly discuss the two images "Worse Than Slavery" (4.16.1) and "Visit of the Ku Klux" (4.16.2).

❖ What is the phenomenon depicted in the prints?
❖ What does the text in "Visit of the Ku Klux" tell you about its subject matter?
❖ What do you think the creators of the images thought of the phenomena they depicted?
❖ What specific elements of the prints lead you to this conclusion?

Now read the testimony of Maria Carter (4.16.3).

❖ Do you think the artists who made the images would have been sympathetic with the freedperson testifying?
❖ What does this document tell us about (1) what the Ku Klux Klan wanted, and (2) how it tried to achieve those aims.

Activity 3   **Debating the Federal Role**

Students should prepare for the exercise by scanning the handout "Efforts to secure civil rights for freedpeople, with responses" (Item 4.16.B). Divide the class into six groups. Each group will represent a different interest group during Reconstruction with a perspective on the issue of black civil rights. The perspective of each group is represented in a document:

1. African Americans: Frances E. W. Harper, "The Great Problem To Be Solved" (4.16.7)
2. African Americans: P. B. S. Pinchback's address during the Presidential campaign of 1880 (4.16.10)
3. Radical Republicans: Daniel Chamberlain, "On Hayes's Southern Policy" (4.16.8)
4. Liberal Republicans: Carl Schurz, "Why Anti-Grant and Pro-Greeley" (4.16.5)
5. Southern Democrats: George Fitzhugh, "The Freedman and His Future" (4.16.4)
6. Southern Democrats: "The Mississippi Plan in Action" (4.16.6)

Each group should read its document, complete the questions on Study Sheet 1 (Item 4.16.D), and be prepared to report back to the class. After all groups have reported, each group should suggest which of the other groups it would most agree and disagree with, and why.

Discussion—The End of Reconstruction

Activity 4

As a class, read the document "The Result in South Carolina" (4.16.9). Discuss:

- What were the consequences of Republican defeat for southern African Americans?
- Should the federal government have maintained troops in the South to prevent the electoral frauds of the Democrats? If yes, why didn't the federal government do so?

Interpretations of Reconstruction

Activity 5

Ask students to read an account of Reconstruction in a textbook from 1956 (Item 4.16.C). Using Study Sheet 2 (Item 4.16.E), students should list key points in the account. Then, students should take out their textbook assigned for the course and read its account of Reconstruction. (If no textbook is available, any account from a recent high school text will serve.) Students should compare the textbook account of Reconstruction in 1956 with the account of Reconstruction from their textbook, listing on the handout how their textbook treats issues raised in the older textbook. The class may then discuss key points of difference between the older, "traditional" view of Radical Reconstruction and the newer, "revisionist" version.

Further Student and Teacher Resources

Foner, Eric. "Reconstruction Revisited," *Reviews in American History*, 10: 4 (December 1982): 82–100.

Rable, George C. *And There Was No Peace: The Role of Violence in the Politics of Reconstruction.* Athens: University of Georgia Press, 1984.

Wharton, V. L. "The Negro and Politics, 1870–1875," in Kenneth M. Stampp and Leon F. Litwack, eds., *Reconstruction: An Anthology of Revisionist Writings.* Baton Rouge: Louisiana State University Press, 1969.

Video

Reconstruction: The Second Civil War, 2004, PBS DVD Video, 180 minutes. Available at **www.pbs.org**

Websites

Fifteenth Amendment to the Constitution: Voting Rights (1870). Our Documents, National Archives and Records Administration, Washington, DC
www.ourdocuments.gov/content.php?page=document&doc=44

Harper's Weekly: Reconstruction II: 1872–1877. HarpWeek
www.harpweek.com/04Products/products-recon2.htm

Contemporary Connection

⨯

Preventing Disenfranchisement

In recent years, disenfranchisement has once again surfaced in the South, this time primarily in Florida's southern region. During the 2000 presidential election, several thousand people were refused the right to vote based on falsified accusations of criminal history. The State of Florida does not, by law, permit convicted felons to participate in presidential votes. However, in Florida, 8,000 people convicted of misdemeanors, who should have been allowed to vote, were turned away at the polls. Disproportionately penalized were African American voters. "Blacks were out to vote in record numbers in Florida this year, but large numbers were systematically turned away for one reason or another," said Bob Herbert, a columnist for the *New York Times*.

In response to this voter fraud, the NAACP sued the State of Florida on discrimination charges. During the investigation, it was determined that three lists had been compiled by the office of the Governor. These lists contained the names of all citizens that were to be banned from voting based on prior criminal records. However, many voters with no convictions at all were selected because their name, gender, race, and/or birth date matched—or nearly matched—that of a convicted ex-felon. Thirteen percent of the names on those lists belonged to African Americans; more than half of the names were placed on the list due to false information.

In March of 2001, John Conyers Jr., Democratic congressman from Michigan, joined with colleagues to introduce federal legislation—the Equal Protection of Voting Rights Act. In October of 2002, the Help America Vote Act was signed into law by President George W. Bush. The new law establishes minimum federal standards intended to prevent fraud and end ballot disputes such as those seen in Florida in 2000. The legislation is technology focused, authorizing money to states to upgrade their voting technologies—things such as punch cards and voter lever machines. For more information see *www.reformelections.org*.

What ideas do students have for assuring that everyone who wants to vote can do so? What role can technology play in equalizing voting conditions across all of the states? What information is available about what each state is doing to modernize its voting system?

Primary Source Materials for Lesson 16

4.16.1

Cartoon by Thomas Nast, "Worse Than Slavery,"
Harper's Weekly, October 24, 1874

Library of Congress

4.16.2

Illustration and text, "Visit of the Ku Klux," *Harper's Weekly*, February 24, 1872

This text accompanied the illustration by Frank Bellew: "The artist pictures an outrage of frequent occurrence in some of the most turbulent districts of the Southern States. The scene is the interior of a Negro cabin, where the little family—fearing no evil—is gathered after the work of the day is over. Suddenly the door is opened, and a member of the Ku-Klux Klan appears, with gun in hand, to take the life of the harmless old man who sits at the fire-place, and whose only 'crime' is his color. It is to be hoped that under a rigorous administration of the laws these deeds of violence will soon cease forever."

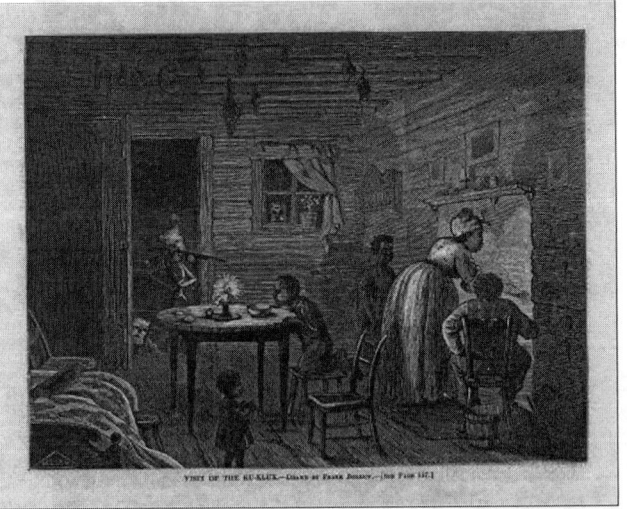

Library of Congress

4.16.3

Testimony taken by the Joint Select Committee to inquire into the condition of affairs in the late insurrectionary states, Atlanta, Georgia, October 21, 1871

Question. Did any persons come to your house that night?
Answer. Yes, sir, lots of them; I expect about forty or fifty of them.

Question. What did they do at your house?
Answer. They just came there and called; we did not get up when they first called We heard them talking as they got over the fence They came hollering and knocking

at the door, and they scared my husband so bad he could not speak when they first came I answered them They hollered, "Open the door: I said, "Yes, sir" They were at the other door, and they said, "Kindle a light" My husband went to kindle a light, and they busted both doors open and ran in-two in one door and two in the other I heard the others coming on behind them, jumping over the fence in the yard. One put his gun down to him and said, "Is this John Walthall?" They had been hunting him a long time. They had gone to my brother-in-law's hunting him, and had whipped one of my sisters-in-law powerfully and two more men on account of him. They said they were going to kill him when they got hold of him. They asked my husband if he was John Walthall. He was so scared he could not say anything. I said, "No" I never got up at all. They asked where he was, and we told them he was up to the next house, they jerked my husband up and said that he had to go up there. I heard them up there hollering "Open the door," and I heard them break the door down. . . .

The full text of Document 4.16.3 is available on the CD-ROM.

4.16.4

Excerpts from "The Freedman and His Future: A Rejoinder," by George Fitzhugh, *Lippincott's Magazine*, February 1870

Let not our Northern friends, then, fear to turn the freedmen over to us. It is in our interest to treat them well, and our feelings and sympathies coincide with our interests. We see every day around us the bad effects of improper education of negroes. Those who when slaves were accustomed to field-work are better laborers than ever, and are contented, honest and doing well. Those brought up as house-servants, mechanics, etc., are half their time out of employment, thievish, half starved and discontented. The pampered menials of *ante-bellum* days have become ragged, starving mendicants and thieves. . . .

The full text of Document 4.16.4 is available on the CD-ROM.

4.16.5

Excerpts from a speech by U.S. Senator from Missouri Carl Schurz, July 22, 1872

Look over the legislation of Congress touching the late insurrectionary States. Study it attentively,—the bayonet law, the Ku-Klux law . . . Not only did they, in protecting the rights of some, break down the bulwarks of the citizen against arbitrary authority, and by transgressing all Constitutional limitations of power, endanger the rights of all; . . . but such measures served directly to sustain in power the very adventurers who by their revolting system of plunder were violently keeping alive the spirit of disorder which that legislation was to repress . . .

The full text of Document 4.16.5 is available on the CD-ROM.

4.16.6

Excerpts from editorial, "The Mississippi Plan in Action," *Aberdeen Examiner* (Mississippi), October 7, 1875

The republican journals of the North made a great mistake in regarding the present campaign in Mississippi in the light of a political contest. It is something more earnest and holy than that—it is, so far as the white people and land-owners are concerned, a battle for the control of their own domestic affairs; a struggle to regain mastery that has been ruthlessly torn from them by selfish white schemers and adventurers, through the instrumentality of an ignorant horde of another race which has been as putty in their hands, molded to our detriment and ruin.

The full text of document 4.16.6 is available on the CD-ROM.

4.16.7

Excerpts from a speech by Frances E. W. Harper, "The Great Problem to Be Solved," given during the centennial anniversary of the Pennsylvania Society for Promoting the Abolition of Slavery, April 1875

Ladies and Gentlemen: The great problem to be solved by the American people, if I understand it, is this: Whether or not there is strength enough in democracy, virtue enough in our civilization, and power enough in our religion to have mercy and deal justly with four millions of people but lately translated from the old oligarchy of slavery to the new commonwealth of freedom; and upon the right solution of this question depends in a large measure the future strength, progress and durability of our nation. The most important question before us colored people is not simply what the Democratic party may do against us or the Republican party do for us; but what are we going to do for ourselves? What shall we do toward developing our character, adding our quota to the civilization and strength of the country, diversifying our industry, and practising those lordly virtues that conquer success, and turn the world's dread laugh into admiring recognition? . . .

The full text of Document 4.16.7 is available on the CD-ROM.

4.16.8

Excerpts from a speech by Daniel Chamberlain, "On Hayes's Southern Policy," 1877

What is his [President Hayes's] Southern policy? In point of physical or external fact, it consists in withdrawing the military forces of the United States from the points in South Carolina and Louisiana where they had been previously stationed for the protection and support of the lawful Governments of those States.

In point of immediate, foreseen, and intended consequence, it consists in the overthrow and destruction of those State Governments, and the substitution in their stead of certain other organizations called State Governments.

The full text of Document 4.16.8 is available on the CD-ROM.

4.16.9

Excerpts from "The Result in South Carolina," *The Atlantic Monthly*, January 1878

[Since the election] there has been a relentless effort to bring to retribution and get out of the way all those negroes who, without holding office, made themselves obnoxious or dangerous . . . to the whites . . . No whites have been prosecuted in the state courts for the violent crimes of the campaigns . . . But hundreds upon hundreds of negroes, accused of participation in the arsons, the burglaries, the larcenies, the riots, and the murders of the republican rule, and especially of the last canvass and the dual months, have been and are now being prosecuted in the state courts, by the instigation of either grand juries or individuals. . . .

The full text of Document 4.16.9 is available on the CD-ROM.

4.16.10

Excerpts from Pinkney Benton Stewart Pinchback's address given during the Presidential campaign of 1880

Emancipated to cripple the South and enfranchised to strengthen the North, the colored race was freed and its people made citizens in the interest of the Republic. Its fundamental law declares them citizens, and the Fifteenth Amendment expressly states that: "The right of citizens of the United States to vote shall not be denied or abridged by the United States or by any State on account of race, color, or previous condition of servitude." The faith and honor of the Nation are pledged to the rigid enforcement of the law in this, as in every other respect, and the interests of the 40,000,000 white people in the Republic demand it.

If the law, both constitutional and statutory, affecting the rights and privileges of the colored citizens can be defiantly ignored and disobeyed in eleven States of the Union in a matter of such grave import as this—a matter involving the very essence of republican government, i.e., the right of the majority to rule—who can tell where it will end and how long it will be before elections in all of the States will be armed conflicts, to be decided by the greatest prowess and dexterity in the use of the bowie knife, pistol, shotgun and rifle? . . .

The full text of Document 4.16.10 is available on the CD-ROM.

LESSON 17

The Exodusters—Ho for Kansas!

When federal Reconstruction ended abruptly in 1876–1877, the promise of full citizenship for ex-slaves and their children was called into question. African Americans sought equality before the law, access to education, and land of their own. Black people (like white people) knew that property ownership made families independent of others' control and enabled them to defend their liberty. When white political supremacy and economic dominance were restored in one southern state after another, African Americans struggled to exercise and defend their rights as citizens. Those who challenged white rule faced terrorist attacks from the Ku Klux Klan. Black Codes restricted their freedom of movement and their ability to make contracts. It became ever more difficult for African Americans to buy and hold land in the South. Many black families were stuck sharecropping, renting land from white people, and unable to retain the products of their own labor. This position was, they realized, a dead end; black people, who owned no property, had no control over their own lives.

Thousands of African Americans fled west, seeking a livelihood, a better life, and basic freedoms. In the western states and territories, black men became cowboys, miners, soldiers, and merchants. Black families took up homesteads and bought land from developers. Some established all-black communities where they could enjoy autonomy from white control. Wherever they settled, African Americans recreated their community institutions: churches, schools, and activist organizations.

Southern white landowners whose profits depended on cheap black labor tried to prevent this migration. They convinced transportation companies not to sell tickets to African Americans. Black and white men who encouraged this movement faced reprisals. Vagrancy laws were enacted to arrest black travelers on the pretext that they were a threat to public safety. Still, the mass migration continued. To the African Americans who participated in and led the movement, this was not simply a westward migration like that in which many white families were also engaged. It was an "Exodus," a mass escape from the land of slavery to the "Promised Land" of freedom and security.

In 1880, a Congressional committee investigated the accusation that Republican politicians were encouraging black people to go to Kansas to increase the number of Republican voters there. This accusation was not unreasonable, for white as well as black people were well aware of what was at stake there. Some people remembered the bloody civil strife that had taken place in Kansas before the Civil War over whether the territory would become a slave or free state. "Bleeding Kansas" was one of the sites of John Brown's daring raids. By the 1870s, African Americans already had a visible presence and a long activist tradition in Kansas. Southern black people seeking freedom sought to build on and reinforce those strengths.

Two of the leaders of this "colored" migration, Benjamin "Pap" Singleton and Henry Adams, testified before the Congressional committee about the dangerous and repressive conditions African Americans faced in the South: schools were burned, children abused as they worked in the fields, and ex-slaves bound to the land by debts to landowners and merchants. It was these outrages that propelled black families to leave the South, they argued.

Henry Adams was an ex-slave who had fought for freedom with the Union Army in the Civil War. He believed that black people should move away from the old slave states in order to prosper and secure their citizenship rights. Adams was president of the Colonization Council of Caddo Parish, Louisiana. Initially he was interested in emigration abroad, especially to Liberia, the African colony founded before the Civil War by American former slaves. Then he turned his attention to the western United States. (In the mid-nineteenth century, the term colony was applied to any organized group that moved together, held land collectively, and exercised self-government.)

Pap Singleton, a Tennessee-born former slave and skilled carpenter whose nickname suggests the respect he had earned in the black community, helped to form the Edgefield Real Estate and Homestead Association during the early 1870s. The group was unable to buy land in Tennessee because property was too expensive there—especially when black people were trying to buy it from whites. The Association investigated Kansas as a place for settlement and recruited former slaves to migrate. Its first efforts in Cherokee County in southeastern Kansas were unsuccessful; few migrants had the $1,000 it took to start a farm, and newcomers could not find employment. Singleton learned from this experience and tried to prepare new colonists better. He redirected his efforts to Morris County, in east-central Kansas, where land was cheaper. This settlement thrived.

In 1879–1880, six thousand black people departed from Louisiana, Mississippi, and Texas in just a few months. This mass exodus was dubbed "Kansas Fever," as if it were a contagious disease. But participants were not suffering from delirium. This migration had a biblical dimension; African Americans saw themselves as similar to the Israelites who fled from Egyptian bondage in their beloved Old Testament.

Religious motivation was especially important to the people who founded Nicodemus, a community that was intended to exemplify the Christian virtues and the promise of redemption from sin and suffering. The black tradition has many prophets, religiously based liberation movements, and sacred communities; Nicodemus was a westward manifestation of that spirit.

Organizing Idea

After the end of Reconstruction, with few prospects for improving their lives, thousands of African Americans migrated west seeking a livelihood and a better life. They became homesteaders and cowboys, military men, storeowners, and social activists. An important story of black migration may be found in the history of Kansas.

Student Objectives

Students will:

- be able to describe problems that African Americans faced following Reconstruction
- analyze primary source documents, make inferences, and draw conclusions about the process of recruiting freedpeople to go west
- study primary sources for evidence of the importance of family and the value of community in the lives of former slaves
- read the story of one town and the testimonies of two men who were instrumental in the exodus west

Key Questions

- What conditions drove African Americans to move west in the 1870s?
- What can we learn from the testimony of Henry Adams and Pap Singleton before the U.S. Senate committee investigating this movement?
- How were people recruited?
- What problems did migrants face as they relocated?
- What can we learn about the importance of community from studying the town of Nicodemus, Kansas?
- How do people like Pap Singleton become recognized leaders of mass movements?
- What is the legacy of the Exodusters?

Primary Source Materials

DOCUMENT 4.17.1: Homesteaders' poster from the Edgefield Real Estate Association

DOCUMENT 4.17.2: "Ho for Kansas!" poster, 1878

DOCUMENT 4.17.3: "Negro Exodusters en route to Kansas, fleeing from the yellow fever," from *Harper's Weekly*, 1870

DOCUMENT 4.17.4: Photograph of emigrants waiting for a boat to take them west, 1880

DOCUMENT 4.17.5: "A Second Methuselah," *The Arkansas Independent*, April 9, 1875

DOCUMENT 4.17.6: Map of Kansas in 1870

DOCUMENT 4.17.7: "To the Colored Citizens of the United States," an advertisement from the Nicodemus Town Company, 1877

DOCUMENT 4.17.8: Testimony of Benjamin Singleton before the Senate Select Committee Investigating the "Negro Exodus from the Southern States," April 17, 1880

DOCUMENT 4.17.9: Testimony of Henry Adams before the Senate Select Committee Investigating the "Negro Exodus from the Southern States," April 1880

DOCUMENT 4.17.10: Anniversary celebration poster honoring Pap Singleton, 1882

DOCUMENT 4.17.11: Photograph of Pap Singleton

Supplementary Materials

ITEM 4.17.A: Additional vocabulary lists for primary sources

Vocabulary

brethren	emigrants	exodusters	migration
colony	exodus	homesteader	White League

Student Activities

Activity 1 — **Engaging the Students—The Context**

Together in class discussion, students review what they know about the successes and failures of Reconstruction. Ask: What do we know about black families during and after Reconstruction? Do students have stories from their own family histories? What questions come up for students when they consider the sudden need for large numbers of people to make their own way in an economy that favors those who own land?

Introduce the topic of this lesson using ideas from the introduction. What factors forced many blacks to leave the South for unknown lands in the West. How can we use primary sources to learn this history?

Activity 2 — **Comparing Posters**

Distribute copies of both posters (4.17.1 and 4.17.2). Ask students to study the Homesteaders' poster.

❖ What is the message?

- Who wrote it? Who is the anticipated audience?
- What is the Edgefield Real Estate Association asking people to do?
- What do you think of the pledge (in small print)?
- Can you tell from this broadside what the Association intends to do with the money?
- On the basis of the invitation on this broadside, would you invest?

Now, hand out Document 4.17.2, the "Ho for Kansas!" broadside.

- What is this broadside announcing?
- How is it different from the other one?
- What name appears on both announcements?
- What might be meant by the sentence, "Beware of Speculators and Adventurers, as it is a dangerous thing to fall into their hands."
- Would this poster convince you to accept the invitation to go to Kansas? Why or why not?

Discovering Stories in Pictures

Activity 3

Divide the class into small working groups. Each group receives copies of the engraving from *Harper's Weekly* (4.17.3) and the photograph of migrants (4.17.4). Ask students to carefully study the images, paying attention to details. One student in each group should serve as recorder of the group's discussion.

Questions for discussion
- Are people in family groups?
- How are they dressed?
- What can you guess about their emotions from their expressions and/or body posture?
- What kinds of objects do you see (household items, tools, etc.)?
- Can you identify stereotypes in the engraving?
- How do the pictures compare with one another?
- In each picture, does it appear that the people are *going away from* or *looking forward toward* a destination?

Ask each group to share its findings with the class. What can we learn from these pictures about the westward migrations of African Americans?

Writing in Response to an Article

Activity 4

Each student receives a copy of "A Second Methuselah" (4.17.5). For homework, students should read the document carefully and write a paragraph responding to these questions:

- Who was the original Methuselah?
- Why do you think that the newspaper called Fortune Snow by this name?
- What qualities about the man does the writer admire?
- What facts do we learn about Fortune Snow?

Ask students to create a time line for Fortune Snow using the information in the news story. Is it possible that he was really as old as reported? Whether or not he was actually 127 years old, what does this short story tell us about the value freedpeople placed on care for their families?

Activity 5 — Working with Maps

Print a copy for each student of the 1870s map of Kansas (4.17.6). Also print copies of the advertisement for the town of Nicodemus (4.17.7).

Ask students to identify and mark the counties in which we know freedpeople settled—Cherokee county (in southeastern Kansas), Morris county (in the east-central part of the state), and Graham county (in the northwest). Efforts to settle in Cherokee country were not successful. Why might that location have been appealing to settlers, and why do you think it didn't work? (The location is close to the eastern border with Missouri; therefore, it is closer for the travelers but also more expensive.)

The Morris county settlement did succeed. Why was that location better? Notice the location of the Union Pacific Railroad. (By 1870, with the importance of the railroad established, maps showed railroad lines instead of roads.)

On an outline map of the United States, ask students to trace the routes and figure the distances migrants must have taken to travel to Kansas from Tennessee and Kentucky, later from Mississippi, Louisiana, and Texas. What were the transportation options in the 1870s? How does this map work help us to more clearly appreciate the experience of the migrants?

Activity 6 — Creative Extension—A Poster

The town of Nicodemus is in Graham county in the northwest part of the state. Looking at the location on the map and using the advertisement "To the Colored Citizens of the United States" (4.17.7), ask students to identify the prime features described and to create a poster that will advertise Nicodemus. The poster should translate words into pictures and provide a powerful incentive for its intended audience to move to Nicodemus.

Activity 7 — Reading, Analyzing, and Discussing the Testimony

Documents 4.17.8 and 4.17.9 report the testimony of Pap Singleton and Henry Adams to the Senate Select Committee investigating the "Negro Exodus from the Southern States." An accusation had been made that Republican politicians were encouraging freedpeople to go to Kansas to increase the number of Republican voters there. Because of their activism in encouraging blacks to leave the south, Singleton and Adams were called to Washington, D.C., in April of 1880.

Divide the class in half, giving one group copies of Pap Singleton's testimony (4.17.8) and the other group, that of Henry Adams (4.17.9). Working in pairs, students read the testimonies and write a summary of what is being described.

- What do we learn about the two men from their words?
- How do they describe the work in which they are engaged? What were their motives?
- What do we learn about conditions in the South at that time?
- Does the Senate Committee learn anything about the involvement of Republican politicians in the exodus?
- By inference, what do we learn about the people who opposed the Republican party?
- What *does* the committee hear from Singleton and Adams?
- What do you think of these two men who worked so tirelessly on behalf of others?

As a class, have students share what they learned. What was the most powerful message from the testimonies? Do these documents enlarge our understanding of conditions for African Americans after Reconstruction? What do we learn about leadership in southern black communities in the late nineteenth century?

As an extended learning activity, interested students could write and produce a play using the information and words from the Senate Select Committee hearings.

Writing—"You Witness the Celebration" *Activity 8*

Hand out copies of the Anniversary celebration broadside (4.17.10) and the photograph of Pap Singleton (4.17.11). Ask students to read the broadside.

- What is being celebrated?
- Where is it being held?
- Who is being honored and why? Who is invited?
- What events are on the program?
- One group of people will be admitted free. Who are they? Why would they be encouraged to come?

Ask students to think about the description of the celebration as represented on the broadside and study the photograph of Pap Singleton. Then, imagining that they attended the celebration, write an "eyewitness" account of the event and of the man being honored. Use information from the previous activities to enrich the account.

> **Music Connection**
> ⟶❋⟵
>
> The original Nicodemus was a prominent Jew whose belief in Jesus is described in the Christian Bible. Because of this religious connection, he became an important figure in the black church. According to one story, the town of Nicodemus was named after an African-born slave who had the gift of prophecy and foresaw the exodus of people moving west. In the 1870s a song was written about Nicodemus, referencing the Great Solomon Valley in Kansas. Around the same time, Henry C. Work, a white abolitionist, wrote another version, called "Wake Nicodemus." Students can read those lyrics online *http://home.t-online.de/home/pheld/1usa7.htm* (no recording available).
>
> **NICODEMUS**
>
> Nicodemus was a slave of African birth,
> And was bought for a bag full of gold;
> He was reckoned a part of the salt of the earth.
> But he died years ago, very old.
>
> Nicodemus was a prophet, at least he was as wise.
> For he told of the battles to come;
> How we trembled with fear, when he rolled his eyes
> And we heeded the shake of his thumb.
>
> Good time coming, good time coming
> Long, long time on the way;
> Run and tell Elija to hurry up Pomp,
> To meet us under the cottonwood tree.
> In the Great Solomon Valley
> At the first break of day.

Further Resources for Teachers and Students

Chu, Daniel. *Going Home to Nicodemus: The Story of an African American Frontier Town and the Pioneers Who Settled It.* Parsippany, NJ: Messner, 1994.

Emancipation: A Photographic Collage (poster and book). GA: Mandela Publishing, Inc., 1998.

Foner, Philip S. *Black Workers: A Documentary History from Colonial Times to the Present.* Philadelphia: Temple University Press, 1989.

Haskins, James. *The Geography of Hope: Black Exodus from the South after Reconstruction.* Brookfield, CT: Twenty-First Century Books, 1999.

Igus, Toyomi. *Book of Black Heroes, Volume Two: Great Women In The Struggle: An Introduction for Young Readers.* Orange, NJ: Just Us Books, Inc., 1991.

Katz, William L. *The Black West: A Pictorial History.* Seattle, WA: Open Hand Publishing, 1987.

Painter, Nell Irvin. *Exodusters: Black Migration to Kansas After Reconstruction.* New York: Knopf, 1992.

Websites

www.loc.gov/exhibits/african/afam009.html
Contains digital images of archival material from the African-American Mosiac Exhibition at the Library of Congress relating to western migration and homesteading

www.slaveryinamerica.org
Designed "by educators for educators" and provides curriculum resources on the institution of American slavery, focusing on the experience of individuals who were themselves enslaved

www.jimcrowhistory.org
Companion site to www.slaveryinamerica.org, *providing a plethora of classroom resources*

www.coax.net/people/lwf/bawmus.htm
Home site for the Black American West Museum & Heritage Center in Denver, Colorado (The purpose of the Center is to promote understanding of the major role that African American people played in the settling and shaping of the American West.)

www2.netdoor.com/~jgh
Provides historical account of the Louisiana Black Guards

www.emancipation.net
Site of Emancipation, a photographic collage of images of prominent African American figures representing 300 years of African American history

http://historicaltextarchive.com
Resource for viewing archival material; some relevant articles

www.schomburgcenter.org
Homepage for the Schomburg Center for Research in Black Culture at the New York Public Library

www.coax.net/people/lwf/bawmus.htm
Provides some "unknown" facts about the West, but does not have much in the way of documents or pictures

www.washburn.edu/cas/art/cyoho/archive
Under the Kansas travel section, a brief summary of the history of Nicodemus as well as links and pictures

www.kshs.org
The Kansas State Historical Society site; has on display some interesting fliers and pictures from the time of the Exodusters and has a link to the NPS Nicodemus site

www.pbs.org/weta/thewest
Not only has information about the PBS program on the West, but also has some background information, teacher resources, and links

www.historymatters.gmu.edu
Gives specific information on the Exodusters and on the town of Nicodemus when "In Search of Eden" is entered

Contemporary Connection

✥

African Americans are part of the history of most western states. However, within only the last twenty-five or thirty years have state historical societies begun to identify materials in their collections to tell these stories and to make the information available to the public. Because of the Internet, it is becoming easier to discover the history of African Americans both locally and across the country.

Students should look at the internet site for the Kansas State Historical Society to identify the rich resources on African Americans in Kansas and the ways in which this amazing history is being preserved and celebrated (*www.kshs.org*). Further, students should research the resources available in their own state to learn about the experiences of African Americans who moved west (or north) after the Civil War.

Primary Source Materials for Lesson 17

4.17.1

Homesteaders' poster from the Edgefield Real Estate Association

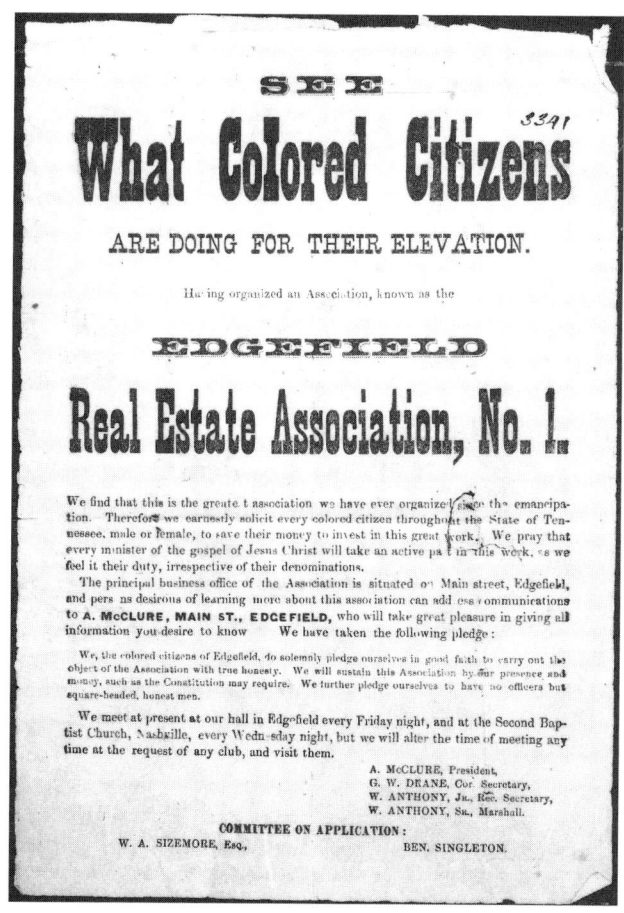

Kansas State Historical Society

4.17.2

"Ho for Kansas!" poster, 1878

Ho for Kansas!

Brethren, Friends, & Fellow Citizens:

I feel thankful to inform you that the

REAL ESTATE AND Homestead Association,

Will Leave Here the

15th of April, 1878,

In pursuit of Homes in the Southwestern Lands of America, at Transportation Rates, cheaper than ever was known before.

For full information inquire of

Benj. Singleton, better known as old Pap,

NO. 5 NORTH FRONT STREET.

Beware of Speculators and Adventurers, as it is a dangerous thing to fall in their hands.

Nashville, Tenn., March 18, 1878.

One of the many posters calling on southern blacks to leave for Kansas.

Kansas State Historical Society

4.17.3

"Negro Exodusters en route to Kansas, fleeing from the yellow fever," from *Harper's Weekly,* 1870

At the time of the Exodus to Kansas, yellow fever ravaged many river towns in Missouri, Mississippi, and Louisiana. Many of the African Americans, traveling by steamboat, train, or horseback, stopped in these towns. Because they were ill, unwashed, and poverty-stricken, city officials assumed that they carried disease. Cities such as St. Louis imposed quarantine measures, hoping to discourage the migrants.

Library of Congress

4.17.4

Photograph of emigrants waiting for a boat to take them west, 1880

In February of 1880, more than nine hundred black families from Mississippi reached St. Louis, on their way to Kansas. Some looked for "conductors" to make travel arrangements for them. Paid in advance, many conductors simply disappeared, leaving the black migrants stranded at docks and train depots.

Library of Congress

4.17.5

"A Second Methuselah," *The Arkansas Independent*, April 9, 1875

Last Wednesday a large crowd of Negroes were at the crossing awaiting a train. They were bound for Arkansas. Among the number was Fortune Snow, perhaps the oldest man in America, and who could well be called a second Methuselah. This old Negro was born in Georgetown, S.C., in the year 1748, and is consequently 127 years old. He was for 6 years a body servant of Capt. Snow in the Revolutionary War. At Capt. Snow's death, he became the property of Nicholas Johnson, who sold him to John A. Adams of Dallas County, Alabama, who at his death gave the old man his freedom. Since then he has resided with his children and grand-children in the 12th District of his county, near Milan, and in consequence of hard times they are emigrating to Arkansas, and take with them the "Old Man."...

The full text of Document 4.17.5 is available on CD-ROM.

4.17.6

Map of Kansas in 1870

Kansas Map Collection, Wichita State University Libraries, Department of Special Collections

4.17.7

"To the Colored Citizens of the United States," an advertisement from the Nicodemus Town Company, 1877

To the Colored Citizens of the United States
Nicodemus, Graham Co., Kan., July 2d. 1877
    We, the Nicodemus Town Company of Graham County, Kan., are now in possession of our lands and the Town Site of Nicodemus, which is beautifully located on the N. W. quarter of Section I Town 8, Range 21 in Graham Co., Kansas, in the great Solomon Valley, 240 miles west of Topeka, and we are proud to say it is the

finest country we ever saw. The soil is of a rich, black, sandy loam. The country is rather rolling, and looks most pleasing to the human eye. The south fork of the Solomon river flows through Graham County, nearly directly east and west and has an abundance of excellent water, while there are numerous springs of living water abounding throughout the Valley. There is an abundance of fine Magnesian stone for building purposes, which is much easier handled than the rough sand or hard stone. There is also some timber; plenty for fire use, while we have no fear but what we will find plenty of coal.

Now is your time to secure your home on Government Land in the Great Solomon Valley of Western Kansas.

The full text of Document 4.17.7 is available on the CD-ROM.

4.17.8

Testimony of Benjamin Singleton before the Senate Select Committee Investigating the "Negro Exodus from the Southern States," April 17, 1880

Q. When did you change your home from Tennessee to Kansas?
A. I have been going there for the last six or seven years, sir.

Q. Going between Tennessee and Kansas, at different times?
A. Yes, sir; several times.

Q. Well, tell us about it?
A. I have been fetching out people; I believe I fetched out 7,432 people.

Q. You have brought out 7,432 people from the South to Kansas?
A. Yes, sir; brought and sent.

Q. That is, they came out to Kansas under your influence?
A. Yes, sir; I was the cause of it.

Q. How long have you been doing that—ever since 1869?
A. Yes, sir; ever since 1869.

Q. Did you go out there yourself in 1869, before you commenced sending them out?
A. No, sir.

Q. How did you happen to send them out?
A. The first cause, do you mean, of them going?

Q. Yes; What was the cause of your going out, and in the first place how did you happen to go there, or to send these people there?
A. Well, my people, for the want of land—we needed land for our children—and their disadvantages—that caused my heart to grieve and sorrow; pity for my race, sir, that was coming down, instead of going up—that caused me to go to work for them. I sent out there perhaps in '66—perhaps so; or in '65, any way—my memory don't recollect which; and they brought back tolerable favorable reports; then I jacked up three or four hundred, and went into Southern Kansas, and found it was a good country, and I thought Southern Kansas was congenial to our nature, sir; and I formed a colony there, and bought about a thousand acres of ground—the colony did—my people.

The full text of Document 4.17.8 is available on the CD-ROM.

4.17.9

Testimony of Henry Adams before the Senate Select Committee Investigating the "Negro Exodus from the Southern States," April 1880

Question: Now, Mr. Adams, you know, probably, more about the causes of the exodus from that country than any other man, from your connection with it; tell us in a few words what you believe to be the causes of these people going away?
Henry Adams: Well, the cause is, in my judgment, and from what information I have received, and what I have seen with my own eyes—it is because the largest majority of the people, of the white people, that held us as slaves treats our people so bad in many respects that it is impossible for them to stand it. Now, in a great many parts of that country there our people most as well be slaves as to be free; because, in the first place, I will state this: that in some times, in times of politics, if they have any idea that the Republicans will carry a parish or ward, or something of that kind, why, they would do anything on God's earth. There ain't nothing too mean for them to do to prevent it; nothing I can make mention of is too mean for them to do. . . .

The full text of Document 4.17.9 is available on the CD-ROM.

4.17.10

Anniversary celebration poster honoring Pap Singleton, 1882

Kansas State Historical Society

4.17.11

Photograph of Pap Singleton

Benjamin "Pap" Singleton (1809–1892), a former slave born in Nashville, Tennessee, became the leader of the "Exoduster Movement" of the 1870s. In later years, his supporters gave him the title "Father of the Exodus."

Library of Congress

Glossary

absolutism: the doctrine or system of government under which the ruler has absolute power.

affidavit: a legal statement made under oath before a notary public or other person authorized to administer oaths.

amiable: friendly and pleasant.

amnesty: a pardon, especially for political offenses against a government; may be issued before a trial and conviction and may be offered to whole classes of people.

antagonism: the state of being opposed to, hostile to another or to each other.

apprentice: traditionally, a young person under legal agreement to learn a skilled trade from a master artisan; in programs for gradual emancipation, a formerly enslaved person bound to serve a master for a term of years; during and after the Civil War, an ex-slave bound to serve for a specific term and not allowed to make his or her own contracts.

artillery: guns of large caliber; mobile cannon.

avaricious: greedy for riches.

brethren: a group of men, a fraternity; also, a term of address used in African American religious organizations, as "brethren and sisteren" (brothers and sisters).

brigade: a large unit of soldiers consisting of two or more regiments.

broadside: a printed notice intended to be posted in a public place.

buccaneer: a pirate, or an adventurous seaman.

carpetbagger: after the Civil War, a white person who came from the North to engage in business in the South; usually with negative connotations, as greedy and untrustworthy.

catspaw : a person used by others to do dangerous, distasteful, or unlawful work; a dupe.

cavalry: combat troops mounted on horses.

citizenship: the status of being a member of a state or nation and enjoying certain rights.

colony: in the nineteenth century, this term applied to any organized group that moved together, held land collectively, and exercised self-government, not just to one country establishing rule over and sending people to settle in another, as in the British North American colonies before the Revolution.

commissioner: an official in charge of a government bureau or appointed to perform a particular function.

conglomerate: a business or bureaucracy with many different companies or subdivisions.

constabulary: the territory under the jurisdiction of a police officer; the force of local police officers.

crop-lien system: in the post–Civil War South, a system by which a tenant farmer obtained credit from a merchant and was required to repay the debt from the proceeds of the crop.

debt peonage: a system by which debtors are required to labor for their creditors and unable to contract freely with another employer.

Democratic Party: before the Civil War, a coalition of diverse groups in various regions that saw itself as the champion of ordinary people against large business interests and advocated local decision making about the future of slavery in the states and territories; dissolved during the Civil War and reformed during Reconstruction to oppose Radical Republicans; in the South, recruited white men to limit black people's rights.

depredation: a predatory, destructive act; an illegitimate violent seizure of property.

despotic: autocratic, tyrannical.

destitute: extremely poor, without property.

diabolical: of the Devil; very wicked or cruel.

disapprobation: disapproval, condemnation.

disenfranchise: [also, disfranchise] to deprive a person of the right to vote.

dispatch [despatch]: to send off or out promptly, usually on a specific errand or business; a note sent from one official to another.

emancipate: to liberate, to set free from bondage.

emasculated: literally, castrated; figuratively, deprived of masculine independence.

emigrant: a person who leaves a place where he or she has been living, usually crossing national or regional boundaries.

emissary: a person or agent sent on a specific mission representing another person or a government.

enfranchise: to give a person or group the right to vote.

enlistment: enrollment for service in a branch of the armed forces.

entice: to attract by offering hope of reward, often deceptively.

exile: a person who is forced to leave his or her homeland to live in another country or region.

exodus: a mass movement of a group of people from a place where they have been oppressed.

"Exodusters": a name popularly applied to African Americans who left the South to settle in the West after the end of Reconstruction.

fatigue duty: noncombat work for the military, such as digging ditches and building fortifications.

fraternizing: associating in a brotherly manner, sometimes against the rules.

"free labor": the idea that working people should be free to make contracts with employers and customers and be paid the full value of their labor and that farmers should own and reap the produce of the land they worked.

fugitive: a person who flees or has fled from danger or capture.

furnishing merchant: a storekeeper who provided goods such as food, seed, and tools on credit to tenant farmers.

homesteader: a person or family who took up land in the West under the Homestead Act and its successors, which required settlers on federally owned land to pay a (relatively low) purchase price, live on the land for several years, and "improve" (clear, cultivate, and/or develop) it in order to obtain a title.

horde: a large group regarded as dangerous.

Iago: the antagonist in the Shakespearean tragedy *Othello*; a clever and evil betrayer.

idol: an image of a god used as an object of worship; an admired person.

immigrant: a person who comes to a new place to live, usually from another nation or region.

immunities: exemption or freedom from public service or other duties; privileges.

improvident: failing to provide for the future; lacking foresight or thrift.

inaugural: (adjective) at the beginning of a series; when taking office.

induce: to lead to some action, condition, or belief; to bring about.

instigation: urging on.

insurgent: rising up against established authority; rebellious.

insurrection: an uprising against established authority, usually with weapons.

jubilee: a time or occasion of rejoicing; in the Judeo-Christian religious tradition, a time of mass redemption from slavery.

legislature: a body of persons officially constituted to make and change laws.

ludicrous: ridiculous; amusing or laughable through obvious absurdity.

mendicants: beggars who travel from place to place.

migrant: a person who moves from one place to another within a nation.

migration: the movement of people within a nation, e.g., to the American West or from South to North.

misdemeanor: an offense for which the law provides a lesser punishment than it does for a felony.

mulatto: a person with mixed African and European ancestry.

odium: hatred or dislike; a bad reputation.

oligarchy: a form of government in which power is held by a wealthy few.

pardon: to forgive someone for an offense; in law, to allow a convicted person freedom from the penalties of his or her crime.

pariah: a person despised or rejected by others; a social outcast.

pathetic: arousing pity, tenderness, or sympathy.

pauper: a person who is extremely poor and may depend on public charity.

peon: a person engaged in menial work, without freedom to control his or her own labor.

perpetuate: to cause to continue or be remembered.

petition: a formal document addressing a request to a person in authority, often signed by a number of people.

proclamation: an official public announcement.

prostrate: literally, lying with face down to the ground in an act of submission; figuratively, without the strength or resources to act for oneself.

provisional: temporary.

Radical Reconstruction: the federal government's efforts to extend power over the former Confederate states, supervising elections and public policies after the state governments had been reestablished.

Radical Republicans: during and after the Civil War, the wing of the Republican Party that favored full citizenship for ex-slaves and civil penalties for former Confederate officials.

rapacious: violently greedy or destructive.

ratify: to approve something in an official way.

rebel: a person who engages in armed resistance against the established government or ruler.

Rebel: during the Civil War, a soldier or supporter of the Confederacy.

reconciliation: the settlement of a quarrel or difference between opposing groups, often after a violent conflict.

Reconstruction: after the Civil War, the process of reorganizing states that had seceded and reestablishing them in the Union and of establishing the citizenship of ex-slaves.

recruit: (verb) to enlist personnel in an army; (noun) a newly enlisted soldier.

redress: to put something right; to remedy.

reformation: the act of forming again, usually in a different way.

refugee: a person who flees his or her homeland and seeks asylum in another country or region.

regiment: a military unit consisting or two or more battalions and forming a basic element of a division.

renunciation: the act of giving up something voluntarily or formally.

refugee: a person who flees his or her homeland and seeks asylum in another country or region.

Republican Party: formed during the early 1850s around the central principle that slavery should not be allowed to expand into the western territories of the United States and the idea of "free labor"; after the Civil War, the party moved toward the recognition that slavery was incompatible with American freedoms and carried out Reconstruction; following the 1876–1877 national election, the party became more conservative and was dominated by white business interests.

scalawag: a southern white person who supported the Republican Party during Reconstruction; usually a derogatory term.

serfdom: feudal servitude; a system by which farm workers are tied to the land and under the control of the landowner.

servile: like or characteristic of a slave or servant; subordinate.

slander: a false statement that deliberately damages another's reputation.

suffrage: the right to vote.

territory: the land and waters under the jurisdiction of a nation, state, or ruler; a large tract of land; a region, district.

treason: violation of the allegiance a citizen owes to the sovereign or nation; betrayal of one's country or government.

Unionist: anyone who supported the federal government during the Civil War.

vagrant: a person who wanders from place to place and is usually poor and unemployed.

venom: literally, a poisonous substance secreted by such animals as snakes, wasps, and scorpions and transmitted through a bite or sting; figuratively, hostility.

veto: the power of a government executive, such as a president or governor, to reject a bill passed by the legislature.

visage: the face, or facial expression.

warrant: (noun) a written authorization giving the holder legal power to search, seize, or arrest; (verb) to authorize or provide sufficient grounds for an action.

White League: a reactionary group of white men organized after the Civil War to restore white supremacy and to repress African Americans who tried to exercise their citizenship rights.

Credits

Documents 4.1.5, 4.2.5, 4.2.6, 4.2.7, 4.2.8, 4.2.9, 4.3.9, 4.3.11, 4.3.12, 4.4.7, 4.7.11, 4.9.1, 4.9.2, 4.12.6, 4.13.2, 4.13.7, 4.15.3, 4.15.4, 4.15.5, 4.15.6, 4.15.7, 4.15.8, 4.15.9, 4.15.10, 4.15.11, 4.16.1, 4.16.2, 4.17.3, 4.17.4, and 4.17.11: Courtesy of the Library of Congress.

Documents 4.2.1, 4.2.2, 4.2.3, 4.2.4, 4.2.10, 4.2.11, 4.3.1, 4.3.4, 4.3.7, 4.5.1, and 4.7.7: Copyright © 1992 *Free At Last: A Documentary History of Slavery, Freedom, and the Civil War*, edited by Ira Berlin et al. Reprinted by permission of The New Press. (800) 233-4830.

Documents 4.2.12, 4.2.13, 4.2.14, and 4.2.15: Family papers and photographs, courtesy of Janice Ross Lorenz, Margaret Elizabeth Ross' great-granddaughter.

Documents 4.3.2, 4.4.11, 4.4.12, 4.4.13, and 4.7.10: From *Freedom: A Documentary History of Emancipation 1861–1867, Series II: The Black Military Experience,* by Ira Berlin (New York: Cambridge University Press, 1982), pp. 79, 244, 539, 557–558, and 665–666. Reprinted with the permission of Cambridge University Press.

Document. 4.3.10: Courtesy of University of North Carolina, North Carolina Collection.

Document 4.3.14: Lydia Maria Child correspondence, 1861–1880. Collection number 4601, Box 6. Courtesy of the Division of Rare and Manuscript Collections, Cornell University Library.

Documents 4.4.5 and 4.14.1: Courtesy of The Granger Collection.

Document 4.4.6: Courtesy of the New York Public Library.

Document 4.4.9: From "War Letters of Charles P. Bowditch," in *Massachusetts Historical Society Proceedings 57* (1923–1924), pp. 431, 434, 436, 444. Used by permission of the Massachusetts Historical Society.

Page 85 and documents 4.13.3, 4.13.4, and 4.14.2: Copyright © 1996 *Freedom's Unfinished Revolution: An Inquiry into the Civil War and Reconstruction,* by the

American Social History Project. Reprinted by permission of The New Press. (800) 233-4830.

Document 4.7.1: Courtesy of Howard University Gallery of Art.

Document 4.7.12: Courtesy of Rare Books and Special Collections Division, McGill University Libraries, Montreal, Canada.

Document 4.9.B: Excerpts from *The Tragic Era* by Claude G. Bowers. Copyright © 1929, and renewed 1957 by Claude G. Bowers. Reprinted by permission of Houghton Mifflin Company. All rights reserved.

Documents 4.10.1, 4.10.3, 4.10.4, 4.10.5, 4.10.6, 4.10.7, 4.10.8, 4.10.9, 4.10.10, 4.10.11, and 4.10.12: From *Black Worker: A Documentary History, Volume II: The Black Worker During the Era of the National Labor Union,* edited by Philip Foner and Ronald L. Lewis. Philadelphia: Temple University Press, 1978. Used by permission of Ronald L. Lewis.

Document 4.11.6: Courtesy of Cornell University Library, Making of America Digital Collection. Barrows, David C., "A Georgia Plantation," *Scribner's Monthly* 21:5 March 1881, pp. 832–833.

Documents: 4.12.1, 4.12.2, 4.12.3, 4.12.4, and 4.12.5: Copyright © 1997 *Families and Freedom: A Documentary History of African American Kinship in the Civil War Era,* edited by Ira Berlin and Leslie S. Rowland. Reprinted by permission of The New Press. (800) 233-4830.

Document 4.13.1: Courtesy of The Chicago Historical Society.

Documents 4.13.5, 4.13.6, 4.13.8, 4.13.9, 4.13.10, 4.13.11, 4.13.12, 4.13.13, 4.13.15, 4.13.17, and 4.13.18: From *The Trouble They Seen: The Story of Reconstruction in the Words of African Americans,* edited by Dorothy Sterling. New York: Doubleday, 1994. Used by permission of Dorothy Sterling.

Document 4.16.C: Thomas A. Bailey. *The American Pageant: A History of the Republic.* Boston: D.C. Heath and Co., 1956. Used by permission of Houghton Mifflin Company.

Documents 4.17.1, 4.17.2, and 4.17.10: Courtesy of The Kansas State Historical Society.

Document 4.17.6: Courtesy of Kansas Map Collection, Wichita State University Libraries, Department of Special Collections.